THE INFLUENCE MINDSET

FOR SALES ACCELERATION

The 7 EQ Brain Hacks
That Get People To Choose You

By

CHRISTIAN
HANSEN

THE INFLUENCE MINDSET FOR SALES ACCELERATION
The 7 EQ Brain Hacks That Get People To Choose You

HANSEN, CHRISTIAN, Author
THE INFLUENCE MINDSET FOR SALES ACCELERATION
CHRISTIAN HANSEN

TheChristianHansen.com

Published by:
ELITE ONLINE PUBLISHING
63 East 11400 South
Suite #230
Sandy, UT 84070
EliteOnlinePublishing.com

Illustrated by Natalie Tutanova

ISBN: 978-1961801851 (Paperback)
ISBN: 978-1961801868 (eBook)

BUS058000
BUS046000
BUS071000

Table of Contents

Why Your Message Matters:

Let's get right to the point:

People don't choose or reject you. They choose or reject their *perception* of you.

That's because no matter your qualifications and abilities, there is a gap between your value and how it's perceived. Your words and behaviors either influence people to choose you or they don't.

The problem is, most people don't know how to communicate their value in a way that bridges the Value/Perception Gap, and so they spin their wheels while their message gets lost in the noise. They lose critical opportunities.

But what if you could present your value in ways that bypass the neural defenses, speak directly to the brain, and influence people to perceive you as the obvious choice?

It turns out you can.

Since the brain is wired to pay attention to certain things, when you communicate and present your message using 7 research-backed strategies, you will rise above the noise, stand out from the crowd, and influence decision-makers to choose you...every time.

This book shows you how.

How To Insult Vikings

To be honest, I never thought a suitcase stuffed with 100 corn tortillas could insult an entire nation. But that's exactly how I (accidentally) declared war on Denmark.

Let's rewind here.

If there is one thing you need to know about me, it's that I grew up working in my family's Mexican restaurant in Los Angeles: *Los Gringos Locos*. Mexican food is my official love language. The other thing you need to know is that my wife, Nathalie, is from the country of Denmark. Think Legos, pastries, and Hans Christian Andersen's *The Little Mermaid*.

So when I flew to meet her family for the FIRST time, how could this American make a good first impression? After thinking long and hard, I took the OBVIOUS approach:

"What better way to break the ice than fresh tacos and enchiladas?"

This was destined to be a "meet-the-in-laws" triumph for the books, I thought. It was herring vs jalapeños, and I was packing the heat.

When I proposed the idea to my (then) girlfriend, she agreed out of politeness, and I mistook her cringe as a smile. I proceeded to enthusiastically pack a suitcase full of dried guajillo chiles, pinto beans, and of course, the 100 corn tortillas. As soon as I arrived at the airport in

Denmark and Nathalie saw my traveling taco stand, her eyes got as big as burritos.

You'd think I was running a Mexican embassy out of Terminal 4.

Oblivious to her worried signals, and carried away by the grand visions in my head (and tummy), we traveled to her hometown, where I commandeered her mother's modest Danish kitchen and began to cook the best damn authentic guajillo salsa roja their village had ever seen. Trays of enchiladas gave way to tacos, and the scent of homemade rice and beans filled the air with comfort-food goodness.

However, as Nathalie's large extended family trickled in and saw Gringo Loco over here cooking away, they were speechless. Why was this American cooking Mexican food? He is so strange! And aren't the tortillas more like pita bread? What did he do to make those so flat? He ruined bread!

Unfortunately, things only got worse. When we sat down to eat, I knew I was in trouble.

Compared to their standard fare of bread, pork, and potatoes, my fiesta was far too spicy. Plates of food I had carefully crafted were left uneaten, and no one even touched the guajillo sauce! They were painfully polite, but I sensed through awkward whispers and glances that I had misjudged the entire affair. I had insulted the ancient Viking ways, and the fiesta was a fiasco.

As the evening ended and her family left, muttering Viking curses under their breath, I wondered, "Where did it all go wrong?"

The food was authentic.

I was organized and efficient.

And the guajillo salsa roja was *chef's kiss* good. I had done everything right!

"There is a disconnect between our efforts and the results that we want."

From my perspective, I had presented my value clearly. I had hoped the quality ingredients, efficient organization, and sincere effort would impress and get them to like me.

But I was wrong.

There was a "gap" between how I presented my value and how it was perceived, and from their perspective, tacos, enchiladas, and guajillo salsa roja might as well have come from outer space. And so, despite my efforts to make a good first impression, this was a "meet-the-in-laws" for the books...but for the wrong reasons.

Why? I was so preoccupied with being impressive that I overlooked what really mattered to them. I got in the way of my own success and had no idea until it was too late.

Gringo Loco indeed.

Have you ever felt the same way? In your career in sales and business development, have you ever presented your best "ingredients," showed your best "skills," and delivered a value proposition that was perfect in every way, but it fell completely flat anyway?

Maybe it was a sales presentation.

Maybe it was an important networking conversation over lunch.

Or maybe you were trying to get that golden prospect over the line.

Whatever the situation, there is a disconnect between our efforts and the results that we want. We may spin our wheels to showcase our value and why it matters, but the prospect still walks out. And you scratch your head wondering why...

One reason? Just like my failed fiesta, we get in our own way (and have no idea).

Why "Higher Value" Does Not Equal "Higher Success"

I work with people and organizations who want to stand out and be the obvious choice.

I got my start about as far away from keynote speaking and consulting as you can get: in university admissions. As I read and reviewed thousands of applicants at the undergraduate level, and later as the associate director of an MBA program (as well as a recruiter in corporate HR), I realized I had a front-row seat in learning how people deal with one of the biggest challenges in life: How do you stand out when everyone else is trying to stand out too?

As I saw thousands of applications with good scores and impressive achievements, here's what I learned:

Most people believe that success happens when they prove they are of high value. And when you think about it, it makes sense.

- In school, if you know the material? You get good grades.
- In sports, if you play hard? You score points and win.
- In work, if you create results? You get paid.

"I work with people and organizations who want to stand out and be the obvious choice."

For years we are taught and trained in school and work that the higher your performance and value, the higher your reward and success. So when people want to succeed, they spin their wheels presenting how high their value is, all the while thinking, "THIS will open the doors of opportunity."

To be fair, this works *most* of the time.

But every so often we encounter situations like sales, networking opportunities (and even meeting your potential Danish in-laws)...where everything is on the line, and we desperately need things to work in our favor.

If we are successful? The doors of opportunity open for us.

If we fail? Back to the drawing board, and start over.

However, what most people don't understand is that in these "Selective Environments," the rules of success have fundamentally changed. Unlike school, sports, or work, success in these situations is not based on how high your value is. Instead, success is REALLY determined by whether people choose YOU over others.

The problem is, when we enter these Selective Environments, something terrible happens. We sense the game has changed but aren't sure why. And so we get nervous, go on auto-pilot, and revert to our song and dance of "look how great my value is."

We showcase our finest ingredients.

We demonstrate our skill and efficiency.

We present our solution that is *chef's kiss* good.

The problem is that everyone else you're being compared to ALSO has great ingredients, skills, and effort. And when you sound just like them, you don't stand out, and your opportunity walks out the door.

Despite these frustrating results, because we have never been taught anything different, we continue to spin our wheels to prove how smart, capable, qualified, and passionate we are, again and again...

Wash,

Rinse,

And repeat.

And yet we keep scratching our heads wondering why we aren't chosen.

To put it simply: We've been taught to behave one way when success demands we behave and communicate another way entirely.

Can you see how we've been trained to get in our own way?

❝We've been taught to behave one way when success demands we behave and communicate another way entirely.❞

Presentation vs Perception

On the other hand, throughout my career reviewing and interviewing thousands of people, I witnessed another group of people who positioned their ingredients, skills, and solutions in ways that influenced decision-makers to choose them.

What was their secret? How did they succeed?

While everyone else was concerned about *presenting their value,* these masterful communicators were *first* concerned about how people *perceived their value.*

True, they had comparable ingredients, skills, and solutions (just like everyone else). But the difference? They engaged in words and behaviors that were designed to influence perception, not merely present their value.

But how did they do this? More importantly, how can YOU communicate your value in a way that is designed to rise above the noise, stand out from the crowd, and make you the obvious choice?

"While everyone else was concerned about *presenting their value*, these masterful communicators were *first* concerned about how people *perceived their value*."

It turns out the answer lies in the brain and how it processes information.

When your message is focused on proving you can perform (just like everyone else), and how smart, capable, qualified, and passionate you are (also, just like everyone else), your message becomes noise.

And the brain is designed to ignore noise.

However, the brain is also wired to pay attention to certain things. And with a little help from the basic principles of neuroscience, you can learn the fundamentals of how to present your value in ways that are designed to bypass the brain's defenses, influence perceptions, and stand out every single time.

Just Like Homemade Salsa

"But wait a second," I hear you say, "I AM just like everyone else. I do the same thing as them, I offer the same service...and I'm not sure what makes me different."

Or, "I know what I'm doing," you might add, "but I'm not sure where to start or how to give my message a more competitive edge."

Even if you aren't sure what your message is, or even if you don't know where to start...this book is for you. That's because, as I read and interviewed thousands of applications and witnessed how master communicators influenced and persuaded groups of people, I discovered that influential communication is NOT a gift reserved for people who are "born that way."

No, after years of studying thousands and thousands of successful communicators, I've found that the ability to influence how people perceive you is a skill that anyone can learn, practice, and improve.

Just like making homemade salsa.

In my first bestselling and LinkedIn Top-Ten ranked book, *The Influence Mindset: The Art & Science of Getting People to Choose You*, I wrote specifically about building a core personal brand narrative that stands out from the crowd. This message strongly resonated with students applying to colleges, career seekers trying to get chosen, and business owners developing their core brand strategy. However, I had many sales and business development professionals (as well as companies) approach me for additional insights on how "The Influence Mindset" could help them appeal to more prospects and stand out from their competition.

Though the book certainly helped, they said, they wanted something more targeted for influence within the context of sales. Which is what we are going to do together in this book.

Relying on firsthand experiences, stories, and (approachable!) neuroscience research, we will learn 7 Emotional Intelligence (EQ) hacks that you can use anywhere, at any time, to bridge the Value/Perception Gap and influence how people perceive you... especially in the context of sales and business development.

Together we are going to break down the fundamental challenges we face and equip you (step by step) with the tools and perspectives you need to position yourself for success. Plus, because this topic is so important and everyone learns differently, at the end of each chapter, I also provide access to extensive bonus material to help you learn the secrets of personal influence and refine your message. There you can get access to training, resources, and additional advanced content not found in the book. Best of all, access to the site is 100% free. Simply go to **(www. TheChristianHansen.com/BookBonus)** to get started!

Imagine What It Would Be Like

Despite my fiesta fiasco, my soon-to-be Danish in-laws realized my plane ticket home wasn't for another week. For the time being, they were stuck with me and gave me a second chance. Their patience and kindness allowed me to try again. This time, however, I focused less on being impressive and instead became a student of connecting on their terms. They graciously welcomed me into their family, and later Nathalie and I married.

However, in the marketplace, second chances to be chosen are rare. Your prospect is faced with an abundance of opportunities to choose from, and their precious time is limited. As the saying goes, "You don't get a second chance at a first impression."

That's because at the end of the day, your words and behaviors either influence people to say "yes" or they don't. They either

"Second chances to be chosen are rare."

persuade people to choose you or they don't. In today's increasingly competitive world, it's time to realize that merely communicating your value is not working. Your success rises or falls on your ability to change your words and behaviors, influence people's perceptions, and get them to choose you. Your influential power is more critical than ever before.

But imagine what it would be like to know you were positioned and prepared to capitalize on the first chance…every time?

Imagine what it would be like to enter a "make it or break it" moment and feel assured that your personal message was engineered to generate results.

More importantly, imagine if you could stand out from the "sameness" of the crowd, capitalize on the opportunities before you, and be seen as the obvious choice.

The truth is, you can!

Welcome to The Influence Mindset: For Sales Acceleration.

Introduction: Key Takeaways

- **Perception is Everything:** There is a gap between your value and how it is perceived. People choose or reject their perception of you, not your actual value. Your message bridges this gap—or it doesn't.

- **Why Messages Fail:** We've been taught to communicate our value, not communicate in ways that influence perception. We sound just like everyone else, our message is noise, and we miss critical opportunities.

- **Influence Can Be Learned:** Crafting an influential message and persuading others to see you as more valuable is a skill anyone can master.

- **Your Opportunity Awaits:** By understanding and applying these strategies, you can consistently position yourself as the obvious choice.

Bonus:

I've created exclusive content to help you apply the principles we cover together in this book. To access them, go to:
www.TheChristianHansen.com/BookBonus

SUMMARY TABLE

(Note: This will be filled in as the book continues. Each "?" represents a key point we will cover.)

?	?	?	?
?	?	?	?
?	?	?	?
?	?	?	?
?	?	?	?
?	?	?	?
?	?		?
?	?	?	?
?	?	?	?
?	?	?	?
?	?	?	?
?	?	?	?
?	?	?	?
?	?	?	?

SECTION 1:

THE FORMULA
FOR INFLUENCE

Bridging the Value/Perception Gap

"We cannot pull people to our side, but we can make
it easier for them to cross."

— Unknown

In the 20th century, as automobile travel became more affordable and popular in Europe, people no longer had to wait on slow and time-consuming trains to get from one place to another. Instead, they could just hop in their car and travel on their own schedule. However, the spread of modernization met some roadblocks in villages where centuries-old thoroughfares had to be widened and paved to become modern roadways.

One of the places that struggled the most was the city of Millau, France. Located in the picturesque Tarn Valley, guarded by steep hills and nurtured by the wandering Tarn river, you would think the quaint medieval city came right out of a fairytale.

Except for one problem: Millau was smack-dab in the middle of the most direct route between Paris and Spain, and every summer, it was clogged with vacationers trying to pass through. Because the streets were ancient, narrow, and crooked, the village couldn't handle the crowds, and the townspeople dreaded the annual onslaught. As for the tourists, the feeling was mutual. It took an enormous amount of time to pass through, they found the traffic jams stressful, and many gave up... avoiding the city entirely.

In the words of architect Norman Foster, Millau was "a valley of extreme beauty which had become one of France's worst bottlenecks." [1] But with no other efficient way to cross the valley, what to do?

That's when someone proposed the idea of a bridge. If people could bypass the city via a convenient overpass, the town would be protected, they said, and tourists would get to where they wanted to go faster. However, most people rejected this idea out of hand because it was simply too hard.

First problem was the distance. The valley was over a mile and a half wide. Such a bridge would have to be roughly the same length as the Golden Gate Bridge in San Francisco. [2]

Next, there was the wind. The tall hills surrounding the valley created a natural funnel that routinely recorded extremely high wind speeds. [3]

And then there was the height! The valley plunged several hundred meters to the Tarn river below, and engineers estimated that such a structure would have to be taller than the Eiffel Tower!

How absurd, the villagers thought. In our little valley? And who would pay for such a thing?

But in 1999, once the French Government's Ministry of Public Works agreed to help with the financing, calls for proposals were sent out, and Eiffage, a French civil engineering company (most famous for the recent completion of the Channel Tunnel between England and France in 1994) was soon granted the winning bid. [1]

How were they going to build a bridge...higher than the Eiffel Tower...and as long as the Golden Gate Bridge? The answer? A technique called "bridge launching," where the bridge is simultaneously built from opposing sides and gradually joined in the middle. And so, in October of 2001, the engineers got to work.

First were the pylons. The 7 massive supporting columns crisscrossing the width of the expanse quickly rose from the ground and towered hundreds of feet above the city. Next was the bridge itself. Two construction sites were created on the highest points of the opposing sides of the valley, and the bridge was slowly built, piece by piece. Then, each pre-built section was carefully inched out over the expanse, anchored to the nearest pylon, and leapfrogged over to the next one. [3, 4]

And so, the villagers and vacationers alike watched expectantly from below as the two sides of the bridge…like two ¾-mile-long extended arms reaching for each other mid-air…slowly stretched their way across, pylon by pylon. Then, in June of 2004, the two halves finally joined in the middle. As a credit to the impressive engineering, when the two sides of the bridge met (hundreds of meters above the ground), they were only a few centimeters off-center.

The sections were joined, and in December of 2004, the Millau Viaduct—floating over the Tarn valley like a cloud—officially opened as the tallest bridge (and one of the most beautiful) in the world. Today, an estimated 10,000–25,000 cars pass over the village daily, and the villagers of Millau take immense pride in the elegantly designed engineering marvel gracing their valley.

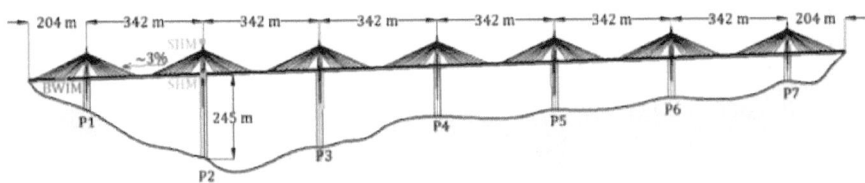

Fig. 1. Scheme of the Millau Viaduct.

Diagram of the Millau Viaduct, Nesterova et al. 2019

The Perception Gap

Just like the Tarn Valley, you face an enormous gap between you and your prospects. From your perspective, you may have the best solution, product, and service. But from the prospect's side of the valley, you are far away, and there are a lot of obstacles to overcome in order for them to understand your value. You are just one option out of many.

I call this the Perception Gap: the gap between your value and how it is perceived.

THE PERCEPTION GAP:

The gap between your value and how it is perceived.

If you get them to cross it? They mentally and emotionally engage with your value, see you as the obvious choice, and your chances of being chosen are significantly higher.

If they don't cross it? They drive on, looking for another way to get where they want to go, pass you up, and you miss a critical opportunity.

Just like the Tarn Valley, your prospect COULD make the drive down, get stuck in traffic, somehow cross the river, and struggle up your side of the hill. They COULD wade through the fine print of your offer, research all the extensive features listed on your website, and meticulously weigh the pros and cons of your merits.

But such an endeavor is enormously costly, energy wasting, and mind-numbing. Ain't nobody got time for that! And so they turn around to look for an option that is easier to understand.

How do you get them to cross the gap? How do you get them to come to your side and perceive you not just as an option but as the obvious choice?

You have to build *a bridge*. However, your bridge has to be constructed with materials of even greater strength and power than steel and concrete. Your bridge of influence must be made of words and behaviors.

"When it comes to influencing people to choose you, what worked back then isn't working now."

Think about it: The language and behaviors you use to position your value are the materials people use to build their perception of you. That means your words either create a more positive perception, or they don't. Your behaviors either invite them to focus on you, or they push your prospects away.

In other words, your words and behaviors either help them to "bridge" the Perception Gap, or they don't.

Which begs the question: Are your words and behaviors getting the results you want? Or, like the dusty tool bag in your garage, are your tools simply there because someone gave them to you?

So often I hear from sales professionals, "That's how I've seen it done."

"That's what so-and-so did."

"If it ain't broke, don't fix it."

If so...they've inherited a tool bag that needs to be examined and replaced. When it comes to influencing people to choose you, what worked back then isn't working now. In our world inundated with click bait, social media, and spam emails, influence has fundamentally

"The language and behaviors you use to position your value are the materials people use to build their perception of you."

changed. If you want the best results, you need the best materials, the best tools, and the best mindset possible.

It's time to give that old bag of tools an upgrade.

The Formula for Influence

So what does it take to build a bridge of words and behaviors that invite people to cross over to your side? Just like the engineers used "bridge launching," the technique of building from two opposing ends of the valley to meet in the middle, we are going to break down the process of building your bridge using this simple formula:

Competence + Connection = Influence

In order to influence people to choose you, you must demonstrate your competence AND create an emotional connection with your prospects.

Just like in Millau, where the bridge was built from both directions, it takes these two opposing (yet complementary) skill sets to build a bridge that influences people to perceive you as the obvious choice. The problem is, most sales professionals are naturally skilled at one of these, but rarely both.

What happens if you are great at establishing your competence but struggle to create connection?

What if you are great at creating connection but have a hard time showing your skills and abilities?

Or what if you're not sure how to do either?

By themselves, as we will soon discover, these skill sets lead to a bridge to nowhere. Prospects turn around and head in another direction.

Which is what we will cover over the next several chapters. We are going to lay the foundation so you can build your own bridge that influences people to perceive you as the obvious choice. Like the engineers, in Chapters 1 and 2 we are going to map out the bridge and first cover the pitfalls we must avoid. There we will dig into the behaviors that get in the way of effectively communicating your value. We will also explore the brain and understand how it is wired and what it is predisposed to pay attention to. Then, we will go over the mindset shifts you can use to increase your chances of success.

Once we have the foundation built and ready to go, in Sections 2 and 3 (Chapters 3–5 and 6–8 respectively), we will break down the strategies of each of the 7 supporting pylons of influence and build them from the ground up, step by step, with research-backed strategies proven to work.

Along the way, we are going to cover specific phrases and tactical tools you can use in any conversation...sales-focused conversations in particular. However, if you would like more resources and scripts on what to say and how to implement the ideas, I recommend you get the

"People need to buy INTO you before they will buy FROM you."

companion field guide *INFLUENCE: Phrases to Get People to Choose You* to help you make the most progress.

The Bridge From Option to Obvious Choice

I frequently tell audiences, "In a world where everyone has comparable skills and abilities, he or she that presents and connects the best...wins." And nowhere else does this apply better than in sales and business development.

People need to buy INTO you before they will buy FROM you. Your personal brand and ability to connect with others has never been more crucial for success than now. Your prospects are looking for solutions. They have problems they need resolved. But in a sea of options, it's hard to pick the best opportunity.

And guess what? Even though everyone else you are being compared to may offer similar value, their bridges that present that value are poorly built or are incomplete. That's because many of your competitors don't understand this fundamental truth: Perception drives behavior. And before you influence people's behaviors in your favor, you must FIRST influence their perceptions.

Which is where you come in.

If you can present and connect with people better than others? You increase your chances.

If you can showcase your value with words and behaviors that are easier to understand? You are more likely to be chosen.

If you can help your prospects bridge the Perception Gap quicker and easier than your competition? You will no longer be just an option. You will be...

...the obvious choice.

Let's start building!

"Perception drives behavior. And before you influence people's behaviors in your favor, you must FIRST influence their perceptions."

Section 1: Key Takeaways

- **The Perception Gap Defined:** The space between your value and how it's perceived by your audience. Your success depends on bridging this gap.

- **Option vs Obvious Choice:** Most people communicate in ways that make them just an option. You want to be seen as the obvious choice.

- **Building the Bridge:** Like the Millau Viaduct, your language and behaviors provide the tools and materials people use to create their perception of you. Are they working?

- **Competence vs Connection:** When communicating your message, the two different skill sets of establishing your competence and creating connection are both essential. Together, they create influence and make you seem like the obvious choice.

Bonus

I've created exclusive content to help you apply the principles we cover together. To access them, go to: **www.TheChristianHansen.com/ BookBonus**

SUMMARY TABLE

INFLUENCE FORMULA:	Competence	(Plus) Connection	(Equals) Influence
?	?	?	?
?	?	?	?
?	?	?	?
?	?	?	?
?	?	?	?
?	?		?
?	?	?	?
?	?	?	?
?	?	?	?
?	?	?	?
?	?	?	?
?	?	?	?
?	?	?	?
?	?		?

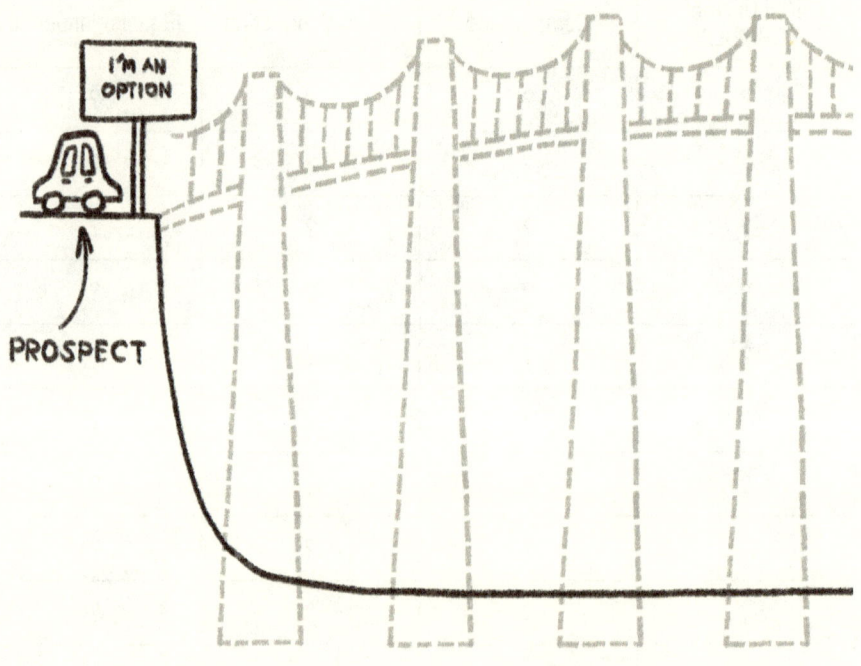

BRIDGE THE PERCEPTION GAP

I'M AN OPTION

PROSPECT

VALLEY OF

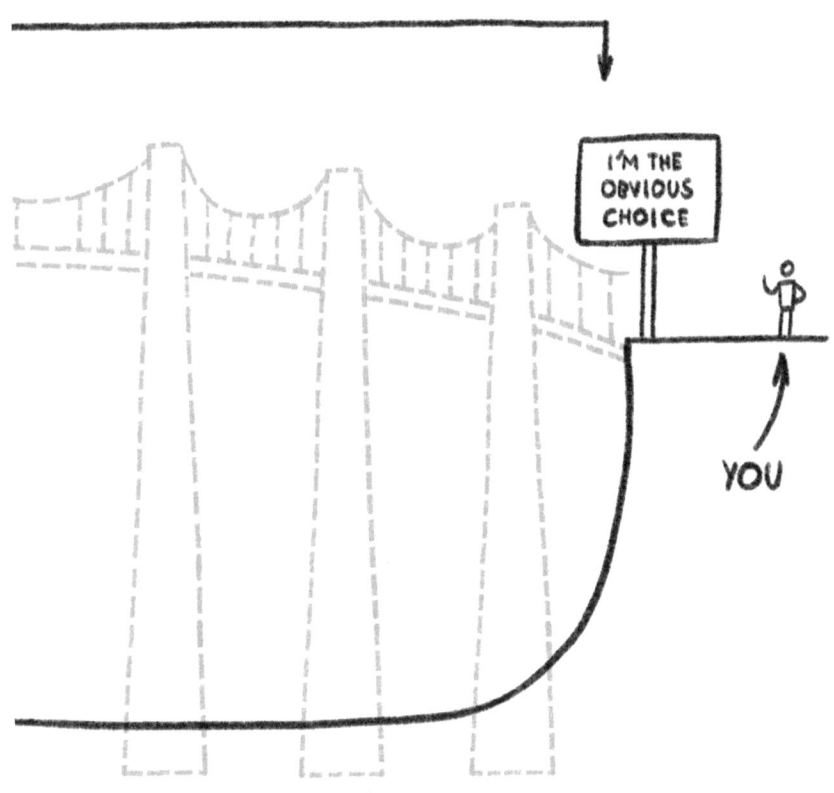

IRRELEVANCE

HOW TO BE IRRELEVANT

"The need to be impressive is the biggest thing stopping you from being influential."

— Leadership Principle

"**W**hy should I choose you?"

I was standing in a boardroom with an executive team sitting around a giant table. Their business had successfully expanded for several decades, but emerging competition from multiple companies was starting to threaten their market position. The leadership team wanted to stand out and grow their market share, and they had brought me in to help.

After letting the question sit for a moment, I asked it again. "If I am your prospective client, why should I choose you over everyone else?"

A director in the back of the room raised their hand and said, "Quality. Our products come from the highest-quality materials."

"Great, thank you," I said. I wrote the word "Quality" on the whiteboard and added a ✓ underneath it. "Alright," I continued, "Why else would you say I should choose your team over others?"

"Service," a team lead said from the right. "We provide the best service possible, and our customers love it."

I wrote the words "Customer Service" on the whiteboard and added a ✓ underneath it.

"Experience," someone chimed in, "we've been doing this for over 30 years, and there is no one better."

"Excellent," I said, writing the word "Experience" on the whiteboard and adding a ✓ underneath it. With the three words, "Quality, Experience, and Customer Service" written on the board, I looked at the group for more responses.

For several more minutes, leaders chimed in with what they would say, and after each comment, I added a ✓ under each corresponding column. Pretty soon, the people in the room were all adding what they felt made them unique, and by the end I had the following list:

Quality ✓✓✓✓✓
Experience ✓✓✓✓✓✓
Customer Service ✓✓✓✓✓

"That's a pretty good list!" I commented. "Do you feel like this represents why people should choose you? You have the highest quality, the most experience, and the best customer service?"

They all nodded.

"For a moment, let's imagine I was your ideal prospective customer." I continued, "I need help and have no idea who to choose between you and your competitors. So I ask around, search online, and compare your websites. If all I have to go on is the messaging I read online, let's see how your messaging sounds compared to your competitors..."

I pulled up their #1 competitor's site, and they all shifted uncomfortably in their seats. Blazoned across the top of their competitor's page it stated: "We have been providing the highest-quality products for over 30 years."

"Hold up," I said, "As a brand-new customer with no idea who to choose, if YOU say you have the highest-quality products and more experience, and your top competitor ALSO says the same thing, how can I decide?" I continued in a facetious tone, "Maybe they offer TERRIBLE customer service..."

I scrolled down further, and there, sure enough, were multiple messages touting Competitor #1's amazing customer service.

"Well, it looks like they offer good service. Who would have thought your competitors were kind humans and wanted their customers to have a good experience too?"

The group chuckled. I then pointed to our list on the board.

"Quality? Check.

"Experience? Check.

"Customer service? Check.

"You both sound exactly the same. But I still don't know who to choose. Let's take a look at your Competitor #2. Maybe they are different."

I pulled up the site of their second competitor, went through the same exercise, and as I suspected, the messaging was almost identical.

"Competitor #2: Quality? Check.

"Experience? Check.

"Customer service? Check. Can you see how you sound exactly the same as your competition? Which brings me back to the original question: 'If you sound just like everyone else, why should I choose you?'"

Now I had their attention.

The Performance Environment

How come BOTH the company I was training AND their competitors all engaged in the same kind of messaging behavior? As I mentioned in the introduction, one reason is because we've all been trained to.

Every day of our lives, we live and work in a world that values and rewards performance.

This is not, by any means, a revolutionary idea.

If you work hard in school? You get an A.

If you complete your tasks at work? You get paid.

If you provide excellent goods and services in a business? Customers return.

We have built a world where success is based on how well you perform. And if you perform well, more and more opportunities are opened to you.

Like I said, this is not rocket science.

Whenever we find ourselves in a situation where performance determines our opportunities, we are in what I call the Performance Environment, where success is based on how well you perform.

THE PERFORMANCE ENVIRONMENT:

Where success is based on how well you perform.

If we live in a world where success is based on how well we perform, we quickly learn how to prove to others that we can perform well. In my first book, I outlined how, on an individual level, we learn to show others that we are smart, capable, qualified, and passionate.[1] However, in sales and business development, people tend to focus on highlighting "Quality," "Experience," and "Service" to their prospects. This is what

I call the Achievement Mindset: The belief that success happens when I prove my value is high.

THE ACHIEVEMENT MINDSET:

Success happens when I prove my value is high.

In the Performance Environment, the Achievement Mindset makes sense. If you know the material, you get good grades. If you deliver results, you get promoted. If your sales numbers are higher, you get the bonus. Hence, we become quite effective and accustomed to proving we are smart, capable, qualified, and passionate and offer quality, experience, and great service.

Which is what happened to this executive team. Can you see how their answers all fell within the Achievement Mindset?

Quality ✓✓✓✓✓
Experience ✓✓✓✓✓✓
Customer Service ✓✓✓✓✓✓

The problem these executives didn't realize is that their competition ALSO had quality, experience, and great customer service, and they sounded just like everyone else.

Their message came across as noise.

That's because if:

Competence + Connection = Influence

Then,

Competence (without Connection) = Noise

"Their competition ALSO had quality, experience, and great customer service, and they sounded just like everyone else."

Because your REAL competitors are ALSO competent. They ALSO have great ingredients, skill, and effort and great quality, experience, and customer service.

When you speak in Achievement Mindset language, your message is noise, and noise is ignored. If you are trying to build a bridge that invites people to come to your side, then the Achievement Mindset ONLY focuses on the FIRST HALF of the bridge that invites people to come and engage. They begin to cross it, but seeing that it's unfinished, realize it sounds like everyone else and turn around.

So what about the other side of the equation, connection? What happens to people who focus mostly on creating connection and fail to establish their competence?

Gutted Over Gutters

A few years ago I was at a local expo wanting to support businesses in my community. As I walked through rows of booths, I came across a representative for a rain-gutter company. You know, as in rain gutters for roofs—the practical stuff most homeowners eventually deal with. The more I thought about it, I realized I actually had some issues with my gutters at home and figured I'd stop by and ask a few questions. Maybe this company could help?

The rep greeted me with a friendly smile, and we started chatting. She asked, "Do you need help with your gutters?" I said, "Actually, yes, I do." So far so good, right? But instead of diving into how her company could solve my problem, she veered in a completely different direction.

She started asking about me—where I was from, my hobbies, and so on. I didn't think much of it at first; after all, a little rapport-building isn't unusual. I answered politely, even cracked a few jokes (that's my default when I feel a little awkward). She laughed and said, "Wow, you're pretty witty!"

I wasn't sure where this was going, but I said, "Well, thanks." Then, out of nowhere, she asked, "Did you do theater in high school?"

I was caught off guard. "Uh, yeah, I actually did," I replied.

"What plays were you in?" she asked eagerly. I rattled off a few, and suddenly she lit up and started listing her own high school theater experiences from years before.

Before I knew it, we were no longer talking about gutters, the problem I needed help with. Instead, we were comparing high school theater productions! What on earth was happening?

At this point, I tried steering the conversation back to my gutters. I asked a couple of specific questions about their services, pricing, and options. But instead of giving me details, she deflected and kept the conversation at the surface level. It quickly became clear she didn't have the answers nor the expertise I needed. Her goal wasn't to solve my problem. Her goal was to get my contact information and set up an appointment with someone else.

And if I was going to solve my problem, I would have to spend more of my time talking to an expert to see if this option was the right opportunity for me. I left the conversation frustrated and confused. My problem wasn't any closer to being resolved, and I felt like my time had been wasted on shallow rapport and surface-level banter.

What had happened? How come this sales rep, for all her social skills, completely lost my interest? Just like the executives in my boardroom training, she thought she was operating in a specific environment. However, instead of the Performance Environment, she thought she was in the OTHER most common environment we find ourselves in... the Relational Environment.

The Relational Environment

Relationships and belonging in social groups is a fundamental part of being human. As we will soon cover, our ability to build and maintain relationships is a core part of our brain's evolution AND fundamental architecture. Accordingly, so much of our lives occur in what I call Relational Environments. For our discussion, I define Relational Environments as places where success is based on how well you connect and work with others.

THE PERFORMANCE ENVIRONMENT:	THE RELATIONAL ENVIRONMENT:
Where success is based on how well you perform.	*Where success is based on how well you connect and work with others.*

Think about friendships, family gatherings, or even casual conversations at a party. In these environments, relationships are the currency. Success isn't measured by how much you know or what you can do—it's about how you make people feel and how well you connect with them. We rely on shared experiences, mutual interests, and emotional bonds to navigate these spaces.

In the Relational Environment, trust and connection are built through empathy, attentiveness, and the ability to relate to others on a personal level. It's where small talk thrives, where inside jokes are formed, and where we build social capital. Whether we're finding common ground, sharing personal stories, or simply making someone laugh, the goal is to strengthen the relationship—not necessarily to solve a problem or make a decision.

Because so much of our lives revolve around Relational Environments, we naturally develop strategies to succeed in them. These instincts often center around creating likability and belonging. I call this mindset the Charismatic Mindset, where success happens when you are likable, relatable, and win people over.

THE ACHIEVEMENT MINDSET:	THE CHARISMATIC MINDSET:
Success happens when I prove my value is high.	*Success happens when I am likable, relatable, and win people over.*

In Relational Environments, this mindset works. If you're meeting new friends or bonding with colleagues, charm and commonality can be incredibly effective [2]. They create a sense of familiarity, making others feel at ease and appreciated. And just like the Achievement Mindset in Performance Environments, through the course of our lives, we become very good at developing the Charismatic Mindset in our most important Relational Environments.

If you crack a joke? People laugh. If you share a relatable story? Heads nod in agreement. If you highlight common ground? Conversations flow easily, and they warm up to you.

Again, this isn't rocket science.

The problem is, in sales situations when you are trying to influence people to choose you over others? An overemphasis in the Charismatic Mindset falls short. Just like the sales rep at the business expo, focusing mostly on connection and failing to establish your credibility and competence can leave prospects feeling frustrated.

If

Competence + Connection = Influence

And,

Competence (without Connection) = Noise

Then,

Connection (without Competence) = Charm

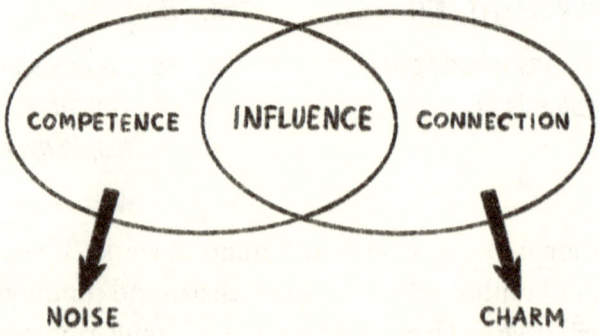

Which is exactly what happened at the business expo. She was charming, witty, fun, and engaging. She thought winning me over was a winning strategy. But what I needed wasn't a new theater buddy. I needed help with my gutters.

And her chances of being chosen...went down the drain. If only my gutters worked that well too...

In sales situations, connection isn't about charm or commonality—it's about trust [3]. Decision-makers don't need you to be their new best friend; they need you to guide them toward a solution [4]. The Charismatic Mindset might help you start the conversation, but without competence and value, it won't help you close the deal.

Have you ever encountered a similar situation? Have you ever met someone who was high on connection but low on competence and credibility? How did it make you feel? Like me, you probably felt that person was delightful and fun to talk to, but ultimately unable to fix what really mattered to you.

They were charming, but irrelevant. And just like I did, you probably walked away. Similar to the bridge in Millau, it takes BOTH sides (competence and connection) to meet in the middle to influence people. And if you ONLY lead with connection, or if you ONLY lead with competence, your prospects will be confused by charm and noise and get stuck in the Valley of Irrelevance.

And if something is irrelevant, why should they invest more energy to understand its value?

They turn around and go somewhere else.

Why Do We Do This?

How come we routinely fall victim to the Achievement Mindset OR the Charismatic Mindset? Like the executive team trying to stand out from the competition, why do we go WAY TOO HARD on competence? Or, like the rain-gutter rep trying to build rapport, why do we lean WAY TOO MUCH on connection?

The reason may surprise you. That's because before we can build your bridge in influencing others to choose you, we have one more critical component of the gap to understand.

How come we get in our own way?

How come we trip over ourselves?

Why do we make the same mistakes over and over again?

It turns out, *our brains are wired to.*

Chapter 1: Key Takeaways

- **The Performance Environment:** Most of the time in our professional lives, we live and work in Performance Environments where success is based on how well you perform.

- **The Achievement Mindset:** To adapt and succeed in these Performance Environments, we develop and perfect the Achievement Mindset where we believe success happens when we prove our value is high.

- **Competence (without Connection) = Noise:** However, when all we do is establish our competence through The Achievement Mindset in sales situations, our message is noise and ignored.

- **The Relational Environment:** In other parts of our life we operate in families, friend groups, and other situations where success is based on how well we connect and work with others.

- **The Charismatic Mindset:** In these situations we develop the Charismatic Mindset, which believes success happens when we are likable, relatable, and win people over.

- **Connection (without Competence) = Charm:** In sales, if all we do is create connection through The Charismatic Mindset, our message is "charm" and ignored.

Bonus

I've created exclusive content to help you apply the principles we cover together. To access them, go to: **www.TheChristianHansen.com/ BookBonus**

SUMMARY TABLE

INFLUENCE FORMULA:	Competence	(Plus) Connection	(Equals) Influence
ENVIRONMENT:	Performance Environment	Relational Environment	?
DEFINITION OF SUCCESS:	Where Success Is Based On How Well You Perform	Where Success Is Based On How Well You Connect & Work With Others	?
STRATEGY:	Achievement Mindset	Charismatic Mindset	?
DEFINITION OF STRATEGY:	Success Happens When I Prove My Value Is High	Success Happens When I Am Likable, Relatable, & Win People Over	?
IF INCOMPLETE?	Competence (Without) Connection = Noise	Connection (Without) Competence = Charm	Competence With Connection = Influence
?	?		?
?	?	?	?
?	?	?	?
?	?	?	?
?	?	?	?
?	?	?	?
?	?	?	?
?	?	?	?
?	?		?

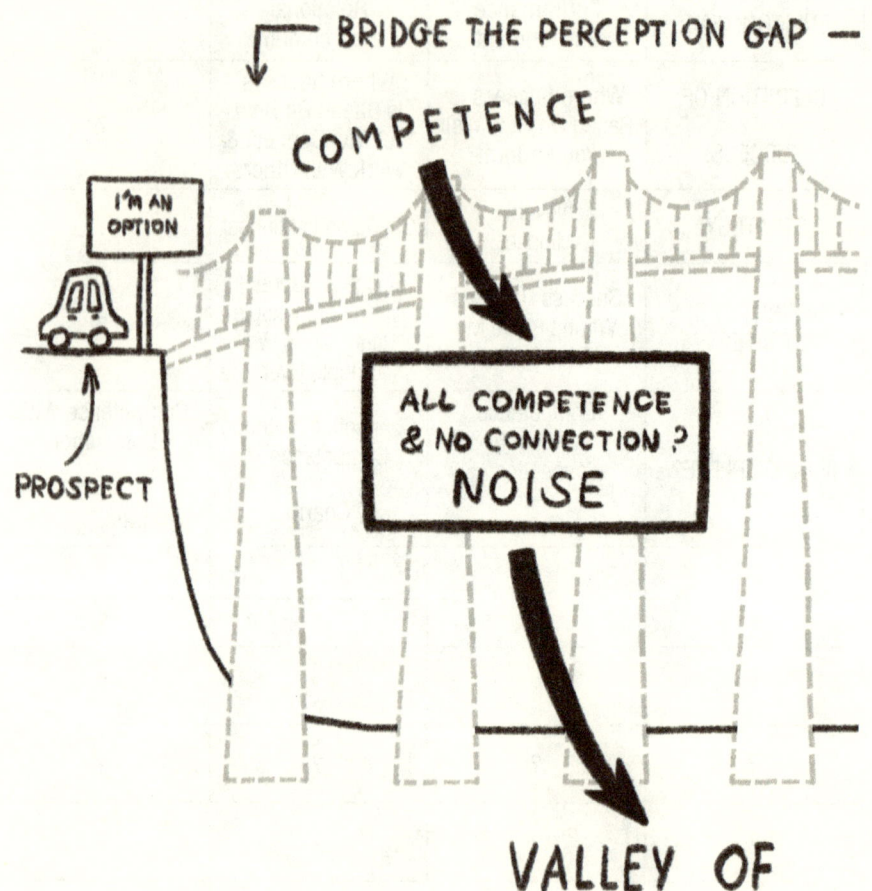

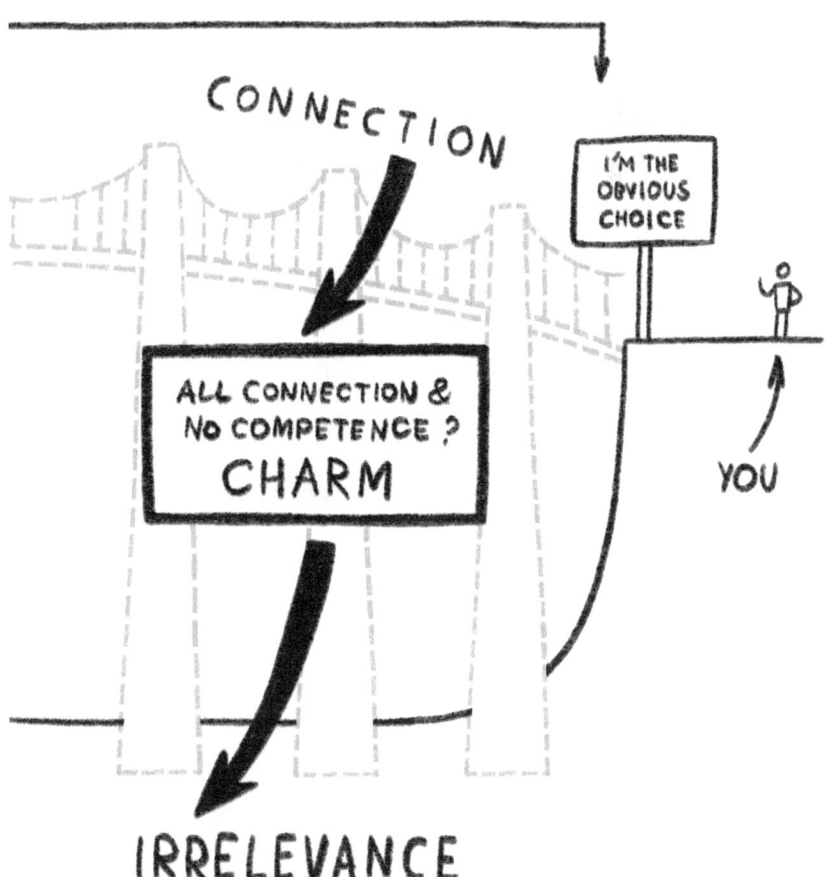

CHAPTER 2

HOW NOT TO CRASH
INTO THE POTOMAC

"No bird soars in a calm."

— **Wilbur Wright**

"Your brain is not designed to make you happy. It's designed
to help you survive."

— **Rick Hanson**

On October 7, 1903, Samuel P. Langley had a disaster on his hands.
Well, to be precise, his "disaster" was sinking in the Potomac river in
front of a huge crowd of onlookers.

All because...he didn't ask the right question.

Let's take a step back for a moment.

Born in Boston in 1834, Langley had been fixated with the sky since
a young age. Initially a gifted mathematician, he became a professor
of astronomy at the University of Pittsburgh and later founded THE
Smithsonian Astrophysical Observatory [1]. But as he gazed at the stars, his
mind became captivated by the more earth-bound question of human
flight.

After studying aeronautics, Langley's first major success came in 1896 when his homemade 25-pound glider flew 3,300 feet after being launched from a boat on the Potomac [2]. Later that year, his next model flew over 5,000 feet. His successes eventually caught the attention of the assistant secretary to the Navy...a young Theodore Roosevelt...who helped orchestrate a $50,000 grant (nearly $2 million today) to develop a full-scale piloted airplane [3].

After years of work and testing, Langley's "Aerodrome" was ready for its maiden launch, and on October 7, 1903, crowds gathered in Washington D.C. to witness history in the making. And who could have doubted it would be successful? He was one of the leading scientists of the time and had recently been appointed as head of the Smithsonian Institute.

Standing on a custom-built houseboat from which to launch the Aerodrome, Langley carefully made sure all the preparations were complete. After helping his test pilot get into position, the moment arrived. The lever was pulled, the Aerodrome picked up speed down the launch track, and finally catapulted free of the boat...only to nosedive right into the river and sink [4].

As onlookers and crew scrambled to rescue the test pilot from the wreckage (thankfully he was safe), Langley looked at his crumpled mass of wings, rope, and propellers and felt his world and reputation sink with it. Even though the craft was salvaged, it failed another flight test a few months later in December [5]. All the money, effort, and fame was gone. Langley's Aerodrome was a disaster.

If the head of the Smithsonian Institute and $50,000 of grant money from the US Government couldn't create human flight, then how on earth did the Wright brothers—two bicycle builders from Dayton, OH—do it for a combined total of less than $1,000 (out of pocket) [6], in Kitty Hawk, NC...nine days later?

One reason? The Wright brothers asked a different question.

While Langley and the rest of the world asked, "How can we create sustained flight?" the Wright brothers asked, "How can we create controlled flight?"

You see, the Wright brothers' genius was creating a control system that allowed a pilot to adapt to the changing circumstances of wind, speed, and power. [7] In fact, their official patent wasn't for a plane, but rather the system of wires and pulleys that enabled the "Wright Flyer" to roll, pitch, and turn to respond to any circumstance [8,9]. The Aerodrome, on the other hand, was only designed to go in one direction, and it couldn't turn or adjust.

In short...while everyone else was simply staying airborne and flying straight, the Wright brothers began by asking a different question. And the answers they found...changed the course of human history.

The Selective Environment

The Wright brothers succeeded because they understood that flight wasn't just about staying in the air—it was about navigating dynamic conditions with control and precision. Similarly, in sales and business development, success isn't just about showing off your skills or charm; it's about influencing decision-makers to choose you in an environment where options abound and the stakes are high.

People that understand this fundamental distinction will beat those who don't every single time.

This unique environment is what I call the Selective Environment. Instead of success being based on how well you perform (the Performance Environment) or how well you connect with others (the Relational Environment), in the Selective Environment success is based on your ability to influence people's perceptions so that they choose you over others.

THE PERFORMANCE ENVIRONMENT:	THE RELATIONAL ENVIRONMENT:	THE SELECTIVE ENVIRONMENT:
Where success is based on how well you perform.	*Where success is based on how well you connect and work with others.*	*Where success is based on influencing people to choose you.*

The problem is, most of the time we are unaware that the game has changed, and so too have the rules of success. We may THINK we are in a Performance Environment and do the song and dance of the Achievement Mindset (and sound just like everyone else). Or, we may THINK we are in a Relational Environment and proceed to mistakenly use the Charismatic Mindset (and convey empty charm).

In either case, our plane takes off with high hopes, only to encounter unexpected wind and turbulence, struggles to adjust, and crashes...and like Langley, we have no idea why. Some people may look around and think their value isn't high enough. Others may think, "It's because people just don't like me." In either case, they are both wrong.

They don't understand that they are in a completely new environment, and they don't know how to change their strategies. Just as flight isn't about simply staying aloft, but rather changing course and adapting in a controlled and intentional way, similarly, in sales and business development situations, the rules of the Selective Environment demand a different approach.

- Like my fiesta fiasco, I needed to first influence the Vikings to see me as the best opportunity for my girlfriend (now wife).
- Just like the Millau Viaduct, we must persuade people to cross our bridge to see us not as an option but as the obvious choice.
- Like the executives and the rain-gutter rep, they needed to influence prospects to choose them over everyone else.

To succeed in the Selective Environment, we need to learn how to develop what I call the Influence Mindset: Success happens when you influence someone to choose you over others.

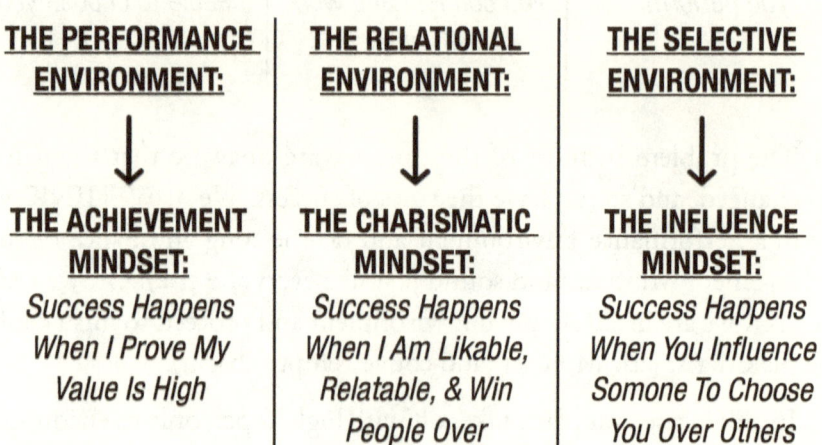

THE PERFORMANCE ENVIRONMENT:	THE RELATIONAL ENVIRONMENT:	THE SELECTIVE ENVIRONMENT:
↓	↓	↓
THE ACHIEVEMENT MINDSET:	THE CHARISMATIC MINDSET:	THE INFLUENCE MINDSET:
Success Happens When I Prove My Value Is High	*Success Happens When I Am Likable, Relatable, & Win People Over*	*Success Happens When You Influence Somone To Choose You Over Others*

However, before we spend the rest of the book digging into the mindsets, words, and behaviors of how to influence people to choose you, we need to understand one final principle. There is a root cause behind why we ultimately get in our own way and frequently fall victim to the twin pitfalls of BOTH the Achievement and Charismatic Mindsets.

If you want to have any hope of ultimately influencing people to choose you, we need to dig deeper and understand the true source of all of these behaviors: our brain.

Your Brain is Like the Aerodrome

Just like Langley's Aerodrome was designed to simply stay aloft through powered flight, your brain is designed to do one job and one job only: keep you alive. Our "Aerodrome Brain" defines success by whether or not we survive, and over the course of millions of years, it has become really good at paying attention to things that help it survive and ignoring things that don't.

The problem is, in our modern world? Success isn't simply about survival. Saber-toothed tigers are gone, and we don't have to be worried about being flattened by a wooly mammoth. Rather, success today (and especially in sales) is defined by whether or not we stand out, are the obvious choice, and are chosen. If our brain is focused on survival, and our conscious mind is focused on "success," can you see how there is conflict between what we want and what our brain wants?

To navigate sales situations better and avoid the pitfalls of the Achievement and Charismatic Mindsets, we need to first understand more about the brain and what it is hardwired to pay attention to. Only then can we use this programming to our advantage when influencing people to see us as the obvious choice.

To start, let's buckle in to take a brief field trip through time and see why this matters.

The Part Where I Condense 4 Billion Years of Neuro-Evolution into a Few Paragraphs

Your brain has had billions of years to figure out how to survive on this planet. [10]

As evolution progressed from one species to another, and as life on earth increased in size and complexity, the brain gradually learned what worked and what didn't. Over time, it adapted and developed to take advantage of the opportunities presented. However, just like Langley's Aerodrome defined "sustained flight" as success, for much of the history of our brain's development, the definition of success was: **consume calories** and **stay safe**[11, 12]. And so, as we evolved from single-celled organisms to backbones, from fish to amphibians, and then onwards to 4-legged animals living on land, our brains became more and more sophisticated in how we **consumed calories** and **stayed safe**.

"We need to first understand more about the brain and what it is hardwired to pay attention to."

Early on, it added a new strategy for survival: seeking novelty. As our habitable world became more and more complex, it was important to explore and seek out NEW ways to obtain food and stay safe. Those that adapted found new opportunities, competed better, and survived. Those that didn't? Failed and died out. Hence, in addition to the proven strategies of **consuming calories** and **staying safe**, the brain now became wired to explore and pay attention to **novelty** [13, 14].

Then, about 300 million years ago, the next major development occurred: Mammals. Instead of leaving offspring in eggs ready to fend for themselves at birth, Mammals instead nurtured their young with milk and formed emotional bonds [15, 16]. Our hardy little ancestors went on to increasingly live in groups and depended on each other. And so, with the advent and evolution of mammals, the brain added a new strategy to its arsenal for survival. In addition to **consuming calories**, **staying safe**, and **seeking novelty,** our brains now focused on **living and surviving in groups** [17].

But wait! It gets better!

As our intrepid ancestors headed for the safety of the treetops, grew opposable thumbs, and became primates, their strategies for survival likewise became more sophisticated. Living and thriving in groups evolved into social hierarchies, cooperation, and even forms of proto communication and language [18]. Now, in addition to the proven strategies of **consuming calories, staying safe, seeking novelty,** and **living in groups,** our brains took an evolutionary leap that changed everything. It began finding ways to assert *status* within these groups [19].

Increased status in a social hierarchy meant increased security, resources, belonging, and access to new things. And so our brain adapted to deal with the incredibly complex world of relationships, language, and intricate societies. To handle this new unprecedented cognitive processing load, about 50 million years ago, evolution started investing in a relatively new part of the brain, the prefrontal cortex [20].

Previously in earlier mammals, the prefrontal cortex supported basic problem-solving and rudimentary social behaviors. However, when the apes swung into existence and began building hierarchical social groups, the prefrontal cortex began significantly expanding in size. Over time, as our primate ancestors increased their levels of intelligence, social behaviors, and proto tool use, the prefrontal cortex increased in size and computing power.

However, it wasn't until the introduction of homo sapiens about 100,000–200,000 years ago that the prefrontal cortex changed everything: It made the greatest leap in computational brain power the world had ever seen.

Survival Brain vs Executive Brain

Located right above your eyes and behind your forehead, today the prefrontal cortex (or PFC) is a grapefruit-sized part of your brain that is responsible for everything that has separated us from our primate relatives. As it grew in size and power, we harnessed fire, created language, art, music, and sent spaceships to the moon. If it had stayed the same? We'd still be peeling bananas and sniffing each other.

Ok, we do that too, but you get my point.

Compared to other primates, humans have a disproportionately large prefrontal cortex. In primates, the PFC takes up an average of 8–12% of total brain mass. In humans? That ratio increases to roughly 17–20% [21]. Research has shown that the PFC is closely tied to our capacity for complex cognitive tasks, emotional regulation, and social interaction—essentially, all the functions that make us uniquely human [22]. As we built increasingly complex societies, our brains adapted, evolved, and expanded along the way.

All this creates an intriguing dilemma.

On the one hand, most of our brain mass is dedicated to fundamental survival functions—securing resources, avoiding threats, and maintaining social bonds. On the other hand, our expanded shiny new piece of cranial kit (the PFC) provides us with unparalleled cognitive abilities, enabling abstract thought, strategic planning, and creativity. This evolutionary tradeoff has made us the most intelligent species in the known universe, yet it also creates constant tension between our primal instincts and our higher reasoning [23, 24].

This is, of course, a gross oversimplification, but for the sake of our discussion, let's divide these functions into the Survival Brain and the Executive Brain. One governs instinctual survival and bodily systems, while the other manages executive functions, abstract thought, and complex decision-making. One favors predictable safety and avoidance of stress, while the other is capable of navigating uncertainty, relationships, and creative problem-solving.

THE SURVIVAL BRAIN:

Survival and bodily functions.

THE EXECUTIVE BRAIN:

Executive functions, abstract thought, and strategic planning.

That is, if it remains in control.

Which raises the question: Between our Survival Brain and our Executive Brain, which one is in charge most of the time? Well, it depends.

When we are rested, fed, not stressed out, and going about our normal day, our Executive Brain and the prefrontal cortex remain in control and we are civilized humans. But the moment we are stressed? Tired? Hungry? Worried? The Survival Brain kicks in, overrides rational thought, takes control, and ensures we live another day. As neuroscience researcher Brian Stetka put it, "Our instincts pull from brain centers both primitive and novel [*ie: newly developed*]; our decisions are divided between animal reactivity and human reason. Despite having far more self control than most species, our primitive brain often wins." [25] (emphasis added).

Like me, and every other human on the planet, you've probably experienced this.

Think about it: Have you ever been in a stressful situation and suddenly your mind went blank? Or maybe you had an important sales opportunity where everything was on the line and all your preparation went out the window? Even worse, you reverted to the Achievement and Charismatic Mindsets (and sounded like everyone else).

In these moments, what happened?

You probably guessed it: Your ancient Survival Brain sensed stress, assumed a saber-toothed tiger was pouncing, and triggered the fight or flight response to stay safe. Physiologically, your Survival Brain decreased energy from the higher thinking abilities of your Executive Brain (prefrontal cortex) and redirected it to the more primal and action-centered areas of your brain. And thus, your words, thoughts, and strategic preparation went out the window [26].

So, even though you have a sophisticated "control system" (like the Wright brothers) that enables you to roll, pitch, and turn to innovate, and navigate situations and relationships with confidence and ease, it is often held hostage by your "Aerodrome" Survival Brain, which has a very different set of goals.

What to do? In these moments, can the Executive Brain regain control? Yes...but only with great practice and effort, which we will cover shortly. But the key takeaway here is: You have two parts of your brain that are in constant struggle with each other.

Even more importantly, so does everyone else you want to influence.

What THEIR Brain Wants

Here's why all this matters: If YOUR brain has been designed by billions of years of evolution to seek out its own survival by paying attention to:

- **Security**
- **Resources**
- **Novelty**
- **Belonging**
- **and Status...**

Then...NEWS FLASH!...this means the people you are trying to influence are ALSO hardwired to pay attention and seek those exact same things. If YOUR brain is in a tug-of-war between reactivity and reason, then THEIR brains are likewise engaged in the exact same struggle.

"If YOUR brain is in a tug-of-war between reactivity and reason, then THEIR brains are likewise engaged in the exact same struggle."

The problem? Often in sales situations, our Survival Brain kicks in and we let OUR needs for security, resources, novelty, belonging and status get in the way of our PROSPECT'S NEEDS for the same things. And if you aren't appealing to the things THEIR brain is wired to pay attention to, you are not perceived as an opportunity, but rather as noise.

Which is why we so often speak in both the Achievement and Charismatic Mindsets. Let's take a moment to break them down:

The **Achievement Mindset** feels like a lifeline to our brain's core needs.

- It appeals to our **security** by creating predictability—when we perform well, we feel like we're in control of the outcomes.
- It promises **resources**, like recognition, money, or opportunities, as a reward for hard work.

- It scratches the itch for **status** by signaling competence and value to others, and it even touches on **belonging** by earning admiration from those who respect achievement.

Simply put, the **Achievement Mindset** makes US feel safe, accomplished, and seen.

Similarly, the **Charismatic Mindset:**

- Plays to our need for **belonging** by focusing on emotional connection—when people like us, we feel accepted and secure.
- Ties into **security**, because social acceptance makes us feel safer in relationships.

"If you aren't appealing to the things THEIR brain is wired to pay attention to, you are not perceived as an opportunity, but rather as noise."

- Fuels our need for **status** by positioning us as likable and relatable, the type of person others look up to or admire.

- Adds a layer of **novelty**, through humor, engaging conversations, and shared experiences that stand out.

But here's the rub: Both mindsets are all about meeting **YOUR** brain's needs, not your prospect's. Can you see how communicating in Achievement and Charismatic Mindset language is really ONLY appealing to YOUR "Aerodrome Brain's" core needs?

Can you see how we are getting in our own way?

All the while, your prospect's ancient Survival Brain continues to drive along searching for solutions elsewhere.

And they pass you by.

THE ACHIEVEMENT MINDSET:	THE CHARISMATIC MINDSET:	THE INFLUENCE MINDSET:

THE SURVIVAL BRAIN:	THE EXECUTIVE BRAIN:
Success = When I meet MY brain's needs for security, resources, novelty, belonging, & status...	*Success = When I meet THEIR brain's needs for security, resources, novelty, belonging, & status...*

Just Like the Wright Brothers

But it doesn't have to be that way. Just like the Wright brothers knew that success was not about staying aloft but rather about controlled flight, in these situations when your immature Survival Brain is raging and fighting for control, it's time to give the reins back to the responsible adult in the room: your Executive Brain.

Just like the Wright brothers' era-defining patent was not a plane but their groundbreaking control system for enabling a pilot to navigate in difficult circumstances, it's time to give the prefrontal cortex control and navigate difficult Selective Environments with confidence and ease.

It's time to stop being controlled by the Aerodrome Brain and its outdated definitions of success for our modern world.

It's time to set your needs for survival to the side and instead intentionally focus on your prospect's needs.

It's time for the Influence Mindset.

Chapter 2: Key Takeaways

- **Sales Situations Are Not Performance Environments or Relational Environments.** Rather, we are in Selective Environments where success is based on influencing people to choose you.

- **To Influence People, We Must Understand That Our Brains Have Developed to Pay Attention to Specific Things.** Namely, security, resources, novelty, belonging, and status.

- **Sometimes We Let OUR Needs Get in The Way of THEIR Needs.** If your brain pays attention to these things, then your prospect's brain pays attention to them as well.

- **Your Survival Brain Can Sometimes Hijack Your Executive Brain** and revert to Achievement and Charismatic Mindset behaviors.

- **You Can Position Your Message and Value** in a way that appeals to their brain needs and influences people to perceive you as the obvious choice.

Bonus

I've created exclusive content to help you apply the principles we cover together. To access them, go to: **www.TheChristianHansen.com/ BookBonus**

SUMMARY TABLE

INFLUENCE FORMULA:	Competence	(Plus) Connection	(Equals) Influence
ENVIRONMENT:	Performance Environment	Relational Environment	Selective Environment
DEFINITION OF SUCCESS:	Where Success Is Based On How Well You Perform	Where Success Is Based On How Well You Connect & Work With Others	Where Success Is Based On Influencing People To Choose You
STRATEGY:	Achievement Mindset	Charismatic Mindset	Influence Mindset
DEFINITION OF STRATEGY:	Success Happens When I Prove My Value Is High	Success Happens When I Am Likable, Relatable, & Win People Over	Success Happens When You Influence Someone To Choose You Over Others
IF INCOMPLETE?	Competence (Without) Connection = Noise	Connection (Without) Competence = Charm	Competence With Connection = Influence
BRAIN'S DEFINITIONS OF SUCCESS:	SURVIVAL BRAIN Success = When I Meet My Brain's Needs For Security, Resources, Novelty, Belonging, & Status…		EXECUTIVE BRAIN Success = When I Meet Their Brain's Needs For Security, (etc.)
?	?	?	?
?	?	?	?
?	?	?	?
?	?	?	?
?	?	?	?
?	?	?	?
?	?	?	?
?	?		?

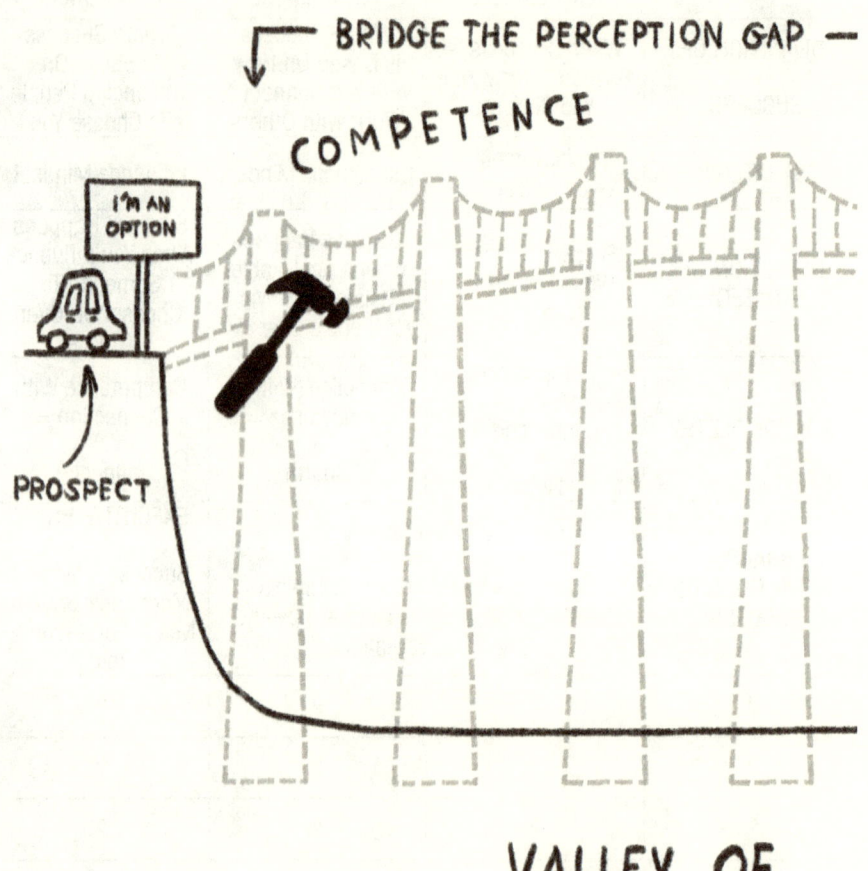

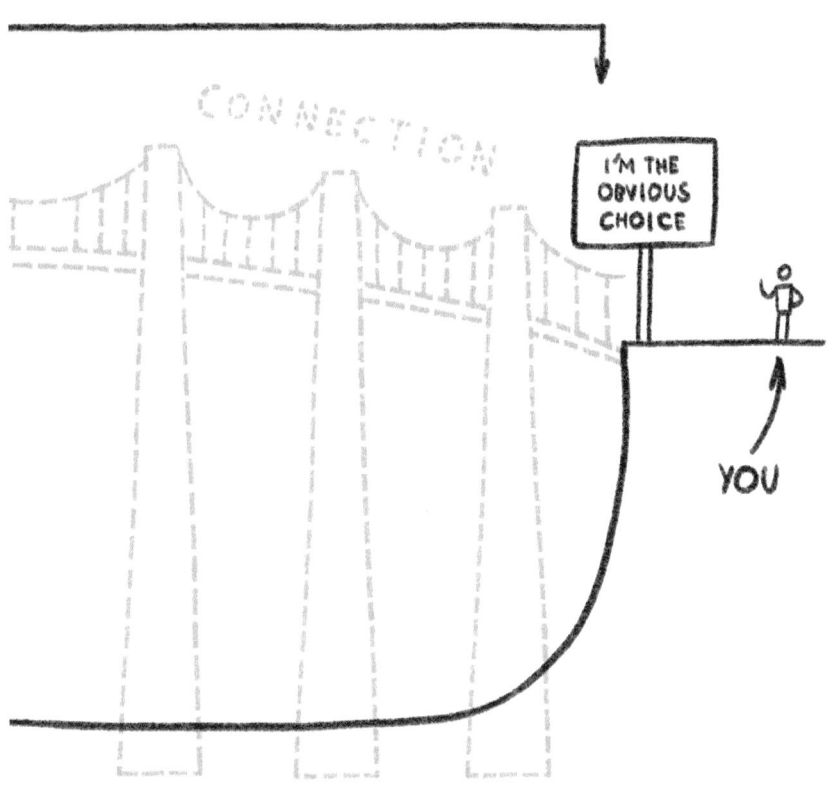

IRRELEVANCE

SECTION 2

POSITIONING YOUR COMPETENCE & CREDIBILITY

Go from Tonic to Iconic

"Perception is reality."

— **Lee Atwater**

In 1886, Dr. John Pemberton woke up like he did everyday: in chronic pain. However, as he picked up the newspaper, he read something that gave him an even greater headache...his business was about to be ruined.

Born in 1831 in Knoxville, Georgia, Pemberton was attracted to chemistry and medicine from a young age and enrolled in the Reform Medical College of Georgia. After graduating with his degree at the age of 19, he moved to Ohio to open up a drugstore. However, when the Civil War broke out, he returned to Georgia and enlisted as a lieutenant colonel in the Confederate Army, where he sustained a life-threatening sabre wound to the chest in April of 1865 [1].

After a slow recovery, Pemberton adjusted to the new daily realities of his chronic pain. When he sought medical help, he was initially prescribed morphine. However, like most veterans at the time who were unaware of morphine's addictive properties, he quickly became dependent on the drug. Wanting to find a solution to manage both his pain AND his troublesome addiction, Pemberton searched for existing medicines that would help.

The problem was, nothing worked. He couldn't find a solution! And so in 1866, desperate for a remedy, Pemberton decided to put his previous medical training and skills as a pharmacist to use and began creating different painkillers and tonics to help. After a series of products with mixed results, Pemberton then experimented with recipes that combined alcohol with extracts of the kola nut...a tropical fruit packed with a recently discovered chemical called...caffeine.

Thus "Pemberton's French Wine Coca" was born, and he quickly advertised it as a cure-all. As his drink expanded in popularity, Pemberton enjoyed modest financial success from his medicinal tonic and eventually returned to Atlanta to expand his business.

However, as Pemberton had been developing his ideas, by the 1880s, alcohol abuse had become a widespread problem in the United States. So much so that religiously driven temperance movements had sprung up around the country advocating tee-totalling abstinence [3]. In Georgia, the fervor was so strong that in 1886, legislators in Atlanta and Fulton County enshrined the movement into law. That's why, when Pemberton read about it in the newspaper that morning, his wonder wine was now illegal, and his business was in jeopardy. Pemberton went back to the drawing board and soon came up with a non-alcoholic version of his medicinal tonic.

What happened next changed the course of beverage history.

Up until this point, his elixir was marketed as a medicine and relied on adding normal water to be consumed. However, with the rise of soda fountains in corner shops around the country, what if the tonic was instead combined with carbonated water and sold as a "refreshing" fountain drink?

That way it would appeal not just to sick people, but to everyone. And so on May 8, 1886, Dr. John Pemberton took a jug of his alcohol-free wonder mix down the street to Jacob's Pharmacy, where it was sampled and placed on sale for 5 cents a glass as a "Delicious and Refreshing" soda fountain drink for all to enjoy [4].

Thus Coca-Cola was born.

Though other brands of "French Wine" were available from other competitors, Pemberton's drink exploded in popularity. As researcher Staci Rogers noted, "By 1887, French Wine Coca was selling 720 bottles a day while, by some estimates, the new Coca-Cola sold around 600 gallons (76,800 drinks) in the weeks before May 1 of the same year." [5]

Compared to the competition, Coca-Cola became the obvious choice.

Fizz to Fortune

Though Pemberton unfortunately faced a tragic death just a few years later, for the purposes of our discussion of influencing people to choose you, the Coca-Cola story provides a masterclass on a critical concept: Positioning.

When he shifted his tonic from being featured as a medicine and added carbonation to make it an enjoyable fountain drink, the ingredients didn't change, the taste didn't change, but how people perceived the drink...did.

Coca-Cola went from tonic to iconic. (Even though it wasn't until 1929 that another key ingredient to the formula...cocaine...was removed from the recipe.)

How can you add "fizz" to how you position your value and change how people perceive it?

This is what we will cover in this section, which will be focused on framing your competence in compelling ways.

In section 1, we talked about the Millau Bridge and how the formula of influence is:

Competence + Connection = Influence

"How can you add "fizz" to how you position your value and change how people perceive it?"

We then explored in Chapter 1 how focusing on "competence" alone leads to the Achievement Mindset, as well as how "connection" by itself leads to the Charismatic Mindset...both being ineffective, as they lead to irrelevant noise and charm.

Over the next several chapters, we are going to revisit the Millau, and just like the bridge is supported by several pylons towering hundreds of feet in the air, we will break down three key skills needed to demonstrate the first part of the formula: your competence and value. However, we will do it in ways that avoid the pitfalls of the Achievement Mindset and instead position you as the obvious choice.

These three skills are:

1. Framing your value in emotion, and not just logic.
2. Speaking in insight and wisdom, not just knowledge and experience.
3. Becoming a guide and letting your prospect see themselves as the hero.

These are the principles that will act as critical pylons for your "bridge of influence." Just like the Millau Viaduct.

Get Ready

How do you speak to what your prospect's brain is wired to pay attention to?

How can you put your Survival Brain at ease and let your Executive Brain take command with confidence?

And just like Dr. John Pemberton, how do you add that unique "fizz" to your message?

Let's begin.

EMOTIONS DRIVE DECISIONS

"If you just meet their service need, you'll create a transaction. If you meet an emotional need, you'll create an advocate."

— Brian Buffini

A few years ago my wife and I needed to find a real-estate agent to help us sell our home. We asked around for referrals, and two realtors were suggested, each with strong recommendations. With such praise, how could we choose which one to work with?

We reached out to both agents and set appointments to meet. Would there be something in their presentation that identified one as the obvious choice?

On the appointed day, the first agent arrived right on time, introduced himself, and proceeded to walk around our house taking notes on a notepad and making keen observations along the way.

- "Let me guess...your property is XYZ square feet, yes? I sold several last year from this development that were the exact same size."
- "I've worked in this neighborhood for over a decade and have sold hundreds of homes. This will be a piece of cake for me to do."

- "My recommendation is that you should list your home for X dollars. That's what comparable properties are going for right now. Did you know that homes one block over are selling for X price? I had a client living there. We actually sold it in X days by the way..."

- "This reminds me of another home I sold earlier this year. In fact, I've sold X number of homes this year and worked with Y number of clients. This will not be a problem at all. I can easily handle this kind of home!"

After he inspected the property, the three of us sat down. He showed us the comparison sheets he had prepared and quickly calculated what our net profits would be. He gave us a timeline of how long he predicted it would take for the home to sell, and after some questions, was on his way to the next appointment.

He was skilled, he was qualified, and he certainly knew his numbers well. But how would that compare to the next agent?

When Agent #2 arrived, instead of immediately walking around the property like Agent #1, she said, "I can tell this is a lovely home, but before I take a look, would it be alright to help me learn more about why you are moving?"

And so as we sat down, Agent #2 asked questions and listened.

- "I can tell this move has a lot at stake for you both. What are some of your concerns?"
- "What are you looking for in an agent? What are you hoping to avoid?"

At this point, instead of scribbling numbers and making calculations like the previous agent, she was carefully writing down our responses on her notepad. Her comments continued:

- "I think you are making a great decision. This is going to open so many opportunities for you. In fact, here's why I think you are making this move at a perfect time..."
- "I can tell you've done your homework, and let me tell you...you are perfectly positioned to make the most out of this...more than a lot of people I meet."

After a few minutes of talking and listening, only THEN did she ask, "Would you mind if I looked around?"

And just like Agent #1, she walked the property and made notes on her clipboard. She even repeated several of the ballpark numbers we had heard before, but as she did so, she added comments like:

- "You guys sure bought this place at a great time."
- "Your bathroom has *this* feature that is very popular right now and will definitely add more value."
- "This room would definitely appeal to XYZ kind of buyer, and I would highlight this in the photography."
- "If you are open to some painting and touching up, I think this one room would really sparkle with a little help. Plus staging it with some additional furniture would be simple. That would, of course, be something I provide at no additional cost. I do that all the time for my clients. It makes such a difference when people tour homes, and I've found it helps sell faster."

She wrapped up our visit with encouraging words and how to get in contact for the next steps. After she left, my wife and I looked at each other and there was no question in our minds. Agent #2 was the obvious choice compared to Agent #1.

But why? They both had comparable experience, they knew the same facts, and could list the same numbers to us. They each knew the area, had sold a similar number of homes, and both came highly recommended. On paper, they were indistinguishable.

Except for one thing: While Agent #1 relied on logic, facts, and figures to present his value, Agent #2 used a combination of logic AND emotional language to influence us to see her as the obvious choice.

Logic vs Emotion

In Performance Environments, logic, facts, and figures are framed as if they rule everything.

In school we are taught that the world is a place of reason, where people make self-interested and rational decisions. In work and in our careers, key performance indicators and analytics govern our promotions, employment reviews, and even the strategic directions companies take. To successfully navigate this performance-driven world, we need to present our messaging with information, logic, and factual evidence. Hence, we learn through years of effort and study that the Achievement Mindset works.

Which is what Agent #1 did.

He illustrated his competence by accurately guessing and assessing our home's value. He rattled off numbers from other properties he had sold and gave us reliable predictions on what we could expect. He was professional, highly experienced, and eminently capable. Back in his broker's office, all these traits were certainly valuable and likely distinguished him from other agents in his "tribe."

But he wasn't operating in a Performance Environment; instead he was really operating in a Selective Environment where he needed to influence us to choose him over others. And the one thing he didn't take into account was that in Selective Environments, emotions play a major role in decision-making.

Emotions and Decisions

For much of the 20th century, academic research on decision-making focused on how "reason" informed and shaped our decisions. Mankind did things rationally, the theories went, and the notion that emotions played a part? Was almost unheard of. Then starting in the late 20th century, a shift began. In 1978, Herbert Simon won the Nobel Prize in Economics for challenging the prevailing belief that humans are purely rational decision-makers [1]. He suggested that our decisions are shaped not just by logic but also by other factors, including...our emotions. When it comes to making decisions, Simon argued, emotions play a critical role [2].

This led to an explosion of research that has only amplified and intensified in the ensuing decades. And the findings have become resoundingly clear: Emotions are not just "noise" interfering with reason but essential tools that guide and inform our choices [3]. And so, when you want to influence people to see you as the obvious choice, your message must combine both logic AND emotion.

Which is what Agent #2 did.

Did you notice her first question?

- "I can tell this move has a lot at stake for you both. What are some of your concerns?"

❝She understood that how we felt mattered just as much as what we perceived she could do.❞

Right out of the gate, she acknowledged that this was a decision fraught with emotional implications ("This move has a lot at stake for you both") and sought to understand what we were most worried about ("What are some of your concerns?"). She understood that how we felt mattered just as much as what we perceived she could do. And if you review the other things she said in our conversation, you will notice how she ingeniously intertwined emotion and logic in her communication.

The result? Compared to Agent #1, she was the obvious choice.

But let's take a look from another angle and see how recognizing and adjusting your message with emotion-filled language can help you win over prospects more easily.

A Problem is Not a Problem Until...

I once worked for a financial services company and woke up one day to an unexpected downward shift in the stock market. I hurried to work, where, upon entering, I saw half of the office running from phone to phone fielding calls from agitated clients. They were reassuring them that our company had everything under control (which we legitimately did).

However, when I came to my side of the office, it was quiet. My email inbox? Normal. My phone? Silent. No panicked messages, no emergency calls.

How come *their* side of the office was in damage-control mode, but our side was calm and business as usual?

I spoke with my boss, the head advisor over our area, and he pointed out something insightful. OUR book of business consisted of accounts of elderly widows and people who had been clients of the company for decades. They were used to market ups and downs and had long ago learned to trust our team.

❝A problem is NOT a problem until someone feels something about it. ❞

The other side of the office? It was filled with new clients. They hadn't experienced market swings with us before, so naturally, they were concerned.

That day, I learned something critical: A problem is NOT a problem until someone feels something about it [4]. Both groups saw the same headline news and had the same set of facts. However, they reacted in wildly different ways.

That's because they felt differently about it.

Think about your own life. There are probably things you KNOW need to be fixed and changed, but they most likely will remain untouched. That is...until you feel something about it. For example, I know my gutters need to be cleaned, but I'm not going to haul out the ladder, climb onto the roof, and cover my hands in muck until either:

1. It begins to rain, the water overflows, and starts ruining the patio I enjoy using.

Or...

1. If I'm AFRAID it will rain, overflow, and start ruining the patio I enjoy using.

In either case, my behavior of ignoring the gutters does not change until something is at risk and an emotion is introduced. And this holds true for most problems we face in life. Signing up for the gym? Getting that insurance? Racing to the store at the butt crack of dawn to get flowers for the anniversary? In each of these cases, there is a clear emotion behind it.

Similarly, if someone is coming to you with a problem to be solved, the problem itself may be the tip of the spear...but the emotion as to why it matters is the shaft behind it, driving it forward [5].

Remember: We decide emotionally and justify our decisions logically.

We must never forget that whenever your prospect is trying to solve something, there is an emotion making it happen. This is why Agent #2 succeeded where Agent #1 failed. She understood that beneath every logical consideration was an emotional driver. Instead of just presenting facts and figures, she wove emotion into her communication:

- "I can tell this move has a lot at stake for you both. What are some of your concerns?"
- "You've done your homework, and let me tell you...you are perfectly positioned to make the most out of this."

Each statement acknowledged both the emotional and logical aspects of the decision. She didn't just address what we were doing—she validated why it mattered to us.

If we know that:

- Emotion plays a significant role in our prospect's decision making...
- We decide emotionally and justify our decisions logically...
- Our prospects are seeking out solutions to emotionally driven problems...

❝If someone is coming to you with a problem to be solved, the problem itself may be the tip of the spear...but the emotion as to why it matters is the shaft behind it, driving it forward.❞

...then what are some strategies we can use to position ourselves for success?

I Thought You'd Never Ask

As we covered in the previous chapter, when our brains enter make-or-break sales situations, the Survival Brain senses stress, freaks out, and grapples for control. It wants to place OUR needs over the needs of our prospect. And so it fights and often wins [6]. However, we know that speaking to the fundamental brain needs of our prospects is the key to success.

"Remember: We decide emotionally and justify our decisions logically."

In these moments, how can we distract the Survival Brain and give strategic power and control to our Executive Brain? How can we "hack" our own brain to go where we want?

Just like the Wright brothers, we begin by asking the right questions.

In moments of stress, or when our thoughts are spiraling, researchers have discovered that asking ourselves intentional questions is a useful tool to stop negative and ineffective thoughts. This is what researchers call "cognitive reappraisal," where we can observe and then intentionally redirect our thought patterns [7]. Just like holding a treat in front of a distracted puppy or clapping in front of an agitated infant disrupts both of their behavior patterns, asking intentional open-ended questions temporarily stops the Survival Brain and lets the Executive Brain regain control.

The only problem is, not all questions are created equal.

In these moments with the Survival Brain raging, the Achievement Mindset has trained us to ask the ineffective question: How can I convince them I'm qualified and capable?

THE ACHIEVEMENT MINDSET:

How can I convince them I'm qualified and capable?

Can you see how this question appeals to OUR brains needs? When we try to "convince" someone of something, it means we marshal our logic and facts and attempt to subdue them to our way of thinking. In these moments, our brain is seeking control, security, and status.

However, if you take a step back, trying to convince someone of your qualifications and capabilities overlooks one critical mistake: In most Selective Environments, a prospect wouldn't even be having the conversation with you if they didn't already accept you as an authority. If they didn't already agree that you had a basis in legitimacy, why would they have wasted their time to schedule a call with you in the first place?

When we contacted Agent #1, it was because of a recommendation from someone we trusted. We already believed he was qualified and capable. And yet his behaviors and language only served to underscore what we already knew.

That's because, when prospects decide to finally have a conversation, it's because they are in an emotionally driven decision-making space. They accept that you are relevant for what they want and are competent (just like everyone else you are being compared against). At this stage, the real question is: How do they feel about you? And yet, like Agent #1, we blunder in rehashing our competencies with logic, facts, and figures, leaving prospects feeling unsatisfied. They were seeking emotionally related information and didn't find it. And so, they turn around and keep looking for another solution.

That's why, when it comes to important sales situations where my Survival Brain is clamoring for control, I have found this Influence-Mindset-inspired question to be most helpful in "hacking" my brain and redirecting my thoughts: How can I also acknowledge this person's emotions right now?

"In most Selective Environments, a prospect wouldn't even be having the conversation with you if they didn't already accept you as an authority."

THE ACHIEVEMENT MINDSET:

How can I convince them I'm capable & qualified?

THE INFLUENCE MINDSET:

How can I also acknowledge this person's emotions right now?

When I'm on a sales call, as I present my value, how can I also acknowledge this person's emotions right now?

When I'm meeting in person and they just shared something meaningful, how can I also acknowledge this person's emotions right now?

When I am presenting my offer to a prospect clearly worried about their situation, how can I also acknowledge this person's emotions right now?

Asking this simple question guides my "cognitive reappraisal" in the direction that I WANT it to go. While the previous Achievement Mindset question ENABLES my Survival Brain, the Influence Mindset question does the opposite. It gives my Survival Brain a chew toy, puts it in time out, and lets my Executive Brain regain control of my behaviors [8]. The moment this happens, I'm able to proceed with greater clarity and communicate my value so it interweaves both emotion and logic in a compelling way. More importantly, it enables my message to appeal to my prospect's brain's needs, and not just my own. And I'm one step closer to being seen as the obvious choice and chosen.

Let's Get Tactical

"This is all well and good," I hear you say, "but how do I actually do this?"

Let's consider and compare some common phrases and how you can implement them.

Example 1:

THE ACHIEVEMENT MINDSET:	THE INFLUENCE MINDSET:
#1: I've worked with X number of companies before, and helped them save X dollars in operating costs (Or insert whatever fact or figure you want).	#1: After working with X number of companies and helping save X in costs, here's why I love working with people in your position...

The difference between these two approaches lies in how they address the emotional undercurrent of the conversation. The **Achievement Mindset** focuses purely on competence—facts, figures, and past accomplishments. While impressive, this statement feels transactional

"When prospects decide to finally have a conversation, it's because they are in an emotionally driven decision-making space."

and can sound overwhelming. It communicates, "Here's what I've done" but doesn't address, "Here's why it matters to you."

On the other hand, the **Influence Mindset** seamlessly integrates emotion by pivoting from "what I've done" to "why I care." This subtle shift validates the prospect's unique situation and signals empathy and connection. By saying, "Here's why I love working with people in your position," you acknowledge their emotional state and their brain's needs for security and belonging. In sales, this approach makes your prospect feel like more than just another client—they feel valued. And when prospects feel valued, they're far more likely to trust you as their solution.

As we covered, people don't just buy based on logic; they buy based on how they feel [9]. The Influence Mindset ensures you are connecting emotionally while also demonstrating competence, creating a powerful message that speaks to both the head and the heart.

Here's How This Applies in Sales Situations

Imagine you're pitching a marketing agency's services to a mid-sized company. Using the **Achievement Mindset**, you might say: *"I've worked with over 50 companies and helped them collectively save millions in advertising costs."* While this demonstrates competence, it risks sounding ego driven and self-centered, leaving the prospect wondering how your expertise applies to their unique situation.

Now consider the **Influence Mindset**: *"After working with over 50 companies and helping save millions in advertising costs, I've found that I love collaborating with teams like yours because the challenges you face and the creative opportunities are really interesting and unique. Can we talk about your goals?"* This approach takes the same facts but personalizes them to resonate emotionally with the prospect. It makes them feel seen and emphasizes that your expertise is a tool to help them specifically—not just a badge of honor you're wearing.

By pivoting from self-focused achievement to prospect-focused influence, you establish trust and build a meaningful connection. This shift can turn a prospect from a passive listener into an engaged partner in the conversation, making them far more likely to move forward with you as their solution.

Example 2:

THE ACHIEVEMENT MINDSET:

#1: "Here's the data that proves our solution is the most effective on the market."

THE INFLUENCE MINDSET:

*#1: "Based on what you've shared, I think this part of our solution **would have the biggest impact for you.** Would it be alright if I explained **how it could solve the challenges you mentioned...**"*

"People don't just buy based on logic; they buy based on how they feel."

In this example, the **Achievement Mindset** leans heavily on logic and assumes that the numbers and data will speak for themselves. While this may seem like a solid approach—after all, facts are important—it often misses the mark because it leaves the prospect to do all the work of connecting those facts to their unique situation. Prospects might feel overwhelmed or disengaged because their emotional needs—the need to feel understood, valued, and prioritized—aren't being addressed.

The Influence Mindset, on the other hand, blends logic with empathy by grounding the conversation in the prospect's specific concerns. Instead of just stating how great your solution is, you connect the dots for them: *"Here's what I heard you say, and here's why this will have the biggest impact."* This approach validates the prospect's feelings and challenges while positioning your solution as the answer they've been looking for. It shifts the focus from your solution's greatness to their problem's resolution, making it far more engaging and emotionally resonant.

Here's How This Applies in Sales Situations

Imagine you're selling a software product to a mid-sized business. The **Achievement Mindset** might lead you to rattle off impressive statistics about how much time your software saves on average, expecting the numbers to wow the prospect. However, the **Influence Mindset** takes it a step further by tailoring the conversation: *"You mentioned earlier that your team is struggling with manual reporting, and it's eating up about 10 hours a week. Here's how our software can automate that process and free up your team to focus on more strategic work."*

By speaking directly to the prospect's situation, the **Influence Mindset** ensures they feel seen and understood. It also frames your solution in a way that aligns with their priorities, reducing resistance and building trust [10]. In the end, it's not just about proving you're the best—it's about helping them see why you're the best choice for their specific needs.

Example 3:

THE ACHIEVEMENT MINDSET:

#1: "We've been in this industry for over 20 years and know exactly how to handle situations like yours."

THE INFLUENCE MINDSET:

#1: "Having worked in this industry for over 20 years, I've learned to never assume I understand someone's motivations for seeking help. What are some of your concerns right now?"

The **Achievement Mindset** focuses on showcasing expertise and authority, which can seem impressive on the surface but risks alienating the prospect. By claiming to "know exactly how to handle situations like yours," the message becomes presumptive and dismissive of the prospect's unique experience. It may leave them feeling like just another client rather than someone with specific challenges and goals that deserve attention. Additionally, this phrasing positions the salesperson as the expert in control, which can inadvertently create a power imbalance that stifles meaningful dialogue.

The **Influence Mindset**, however, acknowledges expertise while emphasizing curiosity and humility. By stating, *"I've learned to never assume,"* it conveys respect for the prospect and opens the door for a collaborative conversation. Asking, *"What are some of your concerns right now?"* invites the prospect to share their thoughts, creating an emotional connection and demonstrating that their input matters. This approach aligns with the principle that people want to feel heard and understood before they can trust someone to solve their problem ".

Here's How This Applies in Sales Situations

Imagine you're meeting with a potential client who's seeking financial planning services. **The Achievement Mindset** might lead you to jump in with, *"With 20 years of experience, I've helped countless clients just like you build their retirement plans."* While this might sound impressive, it assumes you already know their goals, fears, or financial complexities. The prospect might feel you're offering a one-size-fits-all solution without truly understanding their circumstances.

The **Influence Mindset**, on the other hand, would approach the conversation differently: *"Over the past 20 years, I've seen how personal and unique each client's financial journey can be. What are some of the key things on your mind about your retirement plans?"* This repositions your expertise as a tool for collaboration rather than a predefined solution. It conveys curiosity, respect, and a willingness to adapt to their needs—all of which build trust and rapport.

By blending competence with connection, the Influence Mindset ensures that prospects feel valued and understood, making them far more likely to engage and choose you over others. It turns a potentially transactional conversation into a meaningful dialogue filled with competence and connection.

Wrap Up: The Power of Emotionally Intelligent (EQ) Communication

In the end, the choice between the two real-estate agents wasn't about their skills, credentials, or even their track records. Both agents had experience. Both could do the job. But one focused on logic, numbers, and facts—while the other understood that beneath every decision lies an emotional driver.

Agent #2 didn't just sell her services—she connected with us. She didn't just present information—she positioned it in a way that spoke to our concerns, our excitement, and our deeper needs. The result? She became the obvious choice.

This is the essence of the Influence Mindset. People don't just make decisions based on logic; they decide based on how they feel and use logic to justify those feelings. The most effective communicators—those who stand out, build trust, and win over decision-makers—are the ones who can integrate both. They don't just give information; they frame it in a way that acknowledges emotions, fosters connection, and creates an experience where the other person feels seen, understood, and valued.

So as you step into your own Selective Environments, ask yourself: Are you simply presenting facts, or are you combining logic with emotion to make yourself the obvious choice? Because when you master this balance, you won't just communicate your value—you'll make people feel it. And that is what truly sets you apart.

"Are you simply presenting facts, or are you combining logic with emotion to make yourself the obvious choice?"

Chapter 3: Key Takeaways

- **Emotions Are the Hidden Drivers behind Decisions:** While decisions seem logical, emotions influence choices more than facts.

- **We Justify Emotionally-Based Decisions with Logic:** People choose based on feeling first, then look for logical reasons to support it. Ignoring emotions can weaken your message.

- **Emotional Problems Need Emotional Solutions:** Behind every challenge is an emotional driver—frustration, anxiety, or excitement. Solutions must address both the issue and the feeling behind it.

- **Your Survival Brain Can Be Tamed:** Asking intentional questions can override YOUR emotional reactions and allow rational thinking to take control.

- **Balance Emotion with Logic:** The best messages connect emotionally first, then reinforce with logic to create a compelling and persuasive case.

Bonus

I've created exclusive content to help you apply the principles we cover together. To access them, go to: **www.TheChristianHansen.com/BookBonus**

SUMMARY TABLE

INFLUENCE FORMULA:	Competence	(Plus) Connection	(Equals) Influence
ENVIRONMENT:	Performance Environment	Relational Environment	Selective Environment
DEFINITION OF SUCCESS:	Where Success Is Based On How Well You Perform	Where Success Is Based On How Well You Connect & Work With Others	Where Success Is Based On Influencing People To Choose You
STRATEGY:	Achievement Mindset	Charismatic Mindset	Influence Mindset
DEFINITION OF STRATEGY:	Success Happens When I Prove My Value Is High	Success Happens When I Am Likable, Relatable, & Win People Over	Success Happens When You Influence Someone To Choose You Over Others
IF INCOMPLETE?	Competence (Without) Connection = Noise	Connection (Without) Competence = Charm	Competence With Connection = Influence
BRAIN'S DEFINITIONS OF SUCCESS:	SURVIVAL BRAIN Success = When I Meet My Brain's Needs For Security, Resources, Novelty, Belonging, & Status…		EXECUTIVE BRAIN Success = When I Meet Their Brain's Needs For Security, (etc.)
STRATEGIES	ACHIEVEMENT THINKING	CHARISMATIC THINKING	INFLUENCE BRAIN HACKS
Competence Strategy #1: LOGIC VS EMOTION	How Can I Convince Them I'm Qualified And Capable?	N/A	How Can I Also Acknowledge This Person's Emotions Right Now?
?	?	?	?
?	?	?	?
?	?	?	?

?	?	?	?
?	?	?	?
?	?		?

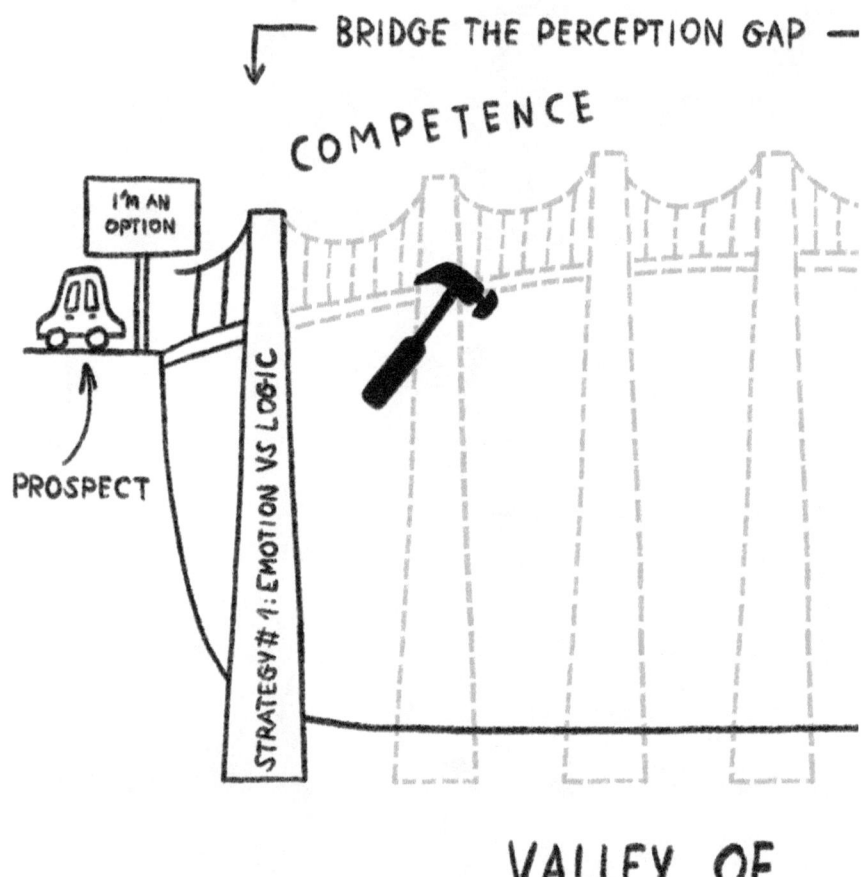

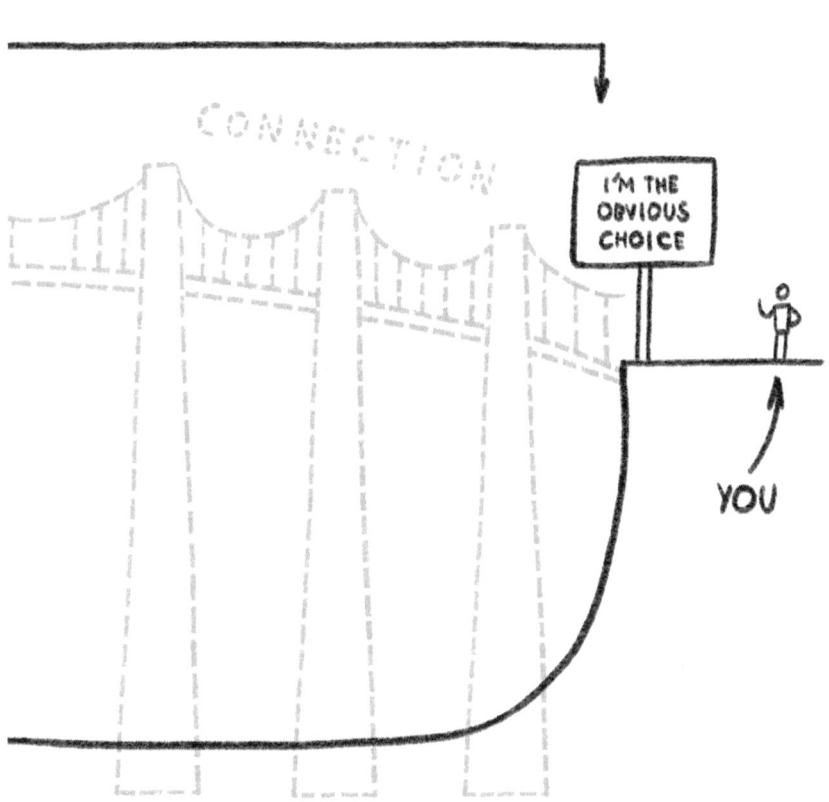

CONNECTION

I'M THE
OBVIOUS
CHOICE

YOU

IRRELEVANCE

THINK "INSIGHT" THE BOX

"A ship earns nothing sitting at a dock."

— **Malcom McLean**

"We do not learn from experience...
we learn from reflecting on experience."

— **John Dewey**

On Thursday April 26, 1956, 100 dignitaries gathered in Newark, New Jersey to witness something revolutionary: a crane loading 58 uniformly sized metal containers onto a cargo ship. As the boxes were stacked with breathtaking speed, two people in the crowd, Malcom McLean and Freddy Fields, watched on with two radically different reactions: elation and horror [1].

McLean was the entrepreneur who had created this moment through years of work and determination. He watched, elated, as his ship embarked on a 6-day voyage to Houston filled with efficiently loaded and stored containers. Fields, on the other hand, a senior leader from the International Longshoremen's Association, watched in horror. He knew his industry was about to be threatened. When someone asked him his thoughts, Fields replied, "I'd like to sink that son of a bitch." [2]

Let's backtrack here and explore what happened and why this connects to influence.

Born in 1913 in Maxton, North Carolina, Malcom McLean had a level of ambition that drove its way into the trucking business. By 1935 at the age of 22, McLean owned a small trucking company with 2 trucks, 1 tractor trailer, and 9 drivers. Ten years later in 1945? "McLean's Trucking" had grown to over 162 trucks with revenues exceeding $2.2 million [3]. Worried about the rising fuel costs from increased highway congestion and obsessed with cutting costs, in 1953 McLean looked to the sea as a way to competitively move freight for cheaper. The problem was, the entire system was a mess. No ship, or port, was designed to efficiently load freight directly from trucks [4].

In the 1950s, shipping goods from one place to another by water was nearly the same as it had been since the time of the Phoenicians nearly 3,000 years ago. Bags, crates, and boxes were loaded by brawny longshoremen who carried and organized disjointed pieces of cargo by hand. Such a process increased the time a ship spent in port, increased the labor fees, and made the cargo prone to theft and damage. All of these hindrances raised the cost of shipping so much that for some commodities, the cost to transport was nearly 25% of the product. By one estimate, "a 4,000-mile voyage for a shipment might consume 50% of its costs" by merely loading and unloading cargo by hand [5].

That meant trade and moving anything from one point to another was often prohibitively expensive.

Enter the cost-conscious Malcom McLean. "What if goods could be stored in intermodal containers that move seamlessly between trains, trucks, and ships?" Such a system would be much more efficient, decrease shipping costs, and be incredibly profitable. And so McLean worked with designers and manufacturers to create aluminum containers, 33 feet in length, that could be stacked and secured efficiently on top of each other because of their uniform shape and size. Compared to other metal boxes commonly used at the time, these containers were nearly 7 times larger and could carry a staggering amount of goods inside [6]. McLean then bought two WW2 oil tankers and retrofitted them to hold his newly fashioned metal containers. But where would these new ships even dock? Most ports were designed for the labor-intensive longshoreman model, and few had cranes that could support his new system.

That's when McLean found the port in Newark, New Jersey. At the time, Newark was a ramshackle, dilapidated affair ignored by many companies in favor of the thriving port of New York and their longshoreman unions across the harbor in Brooklyn. However, Newark was looking to compete and hungry to grow. How could McLean convince them to partner with his revolutionary idea of container shipping? Of all the options, how could McLean be the obvious choice?

The answer? Insight.

Just like the trucking business, where a truck earns money only on the road, "A ship earns money only when she's at sea," Malcom said [7]. His new container system could be loaded in a fraction of the time, he explained to the port authorities, and with no need for each piece of cargo to be carried by hand, a ship could be loaded with a fraction of the man power. That meant ships would spend less time at port, more time at sea, and have significantly decreased costs. Less costs meant more profit, and if Newark made shipping companies more profitable, then those shipping companies would choose Newark over New York. If they chose McLean's plan, this would be the competitive advantage Newark had been searching for all along.

The leaders of New Jersey saw the value behind his argument and agreed. They selected McLean's proposal, and with the help of government funding, McLean redesigned the port of Newark to work with his "containerization" model [8]. And on that day in 1956, 100 dignitaries gathered to witness ships being loaded and unloaded in 1/6th of the time with 1/3rd of the labor [9]. All told, "containerization" would go on to reduce shipping costs across the world by as much as 94% [10].

As for the longshoreman unions, the predictions of Freddy Fields sadly came true. The days of labor intensive longshoreman work were over. Single crane operators replaced entire teams of men who once unloaded the ships by hand. Soon the ports of New York and Brooklyn sank into irrelevance, and across the world new ports opened to meet the increased demand. Oakland supplanted San Francisco, Felixstowe replaced Liverpool, and ports in the Far East like Manila, Incheon, and Hong Kong raced to meet the sudden opportunities of international trade.

Today, we all benefit from McLean's extraordinary vision. His work has made global trade simpler, easier, and much more affordable. Everything from automobile manufacturing, the global adoption of smartphones, and even the Halloween costume you bought for your dog on Amazon...all are made possible because McLean and his containers made shipping radically cheaper. So much so, he has been regarded as one of the "the greatest revolutionar[ies] in the history of maritime trade." [11]

When he passed away in 2001 at the age of 87, container ships around the world blew their deep horns and powerful whistles in his honor [12].

All because he used the power of *insight* to persuade the owners of the port of Newark to see him, and his revolutionary idea, as the obvious choice.

So what exactly is "Insight"? And how does it compare to other forms of communication? To find out, let's go climb one of the pyramids.

The Pyramid of Information

When it comes to showcasing our value, we communicate across four distinct levels of information—but not all levels are created equal. I call this the Pyramid of Information. At the base of the pyramid is **"Knowledge,"** which is simply retained information. If you've read a manual or memorized a fact, congratulations—you have Knowledge. But let's be honest, this is the lowest bar to clear. Nearly anyone with two brain cells to rub together can acquire and communicate Knowledge, which makes it the least compelling way to set yourself apart.

Next up is **"Experience,"** where you take that knowledge and apply it. Experience means you've done something, and perhaps even done it repeatedly. You've been in the trenches, tried your hand at the task, and emerged with something to show for it. You did the thing...but... so have others. That's why "Experience" is a level that's crowded and competitive when trying to stand out.

The real differentiation happens as we move higher up the pyramid. When you take time to reflect on your experience, extracting lessons and patterns, you achieve the third level: **"Insight."** Insight is where you connect the dots, seeing the meaning and value beneath the surface. It's not just what you did, but what you *learned* that others can apply in their *own* journey. Insight is the tipping point where your hard-earned knowledge and experience become valuable to others.

Finally, at the peak of the pyramid is **"Wisdom."** This is where insight becomes transformative, crossing boundaries into other fields and contexts. Wisdom allows you (and those you are trying to influence) to see the bigger picture and speak to universal truths—making it the most powerful, yet rarest, level of communication.

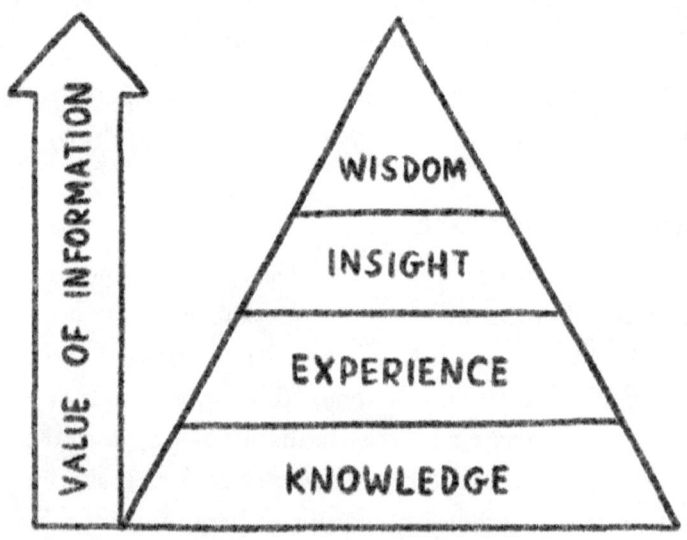

" Insight is the tipping point where your hard-earned knowledge and experience become valuable to others. "

Which is what Malcom McLean did when he convinced the owners of the port of Newark to choose him.

Had he communicated at the level of **Knowledge**, he might have said:

- "I'm here to tell you that 'containerized shipping' is faster and more efficient. A single container can hold X tons of cargo, and containers can be stacked securely on a ship, maximizing space. Using cranes to load and unload containers will reduce the time ships spend in port by up to XYZ%."

Similarly, had he communicated at the level of **Experience**, he might have said:

- "I've spent the last 20 years running and building a successful trucking company. I've expanded from 2 trucks to a fleet of over 160 and have made millions in revenue. Nobody has built anything close to what I have. Trust me when I say, 'I know the trucking business. This is going to work!'"

Both of those statements, while 100% true, fail to influence or persuade. The **Knowledge** approach relies heavily on facts, and the **Experience** approach only serves to bolster McLean's ego. Neither of them appeal to the brains' needs of the people he is trying to influence.

Which is why McLean was so influential when he communicated at the higher levels of **Insight** and **Wisdom**:

- "You know, the shipping business is just like the trucking business. Just like a truck only makes money when it's moving things on the road, a ship only makes money when it moves things from one place to another on the sea. My system will get boats in and out to sea in a fraction of the time, using a fraction of the man power, and ultimately at a fraction of the cost. Thus making the ship owners more money and your port more desirable for business compared to New York."

Can you see the difference between the different levels of communication?

Insight: The Path Forward

Knowledge and Experience, though accurate, would have served *McLean's* brain's needs. They would have reinforced his credibility and capabilities. But the moment when he shifted into the higher levels of Insight and Wisdom? His message began serving his *prospect's* brain's needs. He spoke to *their* wants and desires and showed he understood the issue at a higher level than others.

That's because speaking in Insight and Wisdom leads to a clearer path for *action* on the part of the listener. As we've covered, your

"Speaking in Insight and Wisdom leads to a clearer path for *action* on the part of the listener."

prospects want something and are looking for ways to get there quickly. When you speak in Knowledge or Experience, you leave it up to your prospect to figure out how you are relevant to them.

They wonder, "SO WHAT if you have all that Knowledge and all that Experience? How does that apply to me?"

However, when you speak in Insight and Wisdom, it's like handing them a tool they've been searching for all along. You've made their pathway clearer, the journey simpler, and the goal they've been searching for...suddenly within reach. Simply put, speaking in Insight and Wisdom makes it all about them and where they want to go. Not about you and where you've already been.

Which is what McLean did. He framed his value in a way where it helped the leaders of the port of Newark get to where they wanted to go. And thus his containerization model became the obvious choice.

In a world that is drowning in information and starving for wisdom, the person who can communicate their value at higher levels wins. The only problem is, most people have never been taught how to communicate in this more influential way. Instead, we've been trained to communicate almost exclusively in Knowledge and Experience.

Credibility vs Perspective

In the Performance Environments of school, work, and our careers, we've been taught to demonstrate our competence by communicating what we know and what we've accomplished [13]. And if we are operating in a world where success is based on proving our value is high (in other words, the Achievement Mindset), that approach makes sense. It's rational, logical, and easy to communicate. It also builds our credibility, makes us appear more impressive to others, and meets OUR brain's needs for security, belonging, and status.

That's why, when we enter make-it-or-break-it sales situations, our Survival Brain is asking the question, "How can I prove I'm credible and impressive?"

THE ACHIEVEMENT MINDSET:

How can I prove I'm credible and impressive?

However, as we've covered, this isn't about you. We need to be intentionally thinking about how we can appeal to our prospect's brain's needs when we frame our value. That's why the Influence Mindset uses the following question to "hack" our Survival Brain's insecure power struggle, and allows our Executive Brain to regain control of the situation: What unique insight or perspective speaks directly to their challenges?

THE ACHIEVEMENT MINDSET:

How can I prove I'm credible and impressive?

THE INFLUENCE MINDSET:

What unique insight or perspective speaks directly to their challenges?

"In a world that is drowning in information and starving for wisdom, the person who can communicate their value at higher levels wins. "

Just like McLean's insight changed the way the port authorities saw their problem, so too do your hard earned perspectives make the path easier for your prospects and increase their chances for success. And in a world of comparable options, when you make the path simpler and clearer than anyone else, you will be seen as the obvious choice.

But why? Why is speaking in Insight and Wisdom so powerful compared to Knowledge and Experience? The answer lies...as we have discovered for so many other reasons...in our brain.

The Case for Insight

When you communicate in terms of Insight and Wisdom, you showcase an ability to think strategically.

And you want to be perceived as a strategic thinker.

In 2013, the Management Research Group (MRG) conducted a study of 60,000 executives in 140+ countries, covering 26 industries. Their goal? To find the most effective traits for leaders. They found that being *perceived* as a strategic thinker was the most important skill for being influential. In fact, being perceived as a strategic thinker is twice as important as having strong communication skills and *almost 50 times* more valuable than merely being highly skilled.

To quote directly from the *Harvard Business Review* article, "This doesn't mean that tactical behaviors aren't important, but they don't differentiate the highly effective leaders from everyone else." [14]

Did you catch that? Being highly skilled isn't enough to differentiate you from everyone else.

I find this highly relevant because when we speak in Achievement Mindset language of Knowledge and Experience, we reinforce a perception that we are highly competent and skilled. But as the study shows, that only serves to make you sound just like everyone else. But the moment we communicate in Insight and Wisdom and show we think strategically? We pull the levers of perception in our favor and are perceived as being significantly more valuable.

Nearly 50 times more valuable, in fact.

But the benefits don't end there. When we communicate in Insight and Wisdom, we create paradigm shifts and help people see their problems in new ways.

Aha!

In 2009, researchers John Kounios and Mark Beeman wanted to figure out what happens to our brains when we have an "Aha!" moment. You know: the feeling when something finally clicks, makes sense, or when we have a sudden burst of comprehension...THAT "Aha!" moment. And so they stuck electrodes on people's heads and measured what happened in the brain as they solved different problems [15].

❝When you make the path simpler and clearer than anyone else, you will be seen as the obvious choice.❞

Here's what they found: It turns out the term a "burst" of comprehension isn't far from the truth. When our brains have a moment of insight and realization, a neural firework show occurs. Our brains light up with activity and excitement when it has found a new way to solve a problem. (See diagram.)

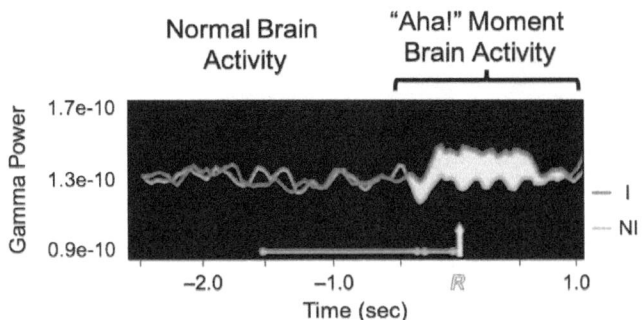

Diagram: Kounios, Beeman 2009. The Aha! Moment,
The Cognitive Neuroscience of Insight

When you speak in Insight and Wisdom, this is the effect you can have. You are providing your prospect's Survival Brain with greater tools to solve the problems they are grappling with, enabling them to navigate the world more effectively. In other words, when you speak with Insight and Wisdom, you enable their Survival Brain to access security, resources, novelty, belonging, and status with greater speed and efficiency. And they pay more attention to you.

If you had the choice between communicating in ways that made you sound just like everyone else (Achievement Mindset: Knowledge and Experience) or in ways that made their brain explode and hunger for more... What would you choose?

But wait, it gets better.

The Part Where You Shield Your Child's Eyes and Ears

If we know that Insight-driven "Aha!" moments create a flurry of activity in the brain, where exactly is this activity happening and can that teach us anything? In 2020, a group of researchers were wondering the same thing. After they stuck more electrodes on people and gave them a series of problems to solve, they discovered that "Aha!" moments lit up the "orbitofrontal cortex, a region associated with reward learning and hedonically pleasurable experiences such as food, positive social experiences, addictive drugs, and orgasm" [16].

Those are the *exact* words of the researchers. And you thought this was a book about sales...

They continued, "These findings support the notion that for many people insight is rewarding... [and] may be a manifestation of an evolutionarily adaptive mechanism for the reinforcement of exploration, problem-solving, and creative cognition." [16]

Did you notice some of the core brain needs?

In other words, when you speak in Insight and Wisdom and create "Aha!" moments for your prospects, their Survival Brain is literally wired by millions of years of evolution to pay more attention to you. And all the while, your competitors are spinning their wheels belaboring their Knowledge and Experience, confused why no one is choosing them.

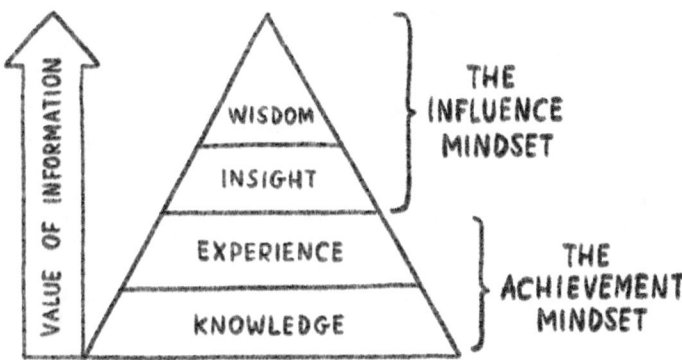

Let's Get Tactical

As entertaining as neuroscience can be, let's consider some Insight- and Wisdom-driven phrases and how you can implement them in everyday sales situations. In this section, we will compare Achievement- vs Influence Mindset-inspired phrases.

Example 1:

THE ACHIEVEMENT MINDSET:	THE INFLUENCE MINDSET:
#1: "I've helped people save X time and Y money with the solution."	#2: "While this solution does save time and money immediately, **the bigger opportunity** is how it positions you to *[long-term or unseen benefit]* over the next few years. Here's why that matters…"

> **"When you speak in Insight and Wisdom and create "Aha!" moments for your prospects, their Survival Brain is literally wired by millions of years of evolution to pay more attention to you."**

Why These Phrases Work (or Don't Work)

The **Achievement Mindset** statement focuses on measurable results—time and money saved. While these outcomes are universally appealing, this approach is purely transactional and surface-level. By emphasizing only short-term benefits, it fails to inspire or connect to the bigger picture the prospect may be striving for, leaving a critical gap in influence.

In contrast, the **Influence Mindset** statement recognizes the immediate benefits (time and money saved) but elevates the conversation to a strategic level. It reframes the solution as a gateway to long-term value or *unseen opportunities*, aligning with the prospect's deeper goals and aspirations. By painting a bigger picture, this phrasing positions you as a trusted guide who not only solves problems but also has a greater strategic vision.

Here's How This Applies in Sales Situations

Imagine you're a financial advisor pitching a retirement-planning service. Using the **Achievement Mindset,** you might say: *"I've helped clients save thousands of dollars in fees and maximize their retirement income."*

While this is an impressive statistic, it frankly sounds generic and self-serving. The prospect might think, *"That's nice, but how does it specifically help me?"* Without connecting the numbers to the prospect's personal goals or challenges, this statement fails to create an emotional connection.

Now let's reframe it with the **Influence Mindset:** *"While I help clients save on fees and maximize income, the bigger opportunity is how it positions you to live the retirement you've envisioned—traveling, spending time with family, or pursuing your passions—without financial stress. Let me show you how this ensures those goals."*

This statement not only delivers the immediate benefits but also paints a vivid picture of how those benefits translate into a better life for the prospect. It connects emotionally by focusing on their dreams and aspirations while positioning you as someone who understands their unique vision of success. This strategic approach builds trust, inspires confidence, and shifts the focus from a transactional relationship to an opportunity for them.

Example 2:

THE ACHIEVEMENT MINDSET:	THE INFLUENCE MINDSET:
#1: *"I've done this successfully for X number of clients over 10 years, so you're in good hands."*	#2: *"In over 10 years of doing this for X number of clients, one **thing I've learned is that success often hinges** on [key unseen factor]."*

Why These Phrases Work (or Don't Work)

The **Achievement Mindset** statement focuses solely on credentials and past experience. While it might build some initial credibility, it risks feeling impersonal and self-serving. It also stops short of demonstrating how that experience benefits the prospect. The lack of a direct connection to their specific needs or challenges makes this approach feel transactional and uninspiring.

On the other hand, the **Influence Mindset** statement leverages the same credentials but reframes them in a way that's outwardly focused. By sharing a key insight learned from experience, it adds immediate value to the conversation. The phrase "success often hinges on [key unseen factor]" invites the prospect to engage with your insight and see how it applies to their unique situation, building trust and connection.

Here's How This Applies in Sales Situations

Imagine you're a real estate agent speaking with a potential home seller. Using the **Achievement Mindset**, you might say: *"I've helped over 100 families sell their homes in this area over the past decade, so you're in good hands."*

While this statement establishes credibility, it doesn't offer anything that distinguishes you from other agents with similar track records. It leaves the prospect to wonder, "How does that help me sell my home faster or for a better price?"

Now let's reframe it with the **Influence Mindset**: *"In over a decade of helping more than 100 families sell their homes, I've found that the most successful sellers focus on [key unseen factor, like staging or pricing strategy]. Let's talk about how that applies to your home."*

This statement uses the same experience to deliver immediate value to the prospect. By sharing an insight gained from your expertise, you demonstrate not only competence but also a deep understanding of the process and the prospect's potential challenges. The addition of a tailored solution—like staging or pricing—makes your expertise actionable and relevant, helping the prospect feel confident that you're the right person to guide them.

This shift from "trust me because I'm experienced" to "here's what my experience has taught me that can help you" transforms the conversation. It creates a sense of partnership rather than a one-sided pitch and establishes you as someone who listens, understands, and is invested in the prospect's success. With the Influence Mindset, you position yourself not just as an expert but as a guide who adds unique value to their journey.

Example 3:

THE ACHIEVEMENT MINDSET:

#1: "I've helped clients navigate difficult markets like this before, and know what it takes."

THE INFLUENCE MINDSET:

#2: "In markets like this, it can be stressful and overwhelming. **But I've found that when clients keep [this thing] in mind,** *time and time again they have been able to get the best results in the end."*

Why These Phrases Work (or Don't Work)

The **Achievement Mindset** phrase leans heavily on the speaker's expertise and past accomplishments. It essentially says, "I've done this before, so you can trust me," but it doesn't create a meaningful connection or instill confidence in how the process applies specifically to them.

The **Influence Mindset** phrase takes a more empathetic and collaborative approach. By acknowledging the emotional challenges of difficult markets ("it can be stressful and overwhelming"), it resonates with the prospect's feelings, building trust and rapport. Then, it shifts to offering a key insight that aligns with their needs, empowering them with a proven strategy. This approach not only conveys competence but also positions you as someone who understands their experience and has actionable wisdom to guide them through it.

Here's How This Applies in Sales Situations

Let's take the example of someone selling a high-end software solution to a company in a turbulent economic climate. Using the **Achievement Mindset**, the salesperson might say:

"I've helped companies navigate market downturns like this before and know how to guide you through it. We've helped hundreds of organizations just like yours."

While this statement highlights experience, it doesn't differentiate the salesperson or their solution from competitors. It also risks sounding generic, as it fails to acknowledge the client's specific concerns or challenges.

Now consider the **Influence Mindset**: *"In times like these, companies often feel torn between cutting costs and pursuing opportunities. But I've found that when teams focus on [a key strategy, like streamlining processes or leveraging specific tools], they consistently emerge stronger and better positioned for the future. Let's explore how that could work for you."*

This phrasing is transformative because it goes beyond competence to address the emotional tension the client may feel. By acknowledging the stress of the market and offering a tailored insight, it builds confidence and positions the salesperson as a collaborative partner who not only understands the client's struggles but also offers a meaningful path forward.

Wrap Up: From Knowledge to Insight: Your Competitive Advantage

Malcom McLean didn't just succeed because he was competent. His competitors were also skilled operators with decades of experience moving goods. What made him stand out was his ability to see a problem differently and articulate a solution that resonated with the deeper goals of the people he was trying to influence [17]. McLean didn't talk about the technical specs of his containers or how they were built; instead, he painted a picture of how his idea would make life easier, simpler, and more profitable for the port of Newark. By communicating in Insight, he built a bridge no one else could match.

This is the shift we must make in our communication. When we default to sharing Knowledge and Experience, we center the conversation on ourselves. And while competence matters, it's not what opens the door to influence. Insight and Wisdom are the tools that allow us to meet our prospects where they are, offering not just answers, but clarity and confidence. When you connect what you know to what your prospects need, you make their path easier—and that's when you become the obvious choice.

Imagine this: Every conversation you have is an opportunity to either reinforce what they already believe about you—or elevate their understanding of your value. Speaking in terms of Knowledge and Experience might get you to the table, but Insight and Wisdom are what will influence their perception of you. In a world drowning in information, what people crave is someone who can make sense of it, simplify their decisions, and guide them forward.

So, as you close this chapter, ask yourself: Are you simply stacking facts, or are you constructing a bridge that connects your expertise to the heart of your prospect's challenges and goals? Because the future isn't won by those who merely know the most—it's won by those who can take what they know and show why it matters to others.

❝Speaking in terms of Knowledge and Experience might get you to the table, but Insight and Wisdom are what will influence their perception of you. ❞

Chapter 4: Key Takeaways

- **Pyramid of Information:** There are 4 levels of information: Knowledge, Experience, Insight, and Wisdom. Most people communicate in the lower levels of Knowledge and Experience, but master communicators frame their value in Insight and Wisdom.

- **While Knowledge and Experience Come across as Noise** (because most people speak on this level), speaking in Insight and Wisdom connects directly to the Survival Brain in ways it is predisposed to pay attention to.

- **Speaking in Insight Creates a Clear Path Forward** for your prospect and helps them get to where they want to go...faster. Knowledge and Experience, while they may speak to YOUR brain's needs, create an additional piece of work for your prospect to figure out why you are relevant to them.

- **The Achievement Mindset Thinks:** "How can I prove I'm credible and impressive?" Whereas the Influence Mindset thinks: "What unique insight or perspective speaks directly to their challenges?"

- **Malcom McLean's Success Wasn't Just in Having a Great Idea;** it was in his ability to communicate its impact in a way that inspired action.

Bonus

I've created exclusive content to help you apply the principles we cover together. To access them, go to: **www.TheChristianHansen.com/ BookBonus**

SUMMARY TABLE

INFLUENCE FORMULA:	Competence	(Plus) Connection	(Equals) Influence
ENVIRONMENT:	Performance Environment	Relational Environment	Selective Environment
DEFINITION OF SUCCESS:	Where Success Is Based On How Well You Perform	Where Success Is Based On How Well You Connect & Work With Others	Where Success Is Based On Influencing People To Choose You
STRATEGY:	Achievement Mindset	Charismatic Mindset	Influence Mindset
DEFINITION OF STRATEGY:	Success Happens When I Prove My Value Is High	Success Happens When I Am Likable, Relatable, & Win People Over	Success Happens When You Influence Someone To Choose You Over Others
IF INCOMPLETE?	Competence (Without) Connection = Noise	Connection (Without) Competence = Charm	Competence With Connection = Influence
BRAIN'S DEFINITIONS OF SUCCESS:	SURVIVAL BRAIN Success = When I Meet My Brain's Needs For Security, Resources, Novelty, Belonging, & Status…		EXECUTIVE BRAIN Success = When I Meet Their Brain's Needs For Security, (etc.)
STRATEGIES	ACHIEVEMENT THINKING	CHARISMATIC THINKING	INFLUENCE BRAIN HACKS
Competence Strategy #1: LOGIC VS EMOTION	*How Can I Convince Them I'm Qualified & Capable?*	*N/A*	How Can I Also Acknowledge This Person's Emotions Right Now?
Competence Strategy #2: KNOWLEDGE VS INSIGHT	*How Can I Prove I'm Credible & Impressive?*	*N/A*	What Unique Insight Or Perspective Speaks Directly To Their Challenges?

?	?	?	?
?	?	?	?
?	?	?	?
?	?	?	?
?	?		?

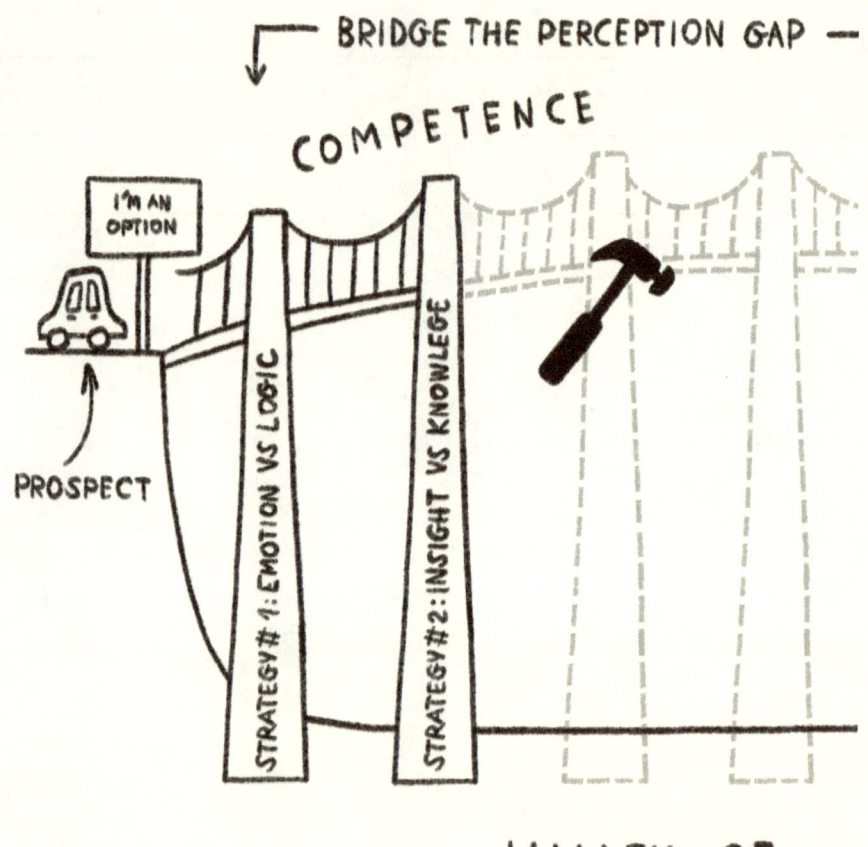

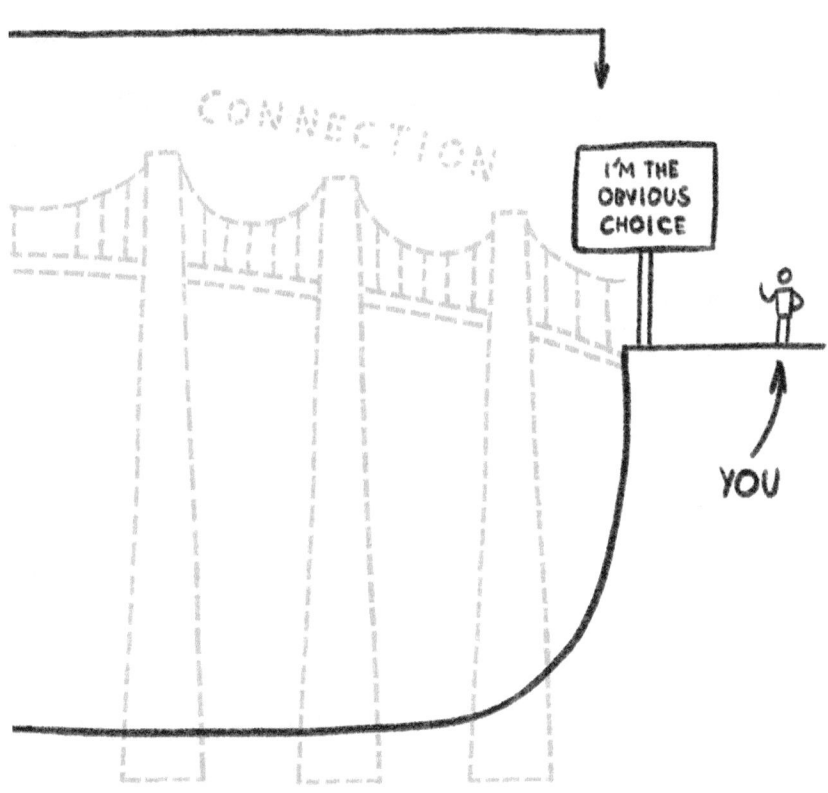

IRRELEVANCE

HOW TO GET A $150-MILLION SHOE

"My mentor said, 'Let's go do it,' not 'You go do it.' How
powerful when someone says, 'Let's!'"

— Jim Rohn

"The mark of a wise man is not in what they say but in what
they enable YOU to say."

— Anonymous

When Deloris Peoples was born in September 1941, few could have
guessed she would become one of the greatest influences in the
history of modern sports. Raised in the small town of Rocky Point,
North Carolina, Deloris was taught to value hard work, determination,
and self-sufficiency; traits she undoubtedly picked up from her father,
Edward Peoples [1].

In a time when most African Americans in the South struggled
against unjust laws and economic systems designed to keep them
disempowered and destitute, Edward Peoples, through years of effort
and personal advancement, was a rare economic success. In contrast to
most tenant farmers and sharecroppers in their town, the Peoples family
proudly owned their own farm and enjoyed modest financial prosperity.

This drive and ambition inherited from her father sustained Deloris through much of her difficult life. At the age of 16, she had her first child, married, and then supported her husband James as he served in the Air Force. [2]. Over the next decade, the young couple moved several times to accommodate James's military deployments, and 4 more children followed. Soon enough, Deloris's singular focus and drive paid off as her growing family enjoyed the financial fruits of her and James's determined efforts. Sadly, however, their marriage was often turbulent with instances of physical abuse.

Despite the obstacles, her devotion to her family and the values she inherited from her father drove her forward. In particular, her fourth son Michael was a gifted athlete. With Deloris's dedication and force of will, Michael excelled both as an athlete and as a student and soon received a scholarship to play basketball for the University of North Carolina at Chapel Hill. There he received the attention of professional scouts, and despite his mother's wishes, put his education on hold to enter the 1984 NBA draft, where he was selected by the Chicago Bulls.

As her son, Michael Jordan, adjusted to his newfound fame, he often turned to Deloris for her guidance and wisdom to make decisions. And her acumen and sharp insight were never more needed than when the Jordan family met a man named Sonny Vaccaro and an obscure shoe company called Nike.

The Mafioso Marketer

When it came to basketball shoes in the 1970s, the two biggest names were undoubtedly Adidas, based in Germany, and Converse, headquartered in Boston. No one would have considered Nike (all the way out in Beaverton, Oregon) as a serious competitor. The reason? Nike made shoes for runners and track and field athletes. However, the scrappy company was looking for ways to grow [3].

Enter Sonny Vaccaro. Originally from Pittsburgh, Vaccaro was a young school teacher who had a love of basketball and a keen eye for opportunities. In 1964 he and a college roommate started the "Dapper Dan Roundball Classic," an amateur basketball tournament showcasing up-and-coming talent. Year after year the tournament grew, and eventually, coaches the likes of John Wooden from UCLA attended to scout recruits. Vaccaro, a master of being in the right place at the right time, networked his way into the highest levels of college basketball and developed valuable relationships with top coaches and players from around the country [4].

Then in 1977, Vaccaro had an idea. "What if I could turn my relationships into revenue?" And what better potential opportunity than with Nike, who was itching to expand into the basketball market. He brazenly called up Nike and proposed a simple plan: If Nike designed a shoe for basketball players, then Vaccaro could work his vast network of college coaches and sign up their programs to wear the shoes. The resulting sponsorship would, in turn, boost Nike's publicity, credibility, and eventual shoe sales. It would also cement Vaccaro as one of the movers and shakers in American basketball.

Nike executives were leary of this guy from Pittsburgh who looked more a mafioso than a marketer, but they decided to give him a try. Vaccaro got to work, and in 1978 when Indiana State's Larry Bird was featured on the cover of *Sports Illustrated*...wearing a pair of Nikes because of Vaccaro... sales exploded. Nike was thrilled with Vaccaro's efforts and poured more money into his strategy. Soon, Adidas and Converse followed suit with their own competing sponsorship campaigns [5].

By the 1980s, Vaccaro was paying millions each year to college programs through Nike sponsorships, and the basketball shoe market was growing. That's when he was introduced to Michael Jordan, one of the rising stars in basketball. Though Vaccaro was impressed with Jordan's talents, at the time UNC Chapel Hill's program was already under contract with Converse. Even so, Jordan was an Adidas fan through and through. During games, he dutifully wore Converse shoes. But in practice? Jordan switched back to Adidas.

Nike wasn't even on his radar.

The Shoe

As the 1984 NBA draft neared, could Vaccaro sign Michael Jordan to wear Nike shoes in the NBA? The problem was that Converse and Adidas were asking the same question. And with Jordan's preference for Adidas, Vaccaro knew he would have to make his offer stand out from all the others. How could he make Nike the obvious choice?

That year, Nike had designated a $2.5-million budget for pro-basketball shoe endorsements and were accustomed to dividing it up among several rising stars. Vaccaro, however, pushed for all of it to be given to Jordan. But he didn't stop there. Vaccaro wanted to have a new shoe line designed in Jordan's name. The name of the new shoe brand? Air Jordan [6].

All these competing opportunities presented a dilemma for Michael Jordan. On one hand, Nike offered equity in the company, ownership of his own brand, and a greater amount of opportunity. But it was a much smaller company with an unknown track record, and he didn't like their shoes. Adidas and Converse, on the other hand, were much bigger companies and had better reputations. But if he chose Adidas or Converse, Jordan would be indistinguishable. He would be just like everyone else in a long line of other sponsored athletes.

What was the better choice?

Enter Deloris.

As the immature and often petulant Michael flip-flopped over which deal to choose, Deloris took charge. In fact, the night before the Jordans were set to fly out to Oregon and meet with Nike in person, Michael phoned his parents, saying he didn't want to go. However, his mother insisted he show up at the airport, and the next morning, show up he did. Once in Beaverton, Deloris was a force to be reckoned with at the negotiating table. She insisted on per-shoe-sale royalties and argued for further gains on behalf of her son. As the meetings with Nike progressed, Vaccaro and other executives were floored at her level of focus and intensity. Vaccaro later said, "I can tell you she is one of the most impressive people I've met in my life, because she was able to negotiate this life for her son." [7]

But what Vaccaro couldn't have known was how Deloris's intense upbringing and ambition instilled from her father were coming to the fore in this moment. Having grown up in the coastal plains of North Carolina, Deloris, like her father, had no intention of ever being a tenant farmer on someone else's land or a sharecropper within someone else's brand—which is essentially what Adidas and Converse were offering. With their companies, the Jordans would be wage earners and voiceless cogs in vast corporate machines. They wouldn't have ownership, they wouldn't have control, and would be disposable the moment Michael wasn't useful anymore. As impressive as the corporate offers were, they fundamentally ran against the deeply held values of independence and advancement that had driven Deloris and her family for so long.

Nike's offer, on the other hand, opened the doors for further opportunity. It resonated with her goals and core narrative for generational growth and security and created a future that aligned with the dreams of her past. Instead of wage earners, the Jordans would join Nike as *partners* with ownership stakes and financial control. Michael would be indispensable, not disposable, and Nike was going all in on the future of her son. In short, Nike enabled the Jordans to be the heroes of their own remarkable family story, not the other way around. This spoke to Deloris on a very deep level. And ultimately, it was that distinction that influenced Deloris Peoples Jordan to convince her son, Michael Jordan, to choose Nike as his official shoe sponsor over the more established and prestigious companies, Adidas and Converse.

Vaccaro later said, "This woman was everything. Michael loved his father, he did. But Deloris ran the show." [8]

The rest, they say, was history. Over the next 3 years, Nike would make an eye-watering $150 million in Air Jordan shoe sales, with Michael Jordan receiving a royalty for each shoe sold. Today, the Air Jordan Brand brings in annual revenues numbering in billions of dollars and made Michael Jordan the first billionaire athlete in history. But even more impactful, Deloris's negotiating prowess changed the landscape for professional athletes and corporate sponsorships, making her one of the greatest influences on modern sport. The power of the personal brand was born, athletes were given more ownership and control, and today "Name, Image, and Likeness" deals have begun to also shape the world of collegiate sports [9].

All because of one remarkable woman from Rocky Point, North Carolina, and her indomitable drive to make her family succeed.

What does this have to do with influencing people to choose you?

Your Prospect is on Their Own Hero's Journey

Whatever field you are in, you must imagine that your prospect is just like Deloris Peoples Jordan. They are trying to get somewhere that is deeply meaningful to them.

Maybe it's a sense of security. Maybe it's a greater sense of belonging. Maybe they are searching for a greater degree of status. Whatever it is, they are deeply motivated to find a solution to help them get there. The question is, are you trying to become part of THEIR success story, like Nike? Or are you trying to make them part of YOUR success story, like Adidas and Converse?

To put it another way, are you trying to make THEM the hero of THEIR own story? Or are YOU trying to be the hero of THEIR story?

"Are you trying to make THEM the hero of THEIR own story? Or are YOU trying to be the hero of THEIR story?"

Here's why this matters so much. One of the most powerful ways that humans make sense of the world is through the lens of storytelling [10]. We often see ourselves on a journey trying to overcome something or on a path towards realizing meaningful goals [11]. In narratology (the science of studying stories), the narrative of a protagonist trying to effect a change through overcoming an obstacle is called "The Hero's Journey."

Let's take a moment to break down a key part of The Hero's Journey and why it matters for influencing people to choose you. And to do that, let me introduce the idea of archetypes.

Archetypes

I look at stories the same way a car mechanic looks at a car engine. In a great story, there are a lot of moving parts, each with a different job to do. If they all work together? You have a story that (like an engine) can create extraordinary power and move people. But if a piece is missing or doesn't do its job properly, then the story sputters and fails to leave an impact.

One of the critical parts to any story are the archetypes, or roles that specific characters play. Let's start with the most common one: the Hero.

Think about any great story you relate to. It is almost always centered around a person trying to get somewhere, obtain something, or accomplish some important achievement. Consider the following examples from popular culture and literature:

- Luke Skywalker is trying to learn how to become a Jedi in order to overthrow the Galactic Empire in *Star Wars: A New Hope*.
- Frodo is trying to destroy the ring in J.R.R. Tolkien's *The Fellowship of the Ring*.
- Moana is trying to save her family's island in the Disney movie *Moana*.
- Even in the Bible, Moses is trying to lead his people out of Egypt.

Luke, Frodo, Moana, and Moses all would fall under the archetype of the "Hero" in each of these stories. From the outset, they are clearly pursuing a worthy ideal we can relate to.

 SOMEONE WHO IS PURSUING A WORTHY GOAL OR IDEAL

However, there are clear things or people that stand in their way... impeding their progress.

- Luke Skywalker must face Darth Vader and the oppressive Galactic Empire, who seek to control the galaxy and crush the Rebel Alliance.

- Frodo is relentlessly pursued by Sauron's dark forces, including the Nazgûl, who will stop at nothing to retrieve the One Ring.

- Moana must overcome the fiery demon Te Kā, who stands between her and restoring the heart of Te Fiti.

- Moses is opposed by Pharaoh, whose hardened heart refuses to let the Israelites go.

In these examples, Darth Vader, Sauron, Te Kā, and Pharaoh (aside from being an intriguing group for a dinner party) are the antagonists, and they all fall under the narrative archetype of Villain. They are the main obstacles for our intrepid Heroes.

 **A PERSON WHO CREATES OBSTACLES FOR THE MAIN CHARACTER OR PROTAGONIST**

And along the way, our Heroes often encounter a third group of people who are suffering or at risk in some way because of the Villains and their actions:

- Luke Skywalker sees the destruction of Alderaan, an entire planet wiped out by the Empire, leaving its people annihilated and Leia as the sole survivor of her family.

- Frodo witnesses the devastation of Middle-earth, with villages burned and lives ruined by Sauron's minions, the Ringwraiths and orcs.

- Moana finds her island's crops dying, the fish disappearing, and her people's way of life threatened by the spreading darkness caused by Te Kā.

- Moses leads the Israelites, who are enslaved and brutalized by Pharaoh's oppressive regime, enduring unimaginable suffering and hardship.

In all these instances, the obliterated people of Alderaan, displaced villagers of Middle-earth, Moana's struggling villagers, and the enslaved Israelites would fall under the narrative archetype we call Victims. We pity their cause and, like the Hero, feel empathy for their plight to the point where action is justified.

VICTIM	A PERSON WHO EXPERIENCES HARM, SUFFERING, OR LOSS DUE TO THE ACTIONS OF ANOTHER CHARACTER OR EXTERNAL FORCES

There are, of course, many other archetypes, but the three most common are those we have covered above: Hero, Villain, and Victim. If you were to ponder the stories you know and love, you could probably provide many additional examples. The truth is, you've been trained through years of reading, listening, and watching stories to quickly identify characters that are playing these archetypal roles in whatever story you encounter. It's likely you have even personally identified with some of them in your own life and related to their struggles and triumphs.

THREE MOST COMMON ARCHETYPES

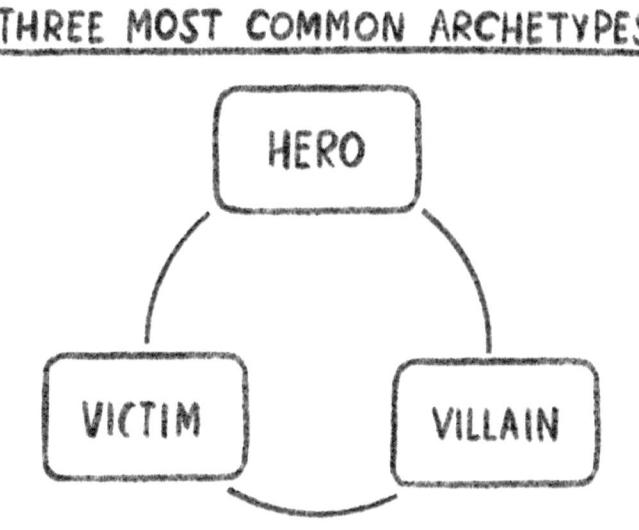

Which brings us to our core problem: If YOU are really good at interpreting the world through the lens of story, and if YOU are good at identifying archetypes and the roles people play, then your prospect is ALSO very good at experiencing their world and reality through story and archetypes.

My question is: In important sales situations, is YOUR story getting in the way of THEIR story?

Wait... If YOU'RE the Hero, Then What About Me?

I once was considering joining a coaching program to help me grow my business. I was attracted to their marketing and content and hoped they had the right solutions for my needs at the time. I had had calls with their sales reps, which were all positive, but hadn't felt quite ready to pull the trigger.

A few weeks later, I was traveling and happened to be close to their headquarters. I had heard they welcomed visitors and offered tours of their space, so I reached out to one of my contacts there. I asked if I could stop by and see their space, and they graciously agreed. Maybe going in person would help me decide if this was the right choice for me.

I arrived, and after briefly waiting in the lobby, a younger employee came out to greet me. "Welcome!" he said, "I am excited to show you around!" And he invited me to follow as we walked through some secure doors to their offices and event spaces.

I hadn't met this person before, and despite being very friendly, I found it odd that he didn't take the time to ask any questions about me or what I was looking for in particular. But I followed along regardless, trying to be polite.

As we toured the premises, the person chatted away about how great it was to work there and how great the benefits were for employees. He listed the awards the company had received from their community and

"In important sales situations, is YOUR story getting in the way of THEIR story?"

how wonderful an organization they were. He even departed from what I assumed was a well-rehearsed script to mention how he was a theater major in college and loved giving tours to people because it was a chance for him to finally use his speaking skills. "And it's great helping our customers, because they come here feeling so lost in their business and needing direction."

That's all well and good, I thought to myself, but how does that help me decide if this is the right thing for me and my business?

Several times during the tour, I tried to ask questions about aspects of their program and details of what I was looking for. I was seeking some assurance, some glimmer of hope that I was in the right place. The employee, though friendly and kind, was clearly out of his depth with my questions and suggested I reach out to the sales reps for more details.

Well, he's useless, I thought.

As the tour ended in the lobby right back where we started, the young employee thought he had absolutely nailed it. He was pleased as punch with himself, and after handing me some promotional materials, wished me a good day as he left through the secure doors.

There I stood in the lobby, holding brochures (that I had previously read before as online PDFs), feeling like I had wasted my morning. What on earth just happened? I wondered.

As I drove away, I reflected on my experience. While many aspects of my visit had been off-putting, one of them had to do with archetypes. I originally reached out to this company because I was on MY own Hero's Journey. I was trying to overcome an obstacle, I was trying to get somewhere with my own business, and when I came to the headquarters, I was hoping to get some answers. In a very real way, I was trying to be the Hero of my story by venturing out into the unknown and exploring my options.

Instead, I encountered a young employee who was trying to be the Hero of HIS journey. Giving the tour was the culmination of HIS dreams, not the starting point of mine. He was FINALLY getting to put his theater degree to use and realizing his dream of being someone who speaks in front of others. As a professional speaker myself, I can certainly relate to that narrative. However, in that moment, he was not in a Performance Environment, where his success was based on how well he presented. He was really in a Selective Environment, where I was deciding to choose his company or not.

This brings us to one of the most common pitfalls in sales situations. In Selective Environments, if you are trying to be the Hero of the moment, it doesn't leave any space for your prospect to be the Hero of theirs. Even worse, it forces them to see themselves as something OTHER than the Hero of their own story. Did you notice what my guide said about their customers?

"...It's great helping our customers, because they come here feeling so lost in their business and needing direction."

"If you are trying to be the Hero of the moment, it doesn't leave any space for your prospect to be the Hero of theirs. "

Does that language describe their customer as someone trying to be the Hero of their own story? Or does it describe them as the archetypal Victim who is powerless to effect desired change?

If we all view our lived experiences through the lens of story, and if you are taking center stage as the Hero in that moment, that leaves your prospect in the uncomfortable position of finding another role to see themselves as. And of the main three, if the Hero is taken, all that's left is the Victim or the Villain: the person who is powerless, or the person who is the problem.

And let me tell you, no one likes to see themselves as the Victim or Villain of their story.

Which is exactly what happened when I toured that coaching company. Despite the positive marketing and excellent content, that in-person interaction left me walking away feeling like I was a fool for reaching out for help in the first place. I left feeling like I was powerless, and also ignorant...feelings I don't like feeling at all. In short, it left a very bad taste in my mouth that negatively influenced my perception of their company's value.

If that is how they treated their tour guests, I wondered, what does that say about their coaching experience?

And so I walked away looking for another option—just like Deloris Peoples Jordan left the promising offers of Adidas and Converse on the table.

The Fourth Archetype: The Guide

In Selective Environments, instead of being the Hero, what if you tried a different strategy altogether? Let me introduce you to the fourth most common Archetype: The Guide.

In all great stories, the Guide is the wise person who helps the Hero *become* the Hero. They don't try to steal the spotlight or claim victory for themselves. Instead, their role is to offer insight, encouragement, and the tools the Hero needs to overcome challenges and fulfill their journey. The Guide doesn't accomplish the mission for the Hero—they empower the Hero to rise to the occasion and succeed on their own terms.

The Guide is critical because they bridge the gap between the Hero's potential and their reality. Without the Guide, the Hero may lack the clarity, confidence, or perspective needed to overcome the obstacles in their way. In storytelling, the Guide offers wisdom earned from their own experiences, often presenting a framework or strategy that the Hero must adapt to their unique journey.

GUIDE   A PERSON WHO HELPS THE HERO BECOME THE HERO

"The Guide bridges the gap between the Hero's potential and their reality."

Let's look at how the Guide plays out in the stories we've been discussing:

- Luke Skywalker has Obi-Wan Kenobi as well as Yoda. They both teach him about the Force, show him what it means to be a Jedi, and inspire Luke to embrace his destiny.

- Frodo relies on Gandalf, whose unwavering faith and deep knowledge of Middle-earth provide the guidance and courage Frodo needs to carry the Ring.

- Moana is mentored by Maui, who, despite his initial reluctance, teaches her the skills and resilience needed to restore the heart of Te Fiti and find her inner strength.

- Moses is guided by God, who speaks to him through the burning bush, provides him with miracles, and reassures him that he is capable of leading his people to freedom.

Not one of these Guides overshadow the Hero, instead they equip them with the tools, knowledge, and confidence to take the journey ahead. And in sales situations, learning to position yourself as a Guide can be powerful when influencing people to choose you.

THE FOURTH ARCHETYPE

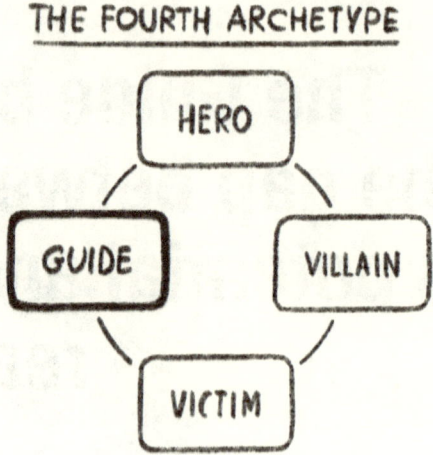

How a Guide Helps You Feel Like the Hero

After the disappointing in-person tour, where it became clear the first coaching program wasn't the right fit, I was reminded of a second program run by a coach I was previously introduced to and trusted. I reached out and scheduled a call to see if his program was a good option.

As our call began, he first listened and then took the time to ask careful questions about my goals and what I was trying to accomplish. Consider the words he used when he spoke with me:

- "I think your instincts are right about your potential market, and I can tell you are headed in the right direction."

- "I think you've definitely seen a gap that no one else is fully addressing. But there are some hidden pitfalls most people stumble over, and I can help you see what those are."

- "Your progress is incredible, and I'm just amazed at everything you have accomplished since we last spoke. You are definitely on the right track."

- "You'd be the perfect fit for our program because there are people in there who would be highly advantageous for you to network with. Plus your perspectives for them would be invaluable and you'd add a lot to our meetings."

- "My goal is for you to walk away from our first coaching session knowing the top three things you should focus on and to have a blueprint for exactly what you should do for the rest of the year."

To me, the experience talking with the second coach was completely different than the first program I toured. Can you see how he subtly positioned himself as the Guide? His language made me feel like I was on the right path for my journey, and he helped create a vision for where I was trying to go. In short, he made me feel like the Hero of my own story, and I felt a more powerful emotional connection with his offer.

Ultimately, I chose his program over the first one.

The Influence Mindset

In each of these examples, Adidas, Converse, and the tour I took with the first coaching company all struggled with the Achievement Mindset, which walks into Selective Environments trying to serve THEIR brain's needs. People with the Achievement Mindset are often thinking: How can I prove I'm the best option they should trust?

THE ACHIEVEMENT MINDSET:

How can I prove I'm the best option they should trust?

In contrast, Nike and the second coaching opportunity I explored insightfully put aside their own insecure brain's needs and used the Influence Mindset, asking: How can I help them feel like the Hero of their story?

THE ACHIEVEMENT MINDSET:

How can I prove I'm the best option they should trust?

THE INFLUENCE MINDSET:

How can I help them feel like the Hero of their story?

This is exactly what Sonny Vaccaro did with the Jordan family. He positioned Nike and himself as Guides helping the Jordans become the Heroes of their own story. He spoke about how Nike was going all in with their long term relationship because they saw something unique in Michael Jordan (that others didn't recognize), and positioned their offer in a way that empowered the Jordans to reach their own dreams. And the rest was history.

Similarly, the second coaching opportunity framed their value in such a way that they had the perspectives and nuggets of insight I needed to reach my next level. I felt like they were sincere in their desire to help me get to where I wanted to go and could relate and understand exactly what I was going through. They also helped me feel like the Hero of my own story.

When you enter the Selective Environment and your Survival Brain is throwing a fit and grasping for control, take the time to ask the brain-hacking question, "How can I help them feel like the Hero of their story?" Your Executive Brain will notice hidden opportunities for influence that most others overlook and will make you one step closer to being the obvious choice compared to everyone else.

But why? Why is speaking and positioning yourself as the Guide so powerful? It turns out the answer lies, as with everything else, in our brain.

Guiding Our Brains

The first reason why positioning yourself as a Guide is so powerful has to do with a concept we've covered previously. Remember the Pyramid of Information and the differences between Knowledge, Experience, Insight, and Wisdom? When Guides speak, they primarily do so at the levels of Insight and Wisdom (higher and more valuable forms of information) compared to Heroes, who tend to speak in Knowledge and Experience. As we've covered, speaking in Insight and Wisdom and being seen as a strategic thinker can increase your perceived value to nearly 50 times more than others who are merely highly skilled [12].

Wouldn't you like to be seen as nearly 50 times more valuable than your competitors who are spinning their wheels being the Hero of the moment?

Second, when Guides speak, they often provide paradigm shifts and enable Heroes to look at problems in unique and novel ways. As we have also covered, speaking in paradigm shifts creates explosive reactions in the reward centers of the brain and empowers Heroes to find novel ways to overcome their difficult challenges [13]. And if you recall, "novelty" is one of our brain's core evolutionary needs it is wired to pay attention to.

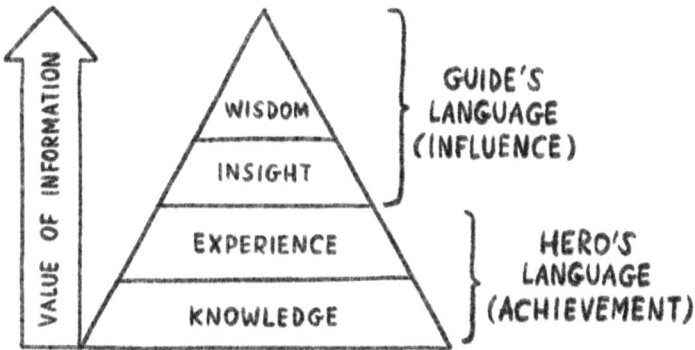

But the benefits run much deeper.

Ain't No Mountain High, Ain't No Valley Low

In 2008, researchers at the University of Virginia took a group of students to a hill located nearby campus and asked a simple question: Can you describe how high you think that hill is?

"When we have people we trust standing by our side, our perception of the world literally changes for the better. "

What they discovered is fascinating:

When students were alone and standing by themselves, they tended to describe the hill as steep and difficult to climb. However, when students were standing with a trusted friend at their side? They described the hill as being much lower and easier to climb.

Same hill, but completely different perceptions of its height. All influenced by whether *someone was standing next to them or not*. When we have people we trust standing by our side, our perception of the world literally changes for the better.

The researchers then discovered that the same phenomenon occurs when we are assessing a challenge in our lives. When we have the "psychosocial support" of another trusted person, it decreases the perceived difficulty of whatever we are facing. Researchers found that, in these situations, challenges seem less daunting, obstacles less formidable, and opportunities more attainable.

But when we face an obstacle by ourselves with no one next to us? The world is perceived to be a much harder place [14].

Can you see the implications for positioning yourself as the Guide?

In the world of story, Guides walk with the Hero every step of the way. When an obstacle looms? The Guide is right there standing beside the Hero, facing it together. As your prospect faces their own mountain to climb or valley to cross, when you position yourself as the Guide, that mountain is perceived to be less steep, and the valley seems less wide. All of a sudden, that problem is a lot easier to overcome because you are with them.

I guess the classic Marvin Gaye and Tammi Terrel song rings true: That mountain ain't so high, and that valley ain't so low...anymore. All because of you, baby.

And you are one step closer to being the obvious choice.

But when YOU are the Hero, your prospect sees you charging up the mountain or braving the deep valley...leaving them where they started. Standing there all alone, their problem suddenly looks steeper, harder, and uglier than they first realized. And so your prospect feels discouraged and turns around to find a better, less difficult way to get where they want to go.

Your prospect chooses someone else instead of you.

Story Always Makes Things Better

Another group of researchers wanted to find out whether or not helping people see themselves as the protagonist in a Hero's Journey made any difference in their well-being and happiness. So they conducted 8 different studies with hundreds of participants where they first measured people's life satisfaction and sense of meaning. Then they asked the participants to compare their current struggles to those of protagonists in the Hero's Journey, and then followed up by measuring the participants' life satisfaction afterwards.

The researchers essentially created a "story intervention" where they helped people switch their paradigm to suddenly seeing themselves as a protagonist in a larger narrative.

The results confirmed that when you help people see themselves as a Hero journeying towards achieving an important goal, they experience higher rates of "well-being, higher life satisfaction, and lower rates of depression." They also feel they are "flourishing" in their life [15].

This is powerful.

When you walk into a sales situation and intentionally position yourself as a Guide, you have the power to help your prospect suddenly feel like they are on a Hero's journey. As they look at a bewildering world filled with confusion and uncertainty, you can overlay a framework in their lives that provides instantaneous clarity, simplicity, and motivation to move forward. And whether they may currently feel that way or not,

❝ Guides make the Hero feel like the Hero… even if a person may not see themselves as a Hero at first. ❞

your language and behaviors will influence them to feel more purpose, meaning, and less depression.

Again, Guides make the Hero feel like the Hero...even if a person may not see themselves as a Hero at first. That paradigm shift can change everything and make your prospect like, trust, and see you as the obvious choice. All while your competitors are taking the center spot as the Hero, feeding THEIR brain's needs, and leaving their prospects feeling alone, struggling, and lost.

Positioning yourself as the Guide sounds like a no-brainer to me.

Lets Get Tactical

So how do you do this? How can you frame your value in ways that position you as the Guide to your prospects? Let's take a look at several examples and explore why they matter.

Example 1:

THE ACHIEVEMENT MINDSET:	THE INFLUENCE MINDSET:
#1: "I've helped X number of companies/clients and have been doing this for X number of years."	#2: "After helping X companies/clients for X many years, **here's why I think you have a great shot at this.**"

Why These Phrases Work or Don't Work

The **Achievement Mindset** phrase focuses exclusively on the salesperson's experience and accomplishments, which—while impressive—feels self-centered and transactional. This phrase assumes that expertise alone will earn trust, which often isn't enough in sales situations. Instead of building connection, it focuses on the seller's story rather than the buyer's needs.

In contrast, the **Influence Mindset** phrase reframes the salesperson's expertise in terms of its relevance to the prospect's goals. By pivoting to why the prospect has "a great shot at this," the salesperson demonstrates belief in the prospect's potential. This creates a powerful blend of competence and connection, acknowledging both the salesperson's credibility as a Guide and the prospect's unique Hero's Journey. It's a much more emotionally engaging approach, making the prospect feel seen and supported.

Here's How This Applies in Sales Situations

In sales, decision-makers don't just want to know that you're qualified—they want to know how your expertise applies to their specific situation. The **Achievement Mindset** approach can leave prospects feeling like they're just another notch on the salesperson's belt. For instance, a financial advisor might say, *"I've managed portfolios for hundreds of clients over the past decade."* While true, it doesn't engage the client's emotions or build a connection.

On the other hand, the **Influence Mindset** approach personalizes the conversation. That same financial advisor could say, *"After managing portfolios for hundreds of clients over the past decade, I've seen people in your position make incredible strides. Here's why I believe you can too."* This subtle shift signals belief in the client's ability to succeed, which builds trust and inspires action. More importantly it reinforces their world view as the Hero of their own story."

When prospects feel your belief in them, they are far more likely to see you as the obvious choice.

"When prospects feel your belief in them, they are far more likely to see you as the obvious choice."

Example 2:

THE ACHIEVEMENT MINDSET:	THE INFLUENCE MINDSET:
#1: *"In my X years of experience, I can tell you here's what's going wrong, here's what has to be done, and here's what needs to be fixed."*	#2: *"From my years of experience and all the clients I've worked with, **here's why I think you're further along than you think..."***

Why These Phrases Work or Don't Work

The **Achievement Mindset** phrase places the focus squarely on the salesperson's expertise and their ability to diagnose and prescribe solutions. While this can seem confident, it often comes across as patronizing or dismissive of the prospect's efforts or progress so far. It subtly implies that the prospect is doing everything wrong, which can make them feel like the Victim (helpless) or the Villain (the problem).

The **Influence Mindset** phrase flips the narrative, starting with acknowledgment of the prospect's progress rather than their shortcomings. By emphasizing, *"You're further along than you think,"* the salesperson builds confidence and positions themselves as an encouraging guide rather than a critical expert. It creates a safe space for the prospect to engage, explore, and trust the salesperson's insights without feeling judged or criticized.

Here's How This Applies in Sales Situations

When a salesperson operates with the **Achievement Mindset**, they often lead with critique. For example, a business consultant might say, *"Your current operations are inefficient, and here's what needs to change."* While technically accurate, this approach can make the prospect feel small, inadequate, or overwhelmed. It puts the salesperson in the "Hero" role, making the interaction about THEIR ability to fix things rather than the prospect's journey toward success.

The **Influence Mindset**, on the other hand, starts with affirmation, which builds trust and opens the door for constructive collaboration. That same consultant might say, *"From what I've seen in companies like yours, you're further along than most people realize. With just a few key adjustments, you could unlock incredible potential."* This frames the prospect as capable and positions the salesperson as a supportive guide who can help refine their success.

In sales situations, starting with acknowledgment and encouragement disarms defensiveness and creates an emotional connection. By shifting the focus from fixing problems to building on strengths, the **Influence Mindset** fosters trust and positions the salesperson as a trusted partner in the prospect's journey.

Example 3:

THE ACHIEVEMENT MINDSET:	THE INFLUENCE MINDSET:
#1: *"Actually, here's why your approach isn't working, and what you should be doing instead."*	#2: *"**I think your instincts are right about that, and what's most impressive** is how you already have done (or noticed) XYZ…"*

Why These Phrases Work or Don't Work

The **Achievement Mindset** phrase, while potentially well-intentioned, focuses entirely on critique and correction. It positions the salesperson as the all-knowing expert who must "rescue" the prospect from their errors. While the salesperson may genuinely have a better approach, the tone of this phrase dismisses the prospect. Instead of creating trust, it risks making the prospect feel judged or inadequate, which can lead to defensiveness or disengagement.

On the other hand, the **Influence Mindset** phrase starts by validating the prospect's instincts and acknowledging their accomplishments. This immediately disarms defensiveness and reinforces the idea that the prospect is capable and on the right path. By highlighting what the prospect has "already done or noticed," the salesperson builds their confidence while subtly guiding them toward deeper insights.

Here's How This Applies in Sales Situations

When using the **Achievement Mindset**, salespeople often approach conversations with a problem-solving mindset, eager to point out flaws and offer solutions. For example, a fitness coach might say, *"Your current workout routine isn't effective, and you need to change it entirely."* While technically accurate, this approach can leave the client feeling defeated and reluctant to trust the coach's guidance. It makes the conversation about "what's wrong" instead of building on "what's working."

The **Influence Mindset**, however, starts by validating the client's efforts. That same fitness coach might say, *"Your dedication is fantastic, and what really impresses me is how you've already incorporated [specific habit]. From here, we could make some adjustments to unlock even better results."* This approach shifts the focus from critique to collaboration, helping the client feel motivated and empowered to make changes.

In sales, prospects often fear being judged for their current strategies or decisions. The Influence Mindset reassures them by emphasizing their strengths and inviting them into a conversation about what's next. By validating their instincts and progress, salespeople foster trust, build rapport, and make the prospect feel like an active participant in their own success story.

"In sales, prospects often fear being judged for their current strategies or decisions."

Wrap Up: Make Them the Hero

Whether they realize it or not, your prospect is on their own Hero's Journey. Like Deloris Peoples Jordan, they may be fiercely pursuing economic stability and chances for personal advancement. Like me, they may be trying to overcome an obstacle to reach greater opportunities for themselves or their business. We are all living our own stories where we are trying to get somewhere. And whatever it is, you can either get in the way or help along the way.

When you succumb to your Survival Brain's insecure needs and inadvertently position yourself as the Hero, you might feel better in the moment...but it leaves your prospect feeling either like a Victim or a Villain in their own Hero's Journey. And no one likes to feel that way. But when you intentionally embody the archetype of the Guide, you open the pathway for your prospect to get where they want to go and become who they want to be...all with your help.

Your words and behaviors have the power to create this life-altering narrative for them, or your words and behaviors will drive them away... seeking another option. The choice is yours.

As for Deloris Peoples Jordan, ever since 1984 and the Nike deal that changed the landscape of modern sport, she has continued to live a remarkable life. She used her newfound wealth and influence to build upon and spread the cherished values she inherited from her father. She has sat on numerous executive boards, created several foundations, and even became a *New York Times* Bestselling author [16]. As she serves on the board of the Jordan Institute for Families at the University of North Carolina School of Social Work, she was once interviewed about what it took to raise Michael Jordan. Her advice?

"Just try to encourage your son or daughter to be a good, decent human being and work hard to achieve. Set goals for yourself ... and work hard to achieve them." [17]

Sounds like the most important Hero's Journey of them all.

Chapter 5: Key Takeaways

- **The Guide Archetype Empowers Prospects:** Positioning yourself as a Guide in sales situations allows you to empower your prospects to see themselves as the Hero of their own journey. This approach fosters collaboration and positions you as a trusted ally rather than the focus of the story.

- **The Danger of the Hero's Spotlight:** When salespeople assume the Hero role, they unintentionally force their prospects into roles of Victim or Villain, which creates discomfort, erodes trust, and reduces influence.

- **Guide Language Builds Trust and Confidence:** Using phrases that validate prospects' instincts and progress shifts the narrative from critique to collaboration, disarming defensiveness and encouraging trust.

- **Guides Reduce Perceived Challenges:** Like trusted allies in research studies, Guides reduce the psychological perception of challenges, making obstacles feel smaller and opportunities more attainable for prospects.

Bonus

I've created exclusive content to help you apply the principles we cover together. To access them, go to: **www.TheChristianHansen.com/ BookBonus**

SUMMARY TABLE

INFLUENCE FORMULA:	Competence	(Plus) Connection	(Equals) Influence
ENVIRONMENT:	Performance Environment	Relational Environment	Selective Environment
DEFINITION OF SUCCESS:	Where Success Is Based On How Well You Perform	Where Success Is Based On How Well You Connect & Work With Others	Where Success Is Based On Influencing People To Choose You
STRATEGY:	Achievement Mindset	Charismatic Mindset	Influence Mindset
DEFINITION OF STRATEGY:	Success Happens When I Prove My Value Is High	Success Happens When I Am Likable, Relatable, & Win People Over	Success Happens When You Influence Someone To Choose You Over Others
IF INCOMPLETE?	Competence (Without) Connection = Noise	Connection (Without) Competence = Charm	Competence With Connection = Influence
BRAIN'S DEFINITIONS OF SUCCESS:	SURVIVAL BRAIN Success = When I Meet My Brain's Needs For Security, Resources, Novelty, Belonging, & Status…		EXECUTIVE BRAIN Success = When I Meet Their Brain'sNeeds For Security, (etc.)
STRATEGIES	ACHIEVEMENT THINKING	CHARISMATIC THINKING	INFLUENCE BRAIN HACKS
Competence Strategy #1: LOGIC VS EMOTION	*How Can I Convince Them I'm Qualified & Capable?*	*N/A*	How Can I Also Acknowledge This Person's Emotions Right Now?

Competence Strategy #2: KNOWLEDGE VS INSIGHT	*How Can I Prove I'm Credible & Impressive?*	*N/A*	What Unique Insight Or Perspective Speaks Directly To Their Challenges?
Competence Strategy #3: HERO VS GUIDE	*How Can I Prove I'm The Best Option They Should Trust?*	*N/A*	How Can I Help Them Feel Like The Hero Of Their Story?
?	?	?	?
?	?	?	?
?	?	?	?
?	?		?

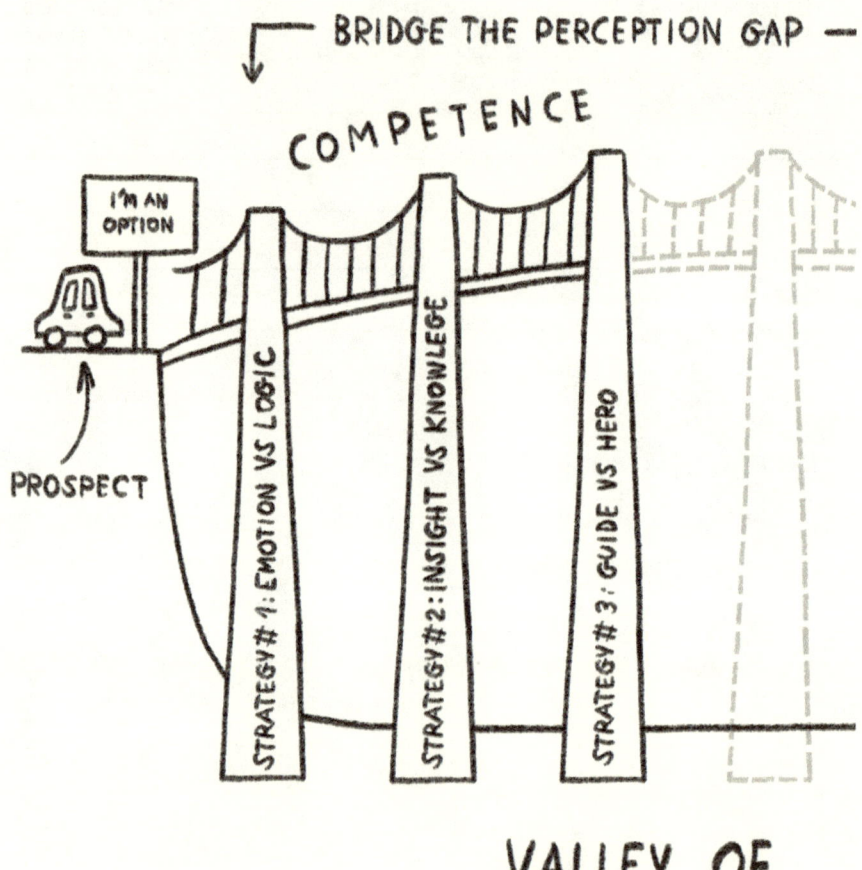

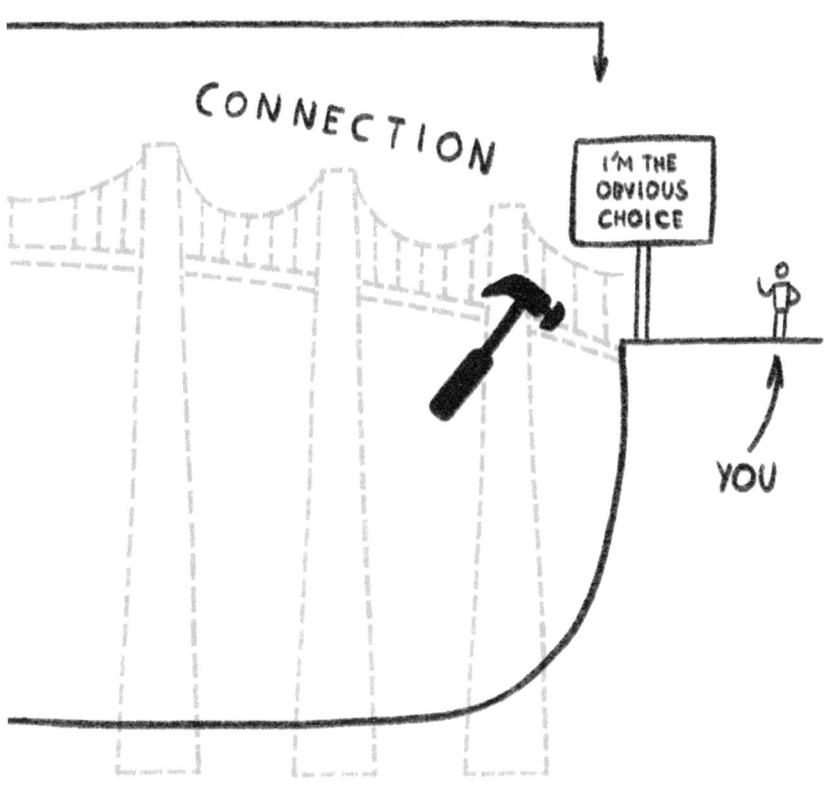

CONNECTION

I'M THE OBVIOUS CHOICE

YOU

IRRELEVANCE

SECTION 3:

ESTABLISHING CONNECTION

The Two Doctors Who Battled an Invisible Killer

"The transmission of disease could be prevented.
I have proved all that I have said, yet nobody heeds me."

— Ignaz Semmelweis

"Chance favors only the prepared mind."

— Louis Pasteur

In the 1800s, if a woman went to a European hospital to give birth, it was practically a death sentence. Women tragically died at alarming rates from "puerperal fever," a deadly infection that seemed to strike without warning in hospitals. It was a problem so pervasive that many expectant mothers tried to have birth in the streets en route to the hospitals to avoid life-threatening infection and additional complications [1]. For one doctor, Ignaz Semmelweis, the senseless loss of life was unbearable.

In 1846, the 28-year-old Semmelweis was a rising star in Vienna's prestigious medical community. His work ethic was unmatched, his observations careful and meticulous. When he began working in the maternity ward of the Vienna General Hospital, he noticed a peculiar trend: Women who delivered with midwives had far lower mortality rates than those who delivered with highly trained doctors. As Semmelweis investigated further, he observed that doctors delivering babies came straight from performing autopsies. The midwives, on the other hand, never came in contact with dead bodies. Could the doctors' unwashed and bloodstained hands carry invisible "cadaverous particles" that spread disease? [2]

That's when Semmelweis proposed a preposterous and revolutionary idea: Whenever doctors moved from one procedure to another, what if they washed their hands with a chlorinated lime solution? Despite the grumblings, the doctors consented, and the results were stunning. In April 1847, before the policy was instituted, the mortality rate was over 18%. In June, just two months later, it was 2.2%. And in July? It dropped to 1.2% [3].

He had found the answer. Or so he thought.

Armed with data, Semmelweis turned to his peers in the wider medical field, expecting celebration. Instead, he was met with skepticism and resistance. Germ theory hadn't been accepted yet in Vienna, and these highly trained doctors were insulted by the suggestion that their hands were unclean. Semmelweis reacted to the rejection poorly. Despite being a brilliant scientist, he struggled with interpersonal relations, and he lashed out at colleagues with frustration. When they resisted further, he even called them murderers for refusing to adopt his methods. The gulf between him and the medical community widened, and few took him seriously. Though his findings were correct, his inability to connect with others and present his idea in a compelling way prevented the medical world from seeing his lifesaving potential. And so, year after year, doctors refused to wash their hands, and thousands of lives continued to be needlessly lost [4].

Tragically for Semmelweiss, his life only got worse. Dismissed from his position, ignored by the medical establishment, and plagued by mental health struggles, he died in an asylum in 1865, his life a tragic testament to a brilliant idea lost due to poor communication.

A Different Path

Several decades later, a Frenchman picked up where Semmelweis had failed. Would he be able to convince the public of the dangers of the "invisible enemy" plaguing hospitals? His name was Louis Pasteur, and at the time, few could have guessed he would forever revolutionize science as we know it.

Though not a doctor, Pasteur was a chemist by training, and in the 1850s, he became intrigued by an unlikely question: Why did wine spoil? Building upon the earlier work of Semmelweis, Pasteur conducted a series of experiments and proposed that microorganisms (later called bacteria) were responsible for ruining wine, milk, and other products. He also discovered that if you heated up liquids to a certain temperature, the microorganisms could be killed, thus extending the shelf life of various foods and drinks. And so, thanks to Louis Pasteur, the field of microbiology, the concept of germ theory, as well as the widespread technique that later became known as pasteurization...were all born.

But Pasteur's curiosity didn't end there. If these microorganisms contaminated food, did they also create disease in animals and humans? This question hit painfully close to his heart. Of their 5 children, Pasteur and his wife had lost 3 to infectious disease as small children. If he could find a way to mitigate the spread of disease through killing off unwanted microorganisms, then he might be able to prevent other families from suffering as he had. So he got to work, and over the course of his career, he created pioneering developments in vaccines, immunology, and...where Semmelweis had first attempted...in medicine and surgical care [5].

But why did Pasteur succeed where Semmelweis had failed? They both advanced similar ideas, namely that small invisible organisms were the cause of disease. However, while Semmelweis struggled in obscurity, Pasteur was (and is) hailed as one of the greatest scientists of all time.

One key reason? Connection.

Pasteur was a master at helping the wider public emotionally connect to his work. He understood that ideas, no matter how brilliant, must be framed in ways that resonate with people's values and fears. He didn't dismiss skeptics—he engaged them. He didn't rely solely on his intellect—he leveraged empathy. Accordingly, he frequently did public demonstrations where crowds gathered to witness the power of vaccines on animals— which people cared for. He even courted the press to tell stories about how his work impacted children and saved lives.

Pasteur also excelled at building alliances. He worked with farmers, physicians, and even politicians to ensure his discoveries had the support they needed to spread. He understood that public trust was just as important as scientific proof, and his ability to unite people around a common vision made his ideas not just influential but transformative [6].

By contrast, Semmelweis, for all his brilliance, berated his peers for their ignorance and failed to create emotional connection. He ranted when people didn't listen and raged when they didn't care. And so, even though he had a world-changing idea, people ignored him.

Today, despite his sad ending, Dr. Semmelweis has been recognized for his pioneering insights on the importance of washing hands and his attempts to create change. However, the question remains: How many more lives could have been saved if he had learned to help people emotionally connect with his world-changing insight?

Think about that the next time you wash your hands.

In the end, it was Pasteur and his ability to connect emotionally with the wider public that made his idea to stop contagion...contagious.

Connection Helps Ideas Spread

Aside from the obvious importance of washing your hands, there are critical lessons to be drawn from the contrasting examples of Louis Pasteur and Ignaz Semmelweis. Namely, your ability to influence people

"How many more lives could have been saved if he had learned to help people emotionally connect with his world-changing insight?"

to see you as the obvious choice depends on your ability to connect with them. Remember: In Selective Environments, how people *feel* about you is just as important as what they *think* about you. On the surface that might seem obvious, but frequently there are things that get in the way of even the best sales people when they are trying to stand out.

In the past several chapters, we have been focusing on how to position your competence in a more compelling way. We've discussed strategies on how to infuse your credibility-filled message with more connection so that you can be more appealing and influential. We used three frameworks in particular to help us do this:

1. Speaking in Emotion vs Logic
2. Framing your value in Insight vs Knowledge
3. Positioning yourself as the Guide vs the Hero

"How people *feel* about you is just as important as what they *think* about you."

As we covered with Dr. John Pemberton and the creation of Coca-Cola, each of these strategies add more "fizz" to your message, thus making you stand out compared to others. But what about connection? How can you establish connection in ways that also bolster the perception of your competence?

That's what we are going to do in this section.

Just as there are simple strategies and "brain hacks" you can use to quiet your Survival Brain and better position your competence, for the next several chapters we will discuss tactics that help you empower your Executive Brain and build connection more effectively. Best of all, these strategies will increase the level of authenticity you bring into *any* conversation and are designed to speak directly to the fundamental brain needs of your prospect.

These strategies can be summarized as:

1. Giving the gift of listening
2. Asking questions with curiosity
3. And giving people a compliment about themselves to live up to

Though highly relevant to sales situations, you'll discover that these simple yet practical strategies will greatly influence ANY relationship you have or want to have. Whether it be with a significant other, a spouse, a child, a work colleague, someone you are networking with for the first time, and even the focus of this book...prospects in sales situations...the chemistry of connection is universal and centers on your ability to help another person feel like you genuinely care.

Though I highly doubt you engage in the disastrous behaviors of Dr. Ignaz Semmelweis, there are things that he could have done that would have prevented the *thinking* that created those behaviors. Like all of us, he had a Survival Brain too, and it tragically took control of many situations he encountered. He didn't understand the importance of connection and influence, and sadly people ignored his idea.

Thankfully, however, we have the example of Louis Pasteur, as well as the advantage of time and greater insights in the art and science of persuasion and how our brain works. And armed with these insights (and knowledge!) we are in a better position than ever to learn how to communicate in ways that truly make our ideas and value...contagious.

Let's begin.

EVERYONE'S FAVORITE GIFT

"We are interested in others when they are interested in us."

— Publilius Syrus, 43 BCE

"Being heard is so close to being loved that for
the average person they are almost indistinguishable."

— David Augsburger

I once was travelling to speak to a major company, and as I landed at the airport, I received a call from the event coordinator. "It just so happens that one of our executives was on the same flight as you." They shared, "We've arranged transportation for her to the hotel, would you like to ride together? It will be about a 45-minute drive." Always looking for the chance to connect, I agreed, and they shared the executive's contact information with me.

After some brief texts to locate each other, we officially met in the baggage claim, and soon, with our luggage in tow, walked to the designated curb to catch our pre-arranged transportation. It was immediately clear she had spent decades in her industry, was highly skilled and intelligent, and best of all, was thoughtful and kind. However, as we loaded into the car, instead of the normal "getting to know you" conversation, I wanted to try something completely different.

For the next 45 minutes, could I focus entirely on her and resist the urge to talk about me and my background? I would of course answer her questions, but for the duration of our trip, could I turn the conversation back to her and give her my full and complete attention?

"I have to say," I initiated, "I've been super impressed with your company as we've been planning this event. How did you first begin working for them?"

And that's how it started.

I switched off my phone, and for the next 45 minutes, I just listened and asked questions. When she shared about unique turns in her career, I asked how it felt to make those major life decisions. When she mentioned her major accomplishments with the company, I asked about the lessons she learned. I did my best to compliment her, identify things I thought were really admirable and impressive, and asked about the company's current challenges and how she felt about them.

Though I was sincere and authentic in my efforts, the process was highly valuable for me as well. I learned a great deal more about the company and made mental notes on how I could adjust my keynote to better serve them and their needs. I also learned more about their industry and gathered important "tribal terms" that were frequently used.

When she asked about me, I answered her questions appropriately but mentioned I would cover it more in depth the following day. I then turned the focus back to her. As the car ride furthered, she continued to open up and felt more and more at ease, all while I gave her my full attention and resisted the urge to talk about myself.

When we reached the hotel, she did something unexpected. She thanked me.

"This has been the most interesting car ride I've had in a long time. You have such fascinating insights, and I'm really excited to hear you speak tomorrow!"

Fascinating insights? I hadn't said a thing. It turns out the less I talk, the smarter people think I am!

But in her mind, I had spoken volumes. She had felt a wealth of connection in our short car ride together.

The next day, it got even better.

Upon my arrival, and without me knowing, she reached out to the event organizers and asked if she could introduce me in front of the company. The organizers agreed, changed the event schedule, and before I took the stage the next day, this highly respected executive stood and read my bio.

Then, in front of the whole company, she said, "On a personal note, I had the privilege to ride with Christian all the way from the airport yesterday, and he is one of the most interesting people I've talked to in a long time. That's why I asked to personally introduce him to all of you. He had the most fascinating insights, and I had several breakthroughs just listening to him. We are so lucky to have him speaking with us today. Will you please stand and give a warm welcome to Christian Hansen..."

Before I said a single word, I had a standing ovation. As a speaker, you can't pay enough money for that kind of introduction.

Now to be clear, this story is not about me and is not intended to make me appear special or that I walk on water. Far from it. But this story is important to demonstrate a critical lesson:

You don't have to be a great conversationalist to help people feel connection. You do, however, have to help them feel heard. And as this experience suggests, helping people feel heard is less about what YOU say, but what you enable THEM to say.

"Helping people feel heard is less about what YOU say, but what you enable THEM to say."

When it comes to influencing people to see you as the obvious choice, never underestimate the power of listening. It isn't just polite—it's strategic.

And when you look at the neuroscience research, it makes sense.

The Power of Being Heard

When we were infants, crying out and being heard was one of the few tools we had to survive.

When we were hungry? We cried.

When we were scared? We cried.

When we were in need of security and comfort? We cried.

And when we did so, others came to us and attended to our needs. That means the earliest way that our brain learned to meet its core needs of security, resources, novelty, and belonging was through crying out and being heard. So it makes sense that feeling heard is one of our deepest needs for security, resources, and belonging [1].

But scientists wanted to better understand why, and so in 2014, researchers set out to explore what happens in our brains when we "feel understood." They began by asking students to record videos of themselves describing significant personal experiences. These videos highlighted moments of joy, such as winning a scholarship, as well as moments of pain, such as a romantic breakup. The researchers then prepared two types of responses—affirming ones like "I understand why that affected you a lot," and disaffirming ones like "I don't understand why you felt that strongly."

Later, these students were shown videos that appeared to feature other people reacting to their stories. Although the participants believed these responses were genuine reactions from other students who had watched their videos, the responses were entirely fabricated and designed to create feelings of being understood or misunderstood. As the participants watched the reactions—some affirming, others dismissive—their brain activity was monitored to uncover the neural mechanisms of feeling understood (or not).

What the researchers found was striking. They discovered that feeling understood activated areas of the brain associated with reward and social connection. These were strongly related to the regions I referenced in the previous chapter about insights and "Aha! moments." However, when someone felt dismissed, it triggered regions linked to social pain and negative emotions.

While feeling heard and understood created a surge of pleasure-inducing dopamine, not feeling understood created very strong negative emotions. Even an acute form of pain [2].

Which would you want to help your prospects feel?

Other (Amazing) Benefits of Feeling Heard

The research provides even more insights into why active listening is so powerful. When someone feels heard and understood:

- They feel closer to the person listening to them, and more satisfied with life [3]
- It increases how much they like and connect to strangers for the first time [4]
- And it even decreases their perception of distance and perceived physical pain [5]

No wonder the executive I shared the car ride with volunteered to give my introduction to her company. Because she felt heard and listened to, the reward part of her brain was on fire, she felt more satisfied with her life, and even momentarily forgot any pain she may have been feeling.

"Far too often we let OUR needs to be heard get in the way of THEIR needs."

And you can have the same impact on people you are trying to influence.

Which brings up our core problem: If YOU have a deep and critical need to be heard, then so does your prospect. If YOUR brain enjoys all the benefits mentioned above, then so too does your prospect's brain. But far too often we let OUR needs to be heard get in the way of THEIR needs.

How can you hear their need to be served if all you do is serve your need to be heard?

Unfortunately, this is exactly what happens with the Charismatic Mindset.

The Charismatic Mindset and Relational Environments

Before we dive into how the Charismatic Mindset falls short, let's step back and remind ourselves about the Relational Environment. In Relational Environments, success isn't measured by performance or competence (like the Performance Environment and the Achievement Mindset)—it's all about connection and how well you get along with others. Whether it's a family gathering, casual conversation, or a

"How can you hear their need to be served if all you do is serve your need to be heard?"

friendship, relationships are the currency that make everything tick. In these settings, we naturally develop strategies to build rapport, foster connection, and create belonging.

The problem is, just like we commonly mistake Selective Environments for Performance Environments, the same thing happens with Relational Environments. In sales situations, many professionals think, "If I can just make this person like me, then I will be chosen." So they engage in ineffective Charismatic Mindset behaviors that fail to influence.

THE CHARISMATIC MINDSET:

How can I make this person like me or see me as interesting?

Which brings us to our second problem.

Whenever we speak with someone else, we need to understand that OUR brain is desperately wanting to feel heard. During the entire car ride with the executive, my Survival Brain was actually jumping up and down wanting to talk about MY experiences and make ME feel important and interesting. But such behaviors would have taken the moment away from her and not achieved my goals of sincerely connecting and also gaining valuable insights about the company. So, I had to focus and intentionally redirect my thoughts to resist the urge to talk about myself.

Similarly, when you enter a Selective Environment, be highly attuned to the fact that YOUR Survival Brian is wanting to do the same through the Charismatic Mindset. It wants to hijack everything your Executive Brain has carefully planned and orchestrated so the Survival Brain can feel safe and secure. Sure, the Charismatic Mindset can lead to surface-level connection (and feel good), but it fails to build the kind of trust and clarity required to guide someone towards choosing you. That's because the Charismatic Mindset misconstrues being liked as being relevant.

The Problem with Commonality

This is exactly what happened with the rain-gutter rep at the business expo in Chapter 1. She believed that leading with commonality would build connection. Her Survival Brain was saying, *"I want you to like me. Let me show you how similar we are."* So she launched into, *"Oh, I used to do the same thing as you! In fact, that reminds me of when I..."* Suddenly, the conversation was about her and HER Survival Brain's needs.

But here's the problem: Commonality is a counterfeit form of connection.

Think about it—there are plenty of people you share things in common with, but does that alone make you want to do business with them? No.

Real connection isn't built on sameness—it's built on feeling heard, valued, and understood. Once those needs are met, THEN commonality

"The Charismatic Mindset misconstrues being liked as being relevant."

can serve as reinforcement. But when you lead with it, it's empty. In my experience, efforts to establish commonality FIRST tend to placate the speaker more than they do the listener. However, intentionally trying to help someone feel heard makes the conversation about the other person...from the start.

Which is what happened to the rain-gutter rep. She mistook building commonality FIRST as a way to build genuine connection. And like many sales professionals, she mistook the Selective Environment for a Relational Environment—and lost the opportunity to influence me.

The Influence Mindset Approach

In contrast, the Influence Mindset flips the script entirely. Instead of focusing on being liked, it focuses on making the other person feel seen, heard, and understood. The Influence Mindset asks a different "brain-hacking" question: How can I help this person feel heard and understood right now? This subtle but profound shift moves the focus from you to them, and it unlocks the kind of trust and connection that actually influences their perception of you.

THE CHARISMATIC MINDSET:	THE INFLUENCE MINDSET:
How can I make this person like me or see me as interesting?	*How can I help this person feel heard & understood right now?*

When you walk into sales situations and focus on repeating this question in your mind, it hacks your brain to redirect the conversation toward serving the prospect's needs instead of your own. You go from being interesting, to interested...which, according to my car ride with the executive, ironically makes you more interesting. And in a Selective Environment, that's the difference between being seen as noise and being seen as the obvious choice.

"Commonality is a counterfeit form of connection."

However, more importantly, when you ask the question, "How can I help this person feel heard and understood right now?" This phrase will wrest control from your insecure Survival Brain and give more power to your Executive Brain, which will focus on what matters most. It literally flips the switch and instantly increases your influence, no matter the situation.

Would you rather be charming or influential? The answer lies in how you listen—and whose needs you prioritize.

And in the Selective Environment, listening (or failing to do so) can make or break critical opportunities.

Stop and Smell the Flowers

A few years ago, an elderly gentleman in San Diego was selling his home of 50 years. He had raised his family there, but his wife had recently passed away, and he wanted to move closer to his children out of state. While he was sad to leave his home, he was devastated to leave his prize-winning rose bushes he and his wife had spent decades growing. They were in the front of the house and were a beautiful compliment to the home and the couple who cared for them.

As his realtor was helping him list and sell the home, they received a call from a successful investor who wanted to see the house. They all toured the home together, and the investor complimented the location, the neighborhood, and the size of the property. It was clear from his comments that the investor intended to tear down the house and build a sleek new addition. However, along the way, the old man paused and proudly pointed out his rose bushes in front of the house and shared that he and his wife had grown them together.

Hearing the words but not listening to the deep sense of pride the man felt for his flowers, the investor carelessly said, "Oh, those will have to go." The old man stiffened when he heard the comment, but the investor didn't notice and continued, "They will get in the way of the new construction. But I'll pay top dollar for this location."

When the investor mentioned the figures he was considering, the seller and agent raised their eyebrows in surprise. It was far higher than they had hoped. The investor said he would have the formal offer in by the end of day, and they thanked him for coming.

As the investor left, the agent turned to the seller and said, "That's probably the best offer you'll receive. That's much higher than the current market value, and I recommend you accept."

The old man hesitated. Though the offer was attractive and would give him the financial security he wanted, the loss of the rose bushes would mean losing his wife's legacy. He wanted something of her memory to live on and someone who would appreciate them.

Later that day, they had a second home viewing. This time it was a teacher who had recently been hired by the local school, and she was looking for a home for her family. As they walked the property, the old man again pointed out his rose bushes, and the teacher, noticing his sense of pride, stopped and listened. She asked questions about them and commented on how beautiful they were. This gave the old man a chance to share some of his memories about his wife, and again the teacher empathized and listened in her natural way.

"I would want to make sure these are cared for because they really are stunning and very special," she added.

The old man's eyes brightened, and he winked at his real-estate agent. The next day when they received the formal offer from the teacher, it was tens of thousands of dollars below what the investor had offered. And yet, the old man didn't hesitate to select the teacher.

Why? One reason is the teacher had listened and noticed the strong connection the man had to his flowers and responded accordingly. She validated him, honored his intentions, and built a deep connection with him. The investor, on the other hand, HEARD the old man's words but had not LISTENED to what the words were really saying. And he missed an important investment opportunity [6].

Even though he gave up an economic advantage, the old man did so for the preservation of an intensely personal and emotional reason: the memory of his wife. Whether that was the right decision isn't the point of the story. Rather, it's to illustrate the chemistry of how emotion-driven reasons play an outsized role for decision-makers in the Selective Environment. Objective reasoning has its part, but never underestimate the power emotions have in decision-making. And like the teacher, the salesperson who learns to listen and adjust their approach accordingly will be the obvious choice compared to those who don't.

Just as the investor heard but failed to listen, what are some other bad habits that frequently get in our way? Let's explore some ineffective listening behaviors that become obstacles in the long run. Then we will move on to strategies to help you avoid these common pitfalls.

Bad Habit #1: Hammer and Nail

I once spoke with a sales rep whose company offered a wide array of software solutions. Their programs were robust, impressive, and had thousands of users. I had reached out to see if they were the right fit for my business and my needs, and scheduled a call. As we spoke, I shared

"Never underestimate the power emotions have in decision-making."

a bit about my business and where I was trying to go. However before I had the chance to truly explain the nuances of the situation, the rep interjected, "Oh, what you need is THIS." And proceeded to explain a featured product and how it would effectively solve a part of the problem I was facing.

"And then we have this upgrade," he continued, "that would make the solution even faster."

I agreed the software was powerful, but I hadn't had the chance to fully explain the full picture and why that program wasn't the right fit for me. As I tried to share more, the rep enthusiastically jumped in again, "What you really should be doing is...and we have a solution that does just that." He then proceeded to tell me about a whizbang feature of another product that...again...addressed *part* of the solution I needed, but not everything.

He was doing what I call the hammer-and-nail approach. "When you're holding a hammer," the saying goes, "everything looks like a nail." In this case, this sales rep looked at my problem as if it were a nail and started hammering away with his predetermined solutions. The problem was (to borrow from the analogy a bit more), I wasn't holding a nail. Had he taken the time to look a bit closer, he would have seen it was a screw. Similar...but totally different.

"If I don't agree with how you see my problem, I likely won't agree with your proposed solution."

He made assumptions and completely misdiagnosed the situation in ways I didn't agree with. And if I don't agree with how you see my problem, I likely won't agree with your proposed solution.

And yet he hammered away, trying to put me in a pre-constructed box while I explained why it didn't fit for me. In the middle of our call I realized, "I am actively selling myself OUT of what he is trying to sell me INTO..." And that is NEVER a good sign.

I left the conversation frustrated.

You've probably had many instances (in and outside the world of sales) where someone has done this to you. Oh, you have this problem? You HAVE to try this medicine—it worked for me! You have to try this exercise! You have to try this product!

Hammer, nail.

Hammer, nail.

Wash, rinse, and repeat.

Many times, peoples' well-meaning Charismatic Mindset and their need to be helpful and friendly overlook our need to be heard. And so we ignore them. However, there is a simple tactic that can help us avoid falling into this common trap. **(Check out The Gift of Listening, Strategy #1.)**

Bad Habit #2: Piggybacking

I once went to lunch with an insurance agent who had put together some quotes for my home and auto rates. We had met at a local business event, and though I was also connecting with other agents to find the best quote, I wanted to get to know him and his business better. Sadly, however, despite looking forward to the lunch, I had an unexpected family tragedy the day before. Though I was personally unharmed, the day of our lunch I was still coming to terms with how life was going to look different moving forward.

When we met up, I apologized for being a bit lower on energy. I shared a snippet about what had happened, and this insurance agent responded by saying, "Oh I remember when that happened to me too..." And they proceeded to talk about their experience.

Was it in his right to share? Absolutely. He can say whatever he wants. But in that moment, I was in a deep amount of pain, and his response seemed tone-deaf. He continued to speak in great detail about how our situations were very similar. Even though I understood his attempt to establish commonality, his well-intentioned efforts missed my needs at that moment.

His need to be heard got in the way of my need to be served.

Eventually, after he ran out of steam, I decided to move the conversation forward. I pivoted to, "So the reason I reached out was to get a better idea of what my insurance options are because we are coming up on a deadline to renew our policies."

"Oh, yeah," he said, "That's a really great idea to contact me. You know, you wouldn't believe what happened to a client who didn't renew their policies on time..." and he proceeded to go into ANOTHER story

" His need to be heard got in the way of my need to be served. "

about someone he knew and the tragedy that befell them and their lapsed insurance.

I was so confused. Wasn't this meeting supposed to be about my family's needs? I didn't mean to be self-centered, but wasn't this about helping me decide on the right option?

Again, he can say whatever he wants, but in this situation he was using the all too common behavior of "piggybacking," where he would use MY comment to launch into his own comment. He "piggybacked" off of what I was saying to simply further the conversation. Now in Relational Environments, this behavior is normal because it is a form of building rapport. The easy back and forth in a friendly exchange brings a sense of harmony and makes for good (albeit sometimes wandering) conversations with people we already feel connected with.

But in Selective Environments, it fails to make a decision-maker feel heard, valued, and understood. Which is exactly what happened.

He behaved as if he was in the Relational Environment and used Charismatic Mindset behaviors of establishing commonality and furthering a directionless conversation. While we talked, I had to wrestle to communicate my needs, and when he continuously failed to respond to them, I eventually gave up.

On the surface, we had a good lunch together and got along, but I did not feel listened to. And despite his competence, I didn't feel a compelling connection. And so I moved on to a different agent, as we will soon cover. **(Look for Parallel Amplifiers, Strategy #2.)**

Bad Habit #3: Minimizing

I once got connected with a loan officer who was recommended by my real-estate agent. At the time, I was trying to buy a property, and though I had a down payment set aside, I needed to get the financing squared away. Despite my preparations, I was a bit nervous. Anyone who has jumped through the hoops for a mortgage knows they are complicated and confusing at the best of times. I had everything I thought I needed pulled up and ready to go, but I still had the nagging feeling that I was missing something.

When the call began, it was clear the guy was very smart, knew his stuff, but was evidently at the end of a long day. His responses were clipped, and it seemed he was trying to get the call over with so he could move on to the next thing. As the call progressed, we got the main things out of the way quickly. However, unfamiliar with the whole process, I said I had questions and needed some clarification. As I went through my prepared list of questions, here are some of the things he said in response:

- "Oh that's not a big deal. You have no need to worry about that."
- "You are stressing too much over that. I've handled way worse cases than yours."
- "That's not something you should be focused on right now."

- "It's all standard stuff, nothing to stress about. That isn't that big of a problem."

As I went through my list of questions, he was able to competently answer them. However, his responses made me feel kind of stupid for asking in the first place. I knew I wasn't as knowledgeable as he was, but I was sincerely anxious and worried about the process. The terms were unfamiliar and the steps never ending, and I didn't feel as confident. Even though his answers may have addressed my concerns, he did so in a way that left a really bad taste in my mouth. That's because he was using a particularly poor way of listening that is called minimizing.

Minimizing happens when we belittle, downplay, or discount a person, their ideas, or their actions. In this case, I had legitimate questions I was worried about, but he downplayed and belittled them. In doing so, he downplayed and belittled me. And no one likes to feel that.

On his end, I don't think he was falling victim to Charismatic Mindset issues...but rather Achievement Mindset problems. He wanted to come across as competent (which he did), but he certainly didn't work at establishing connection. And after our call, I asked my realtor if she had any other recommendations to work with and soon chose someone else instead. Just like with the previous two bad examples, there is a strategy that can help you intentionally avoid this issue. **(Check out The Recall Method, Strategy #3).**

The Foundations of Good Listening

Now that we know that:

- Listening has powerful benefits in our prospects brains
- The Charismatic Mindset (and Achievement Mindset) often get in the way by speaking to OUR needs, and not the needs of our prospect

- And now that we've covered several common examples of BAD listening...

Then what creates good listening? What are the steps we need to take to become better listeners?

Let's break it down.

Reception vs Intention

We need to understand that, while hearing is physiological, listening is psychological. When you "hear" someone, it merely indicates that your ears and auditory receptors are functional, and the information is getting to your brain. When you listen? That's when you take reception and combine it with intention. Entrepreneur Jim Cathcart wisely said, "Listening is wanting to hear." And I find it interesting that some of the best listeners can't hear at all.

My wife and I once went to dinner with some of her friends. As the dinner progressed, I noticed one of them, I'll call her Jenn, repeatedly did something extraordinary. When someone else was speaking, Jenn would turn her entire body to face that person directly. When another person spoke, Jenn swiveled in her chair, squared her shoulders, and faced the speaker with laser-like focus. As she listened, she leaned forward, her eyes taking in every detail with rapt attention. When the conversation

" While hearing is physiological, listening is psychological. "

turned to her, she shared her thoughts, but when someone else took the next step, she attentively turned and faced them once again.

When I contributed to the conversation, Jenn's patient and intent-filled gaze made me feel like I could better express my thoughts. I saw this effect on the others as well. When people shared, Jenn's listening efforts invited them to go deeper and to share more meaningful ideas and insights. Her focus, in turn, influenced us to focus on each speaker as well. Essentially, she was shaping the conversation by saying nothing at all. That's because her attentive and supportive silence said everything.

Halfway through dinner, I paused the conversation and complimented her on how she listened. "I've never seen someone give so much attention to others while speaking," I said. A look of surprise crossed her face. "Really?" she asked.

Then one of her friends nudged her and said, "Tell them about your family."

"Oh!" Jenn relaxed and said, "My parents are deaf, and so are my siblings. That makes me the only hearing person in my family. When we communicate, we HAVE to face each other and give 100% attention because otherwise we might miss something in ASL. I guess that follows me into my 'hearing' conversations too!"

I find it powerful that this extraordinary listener came from a family who couldn't hear at all.

Hearing is a matter of reception, but listening is a matter of intention.

" Hearing is a matter of reception, but listening is a matter of intention. "

Let's Get Tactical: The Three Listening Superpowers Anyone Can Master

If hearing is physiological and listening is psychological, then how can you actually apply these ideas? How can you improve the power of listening to better connect and influence others? Let's talk about strategies you can begin using today to become a better, more influential, listener.

Strategy #1: Give the Gift of Listening

After my poor experience with the sales rep who used the hammer-and-nail approach (Bad Example #1), later that week, I found myself speaking with a prospective client. As I brainstormed over which of my training programs were the right fit for their company, how could I avoid the hammer and nail in my own call? That's when I used what I call the "gift of listening" strategy.

Here's what it is: I imagined a beautifully wrapped gift. In my mind's eye, the gift was a small square box complete with white wrapping paper and a perfect red bow. Next, I imagined this gift being placed between me and the person I was speaking with. I called it, "the gift of listening."

THE GIFT OF LISTENING

Every time my Survival Brain wanted to interject and take control, I focused on this imaginary gift on my desk and said to myself, "How can I FIRST give this person the gift of listening?"

When my Survival Brain wanted to interrupt and say, "Here's the ideal course for you!" I paused, imagined the gift, and asked more questions about how they saw the problem.

When my Survival Brain wanted to jump in and say, "Here's what you're doing wrong, and I can fix it!" my thoughts turned to the gift, and I refocused on the prospect as they were sharing an important part of their story.

Every time, I found that giving the gift of listening gave my insecure Survival Brain a chew toy to grapple with while my Executive Brain maintained control and steered the conversation in the direction I wanted it to go. By the end of our call, several insights came up that would not have been revealed without my attempts to listen and understand.

Better yet, those insights enabled me to put together a solution that fit exactly what they were looking for, and they accepted my proposal. That client turned into a lucrative consulting relationship for that year alone.

All because I used an Influence Mindset "brain hack" to stifle my insecure Survival Brain. In turn, I was seen as the obvious choice.

But why does the gift of listening work so well? As we covered, neuroscience research shows that when someone feels truly heard, their brain releases dopamine—the chemical responsible for feelings of pleasure and reward [2]. In other words, listening isn't just polite; it creates a deep sense of validation and belonging, which our Survival Brain craves. It signals to the other person's brain, "You're safe here. You matter."

On the flip side, when someone feels unheard or dismissed, the brain perceives it as a threat. This activates the same neural pathways as physical pain, leaving them feeling disconnected, frustrated, or even defensive. By pausing, imagining the gift, and focusing on their words rather than your own impulse to respond, you're not just listening—you're creating a space where the other person's brain can relax, trust, and open up. That's the kind of connection that doesn't just make you stand out—it makes you the obvious choice.

"How do you want to give the gift of listening in more of your conversations?"

As for you, how do you want to give the gift of listening in more of your conversations?

Strategy #2: Parallel Amplifiers

After I had the disappointing lunch with the insurance agent who kept "piggybacking" our conversation (Bad Example #2), later that week, I had a phone call with another agent. I still needed new home and auto rates and was looking to choose SOMEONE who could help. In the intervening days, the sharp pain of my family's tragedy had softened, and admittedly, I was in a better place emotionally. However, the topic did come up briefly in the conversation with this new agent nonetheless.

This time, Agent #2 behaved in stark contrast to Agent #1. "Oh my gosh," they said, "how terrible. That must have been a complete shock!"

"Yes, it was," I began, "completely unexpected."

Then, instead of blundering into their own story, they asked questions and compassionately created space for me. With every admission or description I shared, their comments began with "That must have..." or "That must be..."

- That must have been so difficult...
- That must have taken you completely by surprise...
- That must be hard to know that...

Then, as my sharing started to shed light on the positive developments since the tragedy, the phrases changed.

- That must be relieving to know that at least it didn't last long...
- That must have been incredible to see everyone come together like that
- That must have felt good with all that support...

"Parallel amplifiers work for either negative or positive expressions."

- That must be a weight off your shoulders now the situation has changed...

Do you notice a difference?

He was an expert at a technique I call "parallel amplifiers." Instead of diverting the energy of the conversation by "piggybacking" in a completely different direction, he kept his comments parallel to the narrative I was sharing and then amplified the emotion I was expressing. He listened carefully and acknowledged the different turns of my story, always guiding the conversation back to my experience.

Which is what parallel amplifiers do. Notice how the phrases, "That must have..." or "That must be..." work for either negative or positive expressions. Simply listen for the emotion, stay parallel to what they are saying, and amplify the emotion of the story back to them. This demonstrates a level of empathy that is as powerful as it is uncommon in Selective Environments.

Why do "parallel amplifiers" work so well in creating deep connections? The answer lies in how our brains process empathy and emotional validation. As we saw earlier, neuroscientists have found that when we feel our emotions are truly understood, it activates areas of the brain that fosters connection and trust. Essentially, when someone acknowledges and reflects our feelings back to us, this builds a bridge of trust, which is critical in influencing others.

Additionally, the brain's limbic system—the emotional center— releases oxytocin, often referred to as the "bonding hormone." This creates a sense of safety, comfort, and relational warmth [7]. Parallel amplifiers achieve this by keeping the emotional energy of the conversation aligned with what the other person is expressing. Instead of hijacking the narrative or shifting the focus, this approach strengthens the emotional connection and allows the other person's brain to relax, open up, and trust the interaction.

As for me, I felt a deep connection with him, and all the reactions in my brain helped me feel that he would understand me and my needs in the future...regardless of what came up. Like the first agent, he was competent, but his ability to build connection was far superior. And with his competence and connection combined, these two skill sets influenced me to choose him over others.

As for you, how can you notice and amplify the emotions of others as they share important things about themselves?

Strategy #3: The Recall Method

Soon after my emotionally draining conversation with the loan officer who "minimized" my concerns (Bad Example #3), I got in contact with a second loan officer. Right away, this lending professional approached the call differently. He asked open-ended questions to understand my concerns, taking the time to listen carefully to what I had to say. I shared my biggest questions upfront, and he immediately reassured me:

"Don't worry—we'll be sure to address those today."

From there, we dove into the numbers and discussed my financing options. At one point, the conversation shifted toward a specific area

" How can you notice and amplify the emotions of others as they share important things about themselves? "

I had concerns about, but before I had to bring it up again, he said something that caught me off guard (in the best way possible):

"I recall you mentioned earlier that you wanted clarification on XYZ...is that right?"

I was surprised and impressed. He remembered something I had said in passing at the start of the conversation. When I confirmed, he continued:

"I couldn't help but notice that when you brought up that question, it seemed connected to some of your other concerns. Is that fair to say?"

I nodded and opened up more. As I shared additional details, he seamlessly referred back to earlier parts of our conversation:

- "When you mentioned XYZ earlier, I noticed you were curious about how it tied into this process. Let's clear that up."

- "I've been very impressed during our call. From things you've said and the info you've prepared, it's clear that you've done your homework on this. In particular when you made XYZ comment, that showed how much work you put in before our conversation."
- "I also remember you said you were feeling a bit uncertain about XYZ. Let's go through that together."

This was a strategy I call "the recall method" in action. By revisiting key points I'd made earlier, he made me feel heard and valued. He didn't brush aside my concerns or downplay my questions. Instead, he used what I had shared to guide the conversation, creating a sense of trust and partnership.

When you intentionally refer back to something a person said earlier, this approach not only validates their feelings but also demonstrates that you've been paying attention. It creates space for them to express their concerns fully, which helps you build trust and address the root of the issue.

The recall method doesn't just demonstrate attentiveness; it transforms the way people feel in your presence. Specifically, from a neuroscience perspective, it's because this technique aligns with how the brain processes memory and connection. Referencing prior points triggers the brain's recognition systems, creating a sense of continuity and trust. It reassures the prospect that their concerns haven't been forgotten or dismissed, which helps reduce uncertainty—a key driver of stress and hesitation in decision-making [8].

By anchoring the conversation to their own words, the recall method subtly shifts the power dynamic. It's no longer just about presenting solutions; it's about collaborating toward them. This approach is particularly effective in Selective Environments, where your role isn't just to inform but to guide—making your prospect feel confident in the process.

"When you intentionally refer back to something a person said earlier, this approach not only validates their feelings but also demonstrates that you've been paying attention."

How can you practice this in your next conversation? Listen deeply, note the moments when someone shares something important, and circle back to those points at the right time. It's not just a strategy—it's a signal that you see them, you've heard them, and you're invested in their success.

Listening Strategy for Personal Relationships

On a personal note, when my wife and I were first married, I was not a good listener. After a long day's work, she would often come home wanting to share what had happened. The problem was, I (and my insecure Survival Brain) wanted to do the same thing. And so, as she was talking, I would foolishly let MY need to be heard override her need to be heard as I frequently interrupted her and cracked jokes about things she was saying.

To be clear, I wasn't making jokes about her or being unkind, but trying to find good humor in the situations she was describing.

In her infinite patience, she always indulged my ego with a laugh, but would try to pick up where she was in her story. However, it would take a few seconds for her to regain her focus and resume. A few sentences later, sure enough, my Survival Brain's insecure needs would derail her again with another humorous quip.

In retrospect, I must have been really annoying. Understandably, this got pretty tiring for her too, and one day she stopped me mid punchline saying, "Your constant jokes are getting in the way of what I need to say. It's hard for me to share what's important when you keep interrupting me. Can you wait to crack a joke until AFTER I'm done sharing?"

Message heard loud and clear.

As I worked to change, we developed an agreement with one another. Whenever it's clear one of us is sharing something important, the other pauses and asks this question:

"Just so I know, do you need me to:

- Listen and validate?

Or...

- Give advice and get involved?"

The speaker then designates what they need, and from that moment on, it's the listener's job to honor that request. In the ensuing years,

"How can you practice this in your next conversation?"

we've used this agreement to listen and serve each other in important ways, and it's helped create important guidelines as we communicate.

Give it a try, and let me know how it goes!

Wrap Up: Listening: Everyone's Favorite Gift

As I stepped out of that car ride with the executive, I realized something profound. I hadn't offered dazzling advice or shared an impressive story about myself. I simply listened—intently, with curiosity and care. And in doing so, I created space for someone else to feel valued and understood. That moment wasn't about me, yet somehow, it elevated me in her eyes. Why? Because listening is one of the most powerful tools of influence we have, especially in Selective Environments.

Throughout this chapter, we've seen how listening can either strengthen or undermine our ability to connect. When we approach conversations from an Achievement or Charismatic Mindset—trying to prove our value or win others over—we risk serving our own needs at the expense of truly hearing theirs. But by adopting the Influence Mindset and employing strategies like the gift of listening, parallel amplifiers, and the recall method, we flip the script. We demonstrate not only competence but also the connection needed to influence.

"Listening isn't passive; it's an active, intentional act of service. "

Listening isn't passive; it's an active, intentional act of service. It requires us to set aside our Survival Brain's insecurities and focus on helping the other person feel heard and understood. When done well, listening builds trust, fosters clarity, and positions us as a guide who can genuinely help others achieve their goals.

So, as you head into your next sales conversation, remember the executive from the car ride, the teacher who noticed the roses, and the loan officer who used the recall method. Each of these stories illustrates the same truth: The best listeners don't just hear words—they amplify emotions, create trust, and guide others to their desired outcomes. And when you master the art of listening, you won't just be heard—you'll be chosen.

Chapter 6: Key Takeaways

- **Listening is an Act of Service:** True listening is not passive but intentional. It's about creating space for the other person to feel valued, understood, and supported.

- **Avoid Common Listening Pitfalls:** Habits like the hammer-and-nail approach, piggybacking, and minimizing derail conversations and fail to meet your prospect's emotional and informational needs.

- **Use the Gift of Listening:** Imagine giving the other person the gift of listening by focusing entirely on them, quieting your own need to interject, and asking meaningful questions to understand their perspective.

- **Employ Parallel Amplifiers:** Acknowledge and reflect the emotions behind what the other person shares to deepen connection, and show empathy without shifting the focus away from them. *"That must have been... That must be..."*

- **Leverage the Recall Method:** Demonstrate attentiveness and build trust by referring back to previous comments or concerns. This shows your prospect that they are truly heard and that their input matters.

Bonus

I've created exclusive content to help you apply the principles we cover together. To access them, go to: **www.TheChristianHansen.com/BookBonus**

SUMMARY TABLE

INFLUENCE FORMULA:	Competence	(Plus) Connection	(Equals) Influence
ENVIRONMENT:	Performance Environment	Relational Environment	Selective Environment
DEFINITION OF SUCCESS:	Where Success Is Based On How Well You Perform	Where Success Is Based On How Well You Connect & Work With Others	Where Success Is Based On Influencing People To Choose You
STRATEGY:	Achievement Mindset	Charismatic Mindset	Influence Mindset
DEFINITION OF STRATEGY:	Success Happens When I Prove My Value Is High	Success Happens When I Am Likable, Relatable, & Win People Over	Success Happens When You Influence Someone To Choose You Over Others
IF INCOMPLETE?	Competence (Without) Connection = Noise	Connection (Without) Competence = Charm	Competence With Connection = Influence
BRAIN'S DEFINITIONS OF SUCCESS:	SURVIVAL BRAIN Success = When I Meet My Brain's Needs For Security, Resources, Novelty, Belonging, & Status…		EXECUTIVE BRAIN Success = When I Meet Their Brain'sNeeds For Security, (etc.)
STRATEGIES	ACHIEVEMENT THINKING	CHARISMATIC THINKING	INFLUENCE BRAIN HACKS
Competence Strategy #1: LOGIC VS EMOTION	*How Can I Convince Them I'm Qualified & Capable?*	*N/A*	How Can I Also Acknowledge This Person's Emotions Right Now?
Competence Strategy #2: KNOWLEDGE VS INSIGHT	*How Can I Prove I'm Credible & Impressive?*	*N/A*	What Unique Insight Or Perspective Speaks Directly To Their Challenges?

Competence Strategy #3: HERO VS GUIDE	*How Can I Prove I'm The Best Option They Should Trust?*	*N/A*	How Can I Help Them Feel Like The Hero Of Their Story?
Connection Strategy #1: LISTENING	*N/A*	*How Can I Make This Person Like Me Or See Me As Interesting?*	How Can I Help This Person Feel Heard & Understood Right Now?
?	?	?	?
?	?	?	?
?	?		?

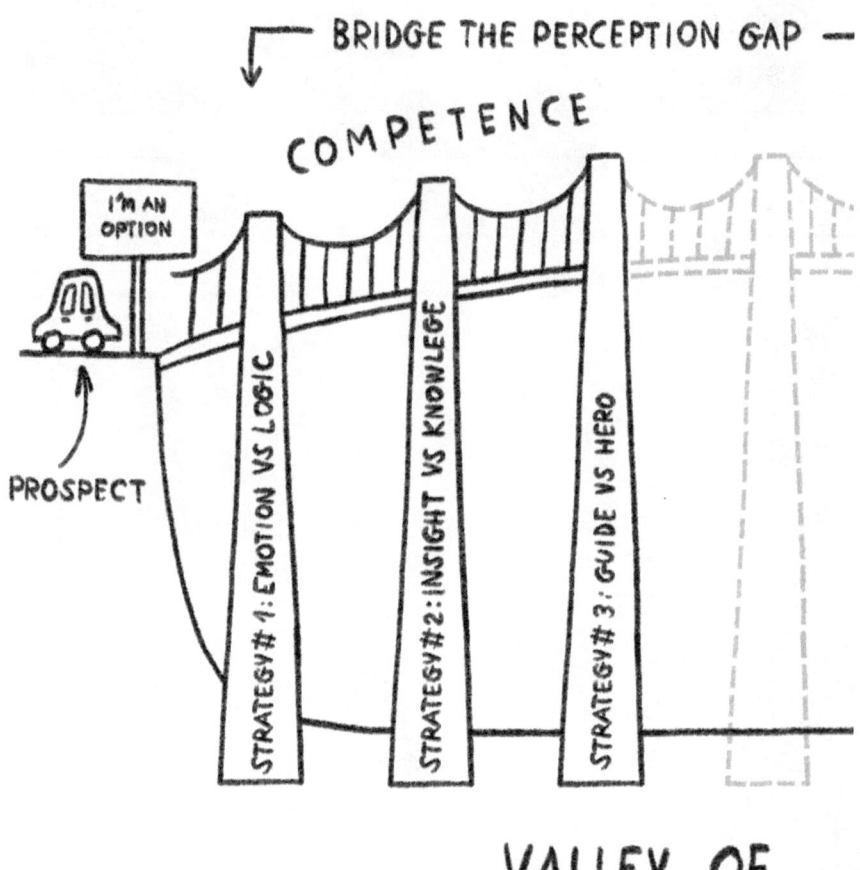

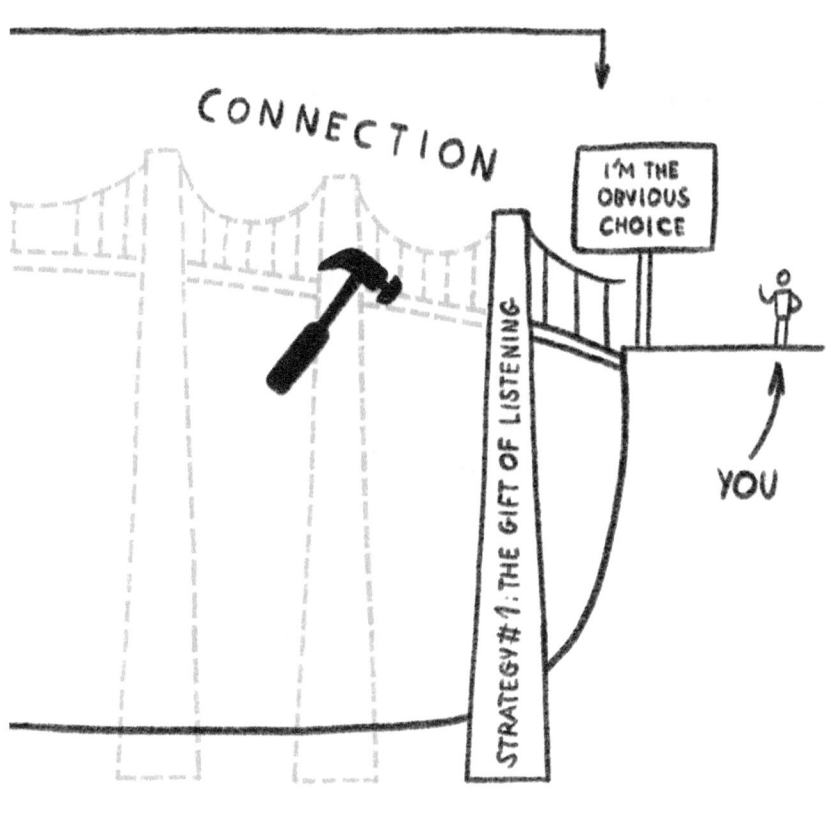

CONNECTION

IRRELEVANCE

I'M THE OBVIOUS CHOICE

STRATEGY #1: THE GIFT OF LISTENING

YOU

HOW TO EXPLORE THE OCEAN FLOOR

"Judge a man by his questions rather than his answers."

— Voltaire

"The whole world was spread out before me. I had a blank canvas to fill with extraordinary possibilities."

— Marie Tharp

In 1952, when Marie Tharp looked at the giant map on her wall, she knew she had just changed the world in a very significant way. The problem was, no one would believe her.

Let's take a step back.

In the 1800s, when explorers discovered identical fossils of the same dinosaur species spread across South America, Africa, and even India... they wondered: Long ago, were all the continents positioned together? If so, what made them separate?

Their best guess? The expanding Earth theory. Here's how scientists thought it worked: At the dawn of time, Earth must have been much smaller, and all the continents were connected. However, for reasons unknown, the earth gradually expanded in size, which pushed the continents apart. And voila, one of the early theories of "continental drift" was born [1].

Enter Marie Tharp. Born in Ypsilanti, Michigan in 1920, she gravitated to the sciences and graduated from the University of Michigan with a Master's degree in Geology in 1944. However, when she became a junior geologist for an oil company in Oklahoma, they made her compile maps and arrange her male colleagues' work trips...instead of allowing a woman to actually complete fieldwork [2].

Luckily for the rest of us, she decided to move on to better opportunities at Columbia University, where she was one of the first women to work for the Lamont Geological Observatory. There, she asked the question that would reshape our world: "If we have maps of every land mass on Earth, what would it be like to have complete maps of the ocean floor?"

The US government wondered the same thing.

At the height of the Cold War, the threat of submarine warfare was ever present, and whichever country knew the ocean floors best would have the advantage. And so, for the next 18 years, with the help of government funding, Marie would take the "bathymetric data" created by ships as they crisscrossed the Atlantic (think: sonar measurements of the ocean floor) and painstakingly aligned them to see what was underneath the water. Despite the prevailing theories, she stayed curious and kept gathering data carefully recorded on giant rolls of paper measuring tens of meters long [3].

What she saw astonished her!

In the middle of the Atlantic Ocean, there was a giant V-shaped rift valley that ran all the way from Greenland to Antarctica. She found matching features in the Pacific and Indian Oceans as well. Could it be that instead of the earth expanding, the continents drifted on plates above the molten magma underneath?

"As humans, we resist curiosity when it threatens our sense of certainty."

Initially her colleagues didn't believe her...that is until she overlayed all the seismic data they had collected to reveal that epicenters of underwater earthquakes perfectly matched the rift valleys running the length of the entire planet. Thus, the mechanism of plate tectonics was confirmed, and the expanding Earth theory was out.

And Marie Tharp was the woman who made it happen.

Regrettably, Marie did not get the credit. Instead, her skeptical colleague Bruce Heezen received all the praise for her work [4]. However, all that changed in 1997 when Marie was invited by the Library of Congress to be recognized as one of the greatest cartographers of the 20th century, and the "Marie Tharp Lamont Research Professor" position was soon created in her honor [5]. At last, she finally received the recognition she deserved all along, and she passed away in 2006 at the age of 86.

Pretty remarkable story, right? But what does this have to do with influence and success?

Curiosity Creates Better Results Than Certainty

Marie Tharp singlehandedly changed the world because when everyone around her persisted in their existing beliefs, she intentionally approached the problem she was trying to solve with openness and curiosity. It would have been much easier to give in and just acquiesce to the theories of the day, but it was her curiosity, that most essential trait of influence, that enabled her to (literally) look beneath the surface and change how we see the world.

On the other hand, her colleagues clung to their beliefs and resisted her findings. Not just that, but in spite of the growing evidence to the contrary, many maintained their *certainty* of the expanding Earth theory. I find it interesting that as humans, we resist curiosity when it threatens our sense of certainty, even though curiosity paves the way to obtain certainty in the first place. Her colleagues' tightly held *assumptions* prevented them from looking underneath the surface. They missed critical insights that could have changed everything.

The thing is, our predisposition for certainty doesn't just get in the way of science, it also gets in the way of your ability to connect and influence. When you connect with people, are you protecting your assumptions like the scientists? Or are you able to cultivate curiosity and look beneath the surface to what's really happening, like Marie Tharp? In no way is this process more impactful in the Selective Environment than in how we ask questions.

That is what we are going to talk about in this chapter.

Thus far in the book, we have covered strategies in what to say and how to outwardly position yourself to others. However, the questions you ask and follow up with are critical to connecting with people. How and what you ask can shape a prospect's perceptions of you (and the experience you provide) just as much as what you say. However, like Marie Tharp's colleagues, are we asking questions

"When you connect with people, are you protecting your assumptions like the scientists? Or are you able to cultivate curiosity and look beneath the surface to what's really happening, like Marie Tharp?"

to preserve OUR sense of control, certainty, and security? Or are we asking questions that are filled with exploration, curiosity, and connection, like Marie?

As you'll soon find out, the questions you ask can change how your prospects look at the world, themselves, and ultimately...how they look at you.

But first, we need to make a stop at the car mechanic shop. Something's wrong with my car...

The Mechanic Who Made Me Feel Stupid

A few years ago, after my wife and I had just moved to a new community, the "check engine" light came on in my car. Just so you know, I'm not the most mechanically gifted "fix it" guy, so I was nervous. Could it be something small, or would I need to buy a whole new transmission? Either way, I knew I had to get it checked out, but I was apprehensive about going.

I decided to support a local mechanic who had positive online reviews. When I pulled in, the owner came out with a kind of brusque, no-nonsense demeanor.

"So," he started, "why'd you bring it in?"

I told him, "There's a check engine light on in my car. It's been on for a few days, and I don't know what's wrong."

"Check engine light?" He frowned. "Well, what do you think the problem is?"

"Uh, I'm not sure," I said, starting to second-guess myself. "There have been some noises. Maybe something's not working or needs replacing?"

"Replacing? The car obviously started and you drove it here, so it can't be that bad," he said, shaking his head at my cluelessness. "Okay, fine. Let's take a look."

After waiting for a while in the lobby, he called me back to the car. He had the hood open and was elbow-deep in the engine. Now for accuracy's sake, the following dialogue may not be 100% technically correct, but I stand by what it sounded like to me and my non-mechanical brain.

"All right, here's your problem," he said, pointing to something. "This right here is the quadratic flux capacitor millennium falcon carbonizer. You know what that is, right?"

An alien descending out of his spaceship would've made more sense. And in an effort to not be a complete fool, I nodded and said I understood. "Uh, yeah...kind of," I lied.

In reality? I felt like a Labrador retriever listening to a human explain taxes. I had no clue what he was talking about.

He gave me a skeptical glance. "Okay, well, since you already know, the carbonizer connects to the transmissionator, which works in tandem with the whizbangle and the reticulating sparken bangenhoffers. You've heard of those, haven't you?"

At this point, I felt like I was trying to pass an advanced calculus test with a broken crayon. "Uh...kind of?" I stammered.

"Well, they're critical," he said, "and trust me, they are going to cause a lot of issues if you don't get them fixed. We could get you on the list for tomorrow if you want." He then handed me a quote that made my wallet cry.

By the time I left, I wasn't just worried about the cost. His questions and explanations didn't help me understand the problem. Instead, they made me feel dumb for even bringing the car in. Rather than building trust and assurance, he used his questions to assert his own expertise and keep control of the conversation. Though I'm sure he was highly competent, his pointed questions failed in creating connection.

So I got back in my struggling car and drove across the street to a national chain instead, hoping someone there would actually listen.

The Mechanic Who Made Me Feel Heard

As I pulled into the national chain, the experience was night and day. The mechanic greeted me with a friendly smile and asked, "What are you coming in for today?"

I explained, "The check engine light came on, and I'm not sure what's going on. I've also noticed some weird noises."

He nodded and asked, "What kind of noises have you heard, exactly? And which lights have popped up on your dashboard?"

I described everything as best I could, and he responded, "Wow, that must have been really concerning." (Notice his parallel amplifier comment from the previous chapter?)

It was the first time in this whole ordeal that someone acknowledged how I was feeling. "Yes, it was," I said, feeling a bit of relief.

He asked, "How do you usually use your car—just around town, or longer trips? And just so I know, have you been on a longer road trip recently?"

When I explained I usually drove around town, he replied, "So hearing those noises while driving around must have been kind of worrying, right?"

"Absolutely," I said, feeling understood. He asked me to wait in the lobby as they figured things out, and after a few minutes, he called me out to the car. He pointed to a part (I believe it was the flux whizbangle carbonizer...) and asked, "Have you ever heard of this?"

"Not really," I admitted.

He smiled and said, "Most people don't—it's not something you usually deal with. Let me show you what it does." He then explained the part in a way that was clear and didn't make me feel dumb.

Finally, he presented me with some options. "Just curious, how would it feel if we took care of the most important issues first? There are other things we could look at later, but this will address the immediate concern. Or," he continued, "We could tackle multiple things at once and knock them out at the same time. Would you like to see a quote for both of those options?"

"Yes!" I said, grateful for the skilled way he was navigating an anxiety-ridden process for me.

Before I walked back to the waiting area, he asked, "And just so I know, are there any other concerns I haven't addressed?"

"That's all for now—thank you for your help!" I said. Even though the quote was expensive, similar to the first mechanic, I was happy to pay it.

The Difference Questions Can Make

Can you see a difference in the questions these two mechanics asked?

The first mechanic's questions made me feel stupid, judged, and ultimately frustrated. His focus was on proving his competence and asserting control of the situation rather than understanding my concerns. More importantly, many of his questions were "assumptive" or flat out assumed I knew the same things he did. They didn't give me any space to admit (with my ego intact) that I didn't have the faintest clue what he was talking about.

Whether he knew it or not, he was serving HIS brain's needs. Not mine. That's because when we assume or cling to our certainty, it can speak to OUR brain's needs for security, belonging, and status. His questions discounted me and made me feel embarrassed.

The second mechanic's questions, however, made me feel heard and respected. He didn't assume and asked questions in a way that increased connection. He spoke to MY brain's core needs for security, belonging, and status. He also came from a place of curiosity as he presented options for me to choose from.

The difference? The second mechanic didn't just fix my car—he fixed my emotional state— and influenced me to become a loyal customer. He knew that when customers come in with their cars, they are often worried and concerned, and his questions met me where I was at...in that moment. Which is what great questions can do.

They decrease what I call "The Asymmetry of Information."

Asking Questions in Selective Environments

When we encounter prospects in the Selective Environment, we need to understand that we are dealing with an "Asymmetry of Information." On one hand, your prospect knows more about their lived experience with their problem than YOU do. On the other hand, you know more about solving the problem than THEY do. In either case, both of you possess critical information the other needs to know, and you must effectively exchange this information so both of you can understand what to do next.

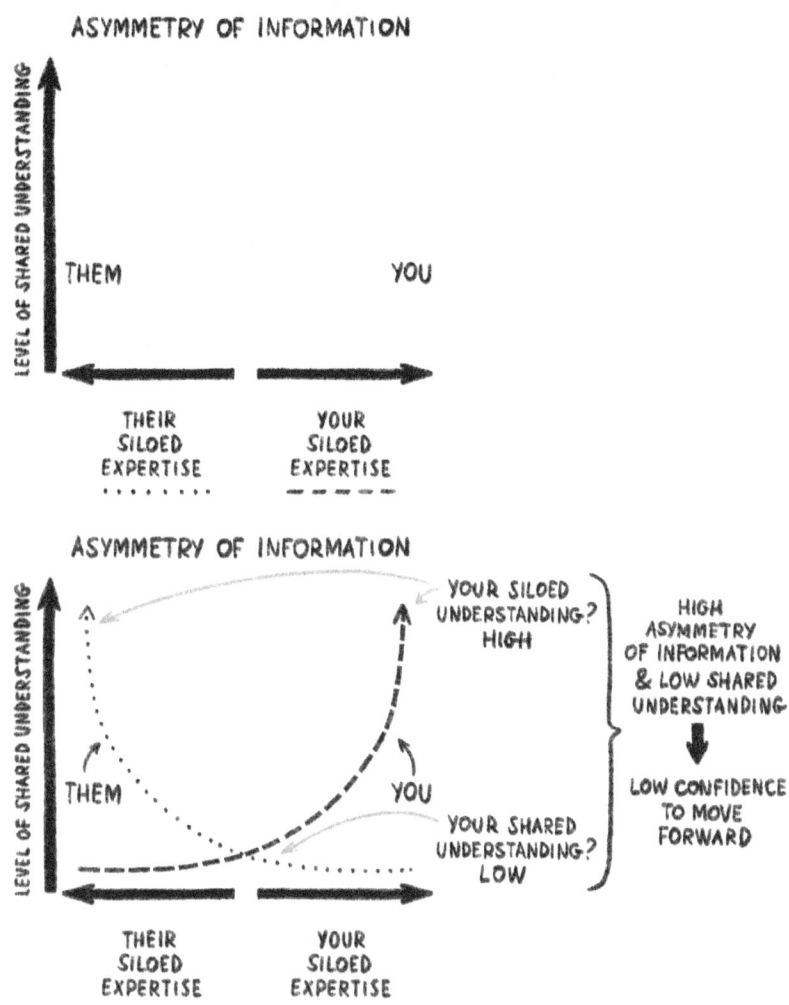

Case in point: When I pulled up to the respective car shops, I knew more about the lights and troubling sounds my car was making than the mechanics did. However, when it came to possible solutions to fixing my car, the mechanics indisputably knew more than me. For both of us to succeed, we had to exchange and negotiate information critical to understanding how to move forward. However, if we cannot navigate this exchange of information, we don't move forward.

When we successfully share information with each other, we overcome the "Asymmetry of Information" and create a "Symmetry of Understanding." This is a state where both parties have enough information to proceed with confidence.

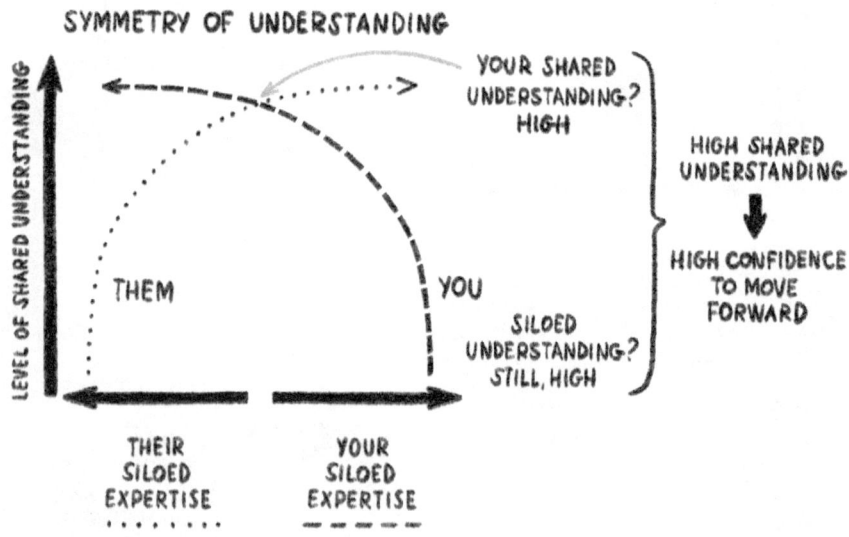

And it's critical. For the car mechanics, it required asking the right questions to uncover my perspective as a driver—what I heard, saw, and experienced. It also involved clearly explaining their expertise and solutions in a way that I could understand and trust.

"When we successfully share information with each other, we create a 'Symmetry of Understanding.' "

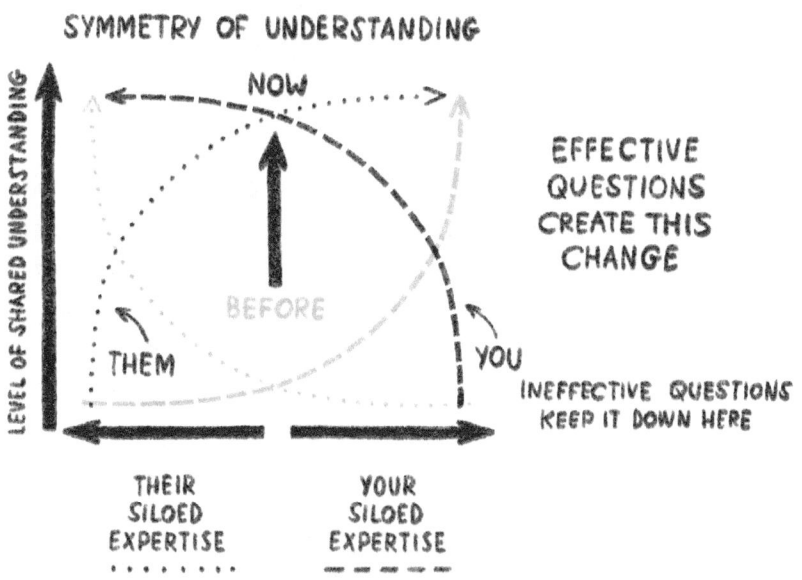

Just like a dance where partners give and take the lead, how you ask questions and participate in this nuanced and delicate exchange of information can make all the difference with a prospect. Good questions reduce the Asymmetry of Information. Poor questions reinforce it. However in this pursuit, not all questions are created equal. Some questions are more influential, while others (like the first mechanic demonstrated) leave a bad taste in the mouth.

To dig into this idea further, let's go watch a baseball game.

Fastball vs Tee-ball Questions

In Major League Baseball when a batter steps up to the plate, everything in that environment is designed to make them fail. There are 9 players spread out over a huge field, hungrily watching a batter's every move, and one of them is looking down from a mound of dirt as they throw fastball pitches. All the batter has in their defense is a wooden baseball bat and their athleticism.

Understandably, when everything is against you, stepping up to home plate can be a bit unnerving. In Major League Baseball when the pitcher throws fastball pitches, the defensive team on the field has every *advantage*, and the batter tapping his cleats and eying the pitcher has every *disadvantage*.

In contrast, consider how we introduce young children to baseball for the first time through the game of Tee-ball. The field is much smaller, and though there are a similar number of players on the field, they are probably distracted by butterflies or waving to their parents in the stands. However, the biggest difference comes in how a young player hits a ball. In Tee-ball, the ball is placed on a "tee" instead of being thrown from a pitcher. This gives every advantage to a young batter and is designed to build confidence and increase their skills.

Even though a young child may be nervous at their first time at bat, soon their confidence grows and they excitedly walk up to the plate

"Good questions reduce the Asymmetry of Information. Poor questions reinforce it. "

when it's their turn. The reason? In Tee-ball, the whole environment is meant to give the *batter* a much *higher* chance of success.

Just like baseball has two very different environments for professionals and beginners, when it comes to asking questions in the Selective Environment and creating a Symmetry of Understanding, I find that most questions can be divided into these two groups: Fastball questions and Tee-ball questions. Fastball questions are designed to give the *inquirer* the advantage and put the *responder* at a disadvantage. In contrast, Tee-ball questions are engineered to give the *responder* more of an advantage, not the inquirer.

Fastball questions are asked with the intent of asserting control, gaining information, and are fueled with assumptions and self-protecting certainty. They may be quick and efficient for the inquirer, but they put the responder at the disadvantage because they increase the amount of cognitive load their brain is trying to process [6]. On one hand, they are trying to answer the question with logic and reason while at the same

"When it comes to asking questions in the Selective Environment most questions can be divided into these two groups: Fastball questions and Tee-ball questions."

time processing their emotional feelings of uncertainty and anxiety. With both logical and emotional thought processes being engaged simultaneously, they experience a heavier cognitive load.

Tee-ball questions, on the other hand, are asked with the purpose of exploration, creating connection, and are filled with curiosity. They may take more time and require more patience from the inquirer, but they create more space and emotional understanding for the responder.

In the car mechanic examples, can you see what kind of questions they each asked?

The first mechanic asked fastball questions that put me at a *disadvantage*. Sure, they helped him quickly find the information he was seeking, and it reasserted his knowledge, but it left little (if any) room for me to feel heard and understood.

The second mechanic, on the other hand, asked Tee-ball questions. Though they took an extra minute or two of his time, they gave me the *advantage*. The questions put me at ease, made me feel understood, and ultimately not stupid. (Confession: I still have no idea what the stupid flux whizbangle-ator does.)

In the nuanced back and forth exchange of information that's necessary to overcome the Asymmetry of Information and create a Symmetry of Understanding, it's critical that you resist the urge to assume, assert, and confirm your certainties and instead intentionally preserve a spirit of curiosity. Researchers call this important state of trust between speakers and listeners psychological safety [7]. And when responders feel safe with your genuine curiosity? You'll create connection more effectively.

Which is exactly what Marie Tharp did at the beginning of this chapter. She didn't try to defend assumptions or outdated beliefs. Instead, she approached her work with curiosity and asked questions that opened the door to discovery. This willingness to explore rather than reinforce gave her the space to uncover truths that changed how we see the world. Her colleagues, by contrast, clung to certainty, asking only the kinds of questions that reaffirmed their existing assumptions and, in doing so, missed the groundbreaking insights right beneath their feet.

Likewise, as you pursue a Symmetry of Understanding in the Selective Environment, the more grace, courtesy, and curiosity you give your conversational dance partner (ie, your prospect), the more you will uncover and the more likely they will feel a greater connection with you [8].More importantly, they are more likely to see you as the obvious choice.

In your own conversations, think about the questions you ask. Are they rooted in certainty, designed to showcase your expertise, or

"In the nuanced back and forth exchange of information it's critical that you resist the urge to assume, assert, and confirm your certainties and instead intentionally preserve a spirit of curiosity. "

are they driven by curiosity to uncover your prospect's deeper needs? Just like Marie Tharp's unflinching curiosity opened a new world of understanding, your ability to ask questions with grace and openness can shape not only the answers you receive but also the way your prospects see you—as the guide they've been searching for.

Which is exactly what the Influence Mindset helps you do.

Asking Questions for Control vs Connection

Though this section of chapters is primarily focused on the Charismatic Mindset and its obstacles, I find that when we find ourselves in Selective

Environments, it's easy to slip into BOTH the Charismatic Mindset as well as the Achievement Mindset. Why? Because in these moments, our brains are often focused on managing how we're perceived.

As for the Achievement Mindset, we want to sound impressive, showcase our competence, and maintain a sense of control over the conversation. That's why the key question the Achievement Mindset asks when it enters sales situations is: How can I ask questions to be more impressive and in control?

THE ACHIEVEMENT MINDSET:

How can I ask questions to be more impressive and in control?

Achievement Mindset questions are often crafted to reinforce our authority or steer the conversation toward a predetermined outcome. Think about the first mechanic in my story. His questions were laser-focused on proving his expertise: "Why do you think there's a problem?" or "You know what that part does, right?"

This is the danger of the Achievement Mindset in the Selective Environment. The focus shifts from understanding the prospect's perspective to showcasing your own competence. While these questions might make you feel more in control, they can leave the other person feeling unheard and dismissed.

The Charismatic Mindset likewise approaches asking questions ineffectively. However, compared to the Achievement Mindset, the Charismatic Mindset asks: How can I ask questions to seem likeable and relatable? This most often appears in the form of questions that establish commonality and mutual interests not related to the core needs of the prospect. The problem is, this strategy usually makes the conversation superficial and not relevant.

THE ACHIEVEMENT MINDSET:	THE CHARISMATIC MINDSET:
How can I ask questions to be more impressive and in control?	*How can I ask questions to be likeable and relatable?*

This is what the rain-gutter rep did in Chapter 1. Though her questions kept the conversation going and built commonality, they failed to actually connect with me and what I was trying to solve. Which is the Charismatic Mindset's key flaw: It spends so much energy trying to be liked and accepted that it misses the needs of the other person.

Remember, the thing people like to talk about most is themselves. Do your questions create a runway for people to talk more about them and their problems? Or are you using sales conversations to inadvertently talk about you and your problems?

The Influence Mindset: Asking Questions for Curiosity

The Influence Mindset flips both of these approaches on their head by asking a simple yet transformative brain-hacking question: How can I ask my next question with more curiosity?

THE ACHIEVEMENT MINDSET:	THE CHARISMATIC MINDSET:	THE INFLUENCE MINDSET:
How can I ask questions to be more impressive & in control?	*How can I ask questions to seem likeable & relatable?*	*How can I ask my next question with more curiosity?*

Intentionally creating a space for curiosity shifts the focus away from you and places it squarely on the person in front of you. Instead of trying to control the conversation or impress the other person, you're opening the door for genuine understanding and connection. The second mechanic from my story exemplified this beautifully. His

" Do your questions create a runway for people to talk more about them and their problems? Or are you using sales conversations to inadvertently talk about you and your problems? "

questions—"What have you noticed about your car?" or "How can we help you today? What's been going on?"—created a space where I felt comfortable sharing more about my concerns.

This approach isn't about sounding smart; it's about making the other person feel understood. By asking questions rooted in curiosity, you signal that their experience matters. And when your prospect feels valued, they're far more likely to trust you as someone who can help solve their problem.

Why This Matters in the Selective Environment

In Selective Environments, your questions are not just tools for gathering information—they're bridges that connect your understanding to your prospect's needs. The Achievement Mindset's need for control builds narrow one-way paths that shut down collaboration. The Charismatic Mindset only asks questions in ways that keep things superficial.

The Influence Mindset, on the other hand, asks questions that create a runway for your prospect to express themselves and feel heard. It enables them to open up in ways that reveal their deeper motivations

"In Selective Environments, your questions are not just tools for gathering information—they're bridges that connect your understanding to your prospect's needs. "

and concerns. And when you truly understand what's driving them, you'll be able to position yourself as the guide they need—someone who can help them achieve their goals.

Let's Get Tactical

Now that we know that the questions we ask are super important, what are examples of fastball questions we should avoid? These are the questions that give YOU the advantage and risk making your prospect feel unheard. While there are many, let's take a moment and break down three common yet ineffective approaches most people use. Then we will explore three proven strategies of asking questions that will help people see you as the obvious choice.

Fastball Question #1: Why?

For starters, questions that start with "why" are the most unhelpful—and often counterproductive—questions you can ask in the initial trust building stages of sales situations. Why? Because "why" questions expose the responder. They are confrontational. They force someone to justify themselves, their choices, or their situation to the inquirer, which puts them on the defensive. In the Selective Environment, the last thing you want is to make your prospect feel cornered. Instead of fostering collaboration and understanding, a poorly timed "why" question can make the other person feel scrutinized, judged, or even attacked.

Here are three examples of "why" questions commonly used in sales and "why" they fall flat:

1. "Why did you reach out?"

This might seem like a harmless way to start a conversation, but from the outset, it subtly places the burden on the prospect to prove why they're worth your time. It can make them feel like they have to *earn* your attention rather than the other way around. Worse, if they're

"The last thing you want is for a prospect to second-guess why they're talking to you in the first place."

not entirely sure what they need yet (which is common), they may feel put on the spot and pull back instead of opening up. The last thing you want is for a prospect to second-guess why they're talking to you in the first place. Your role is to make them feel confident about seeking help—not to make them question whether reaching out was the right move.

2. "Why did you decide to do it this way?"

At first glance, this might seem like a logical question to understand a prospect's reasoning. But to the person on the receiving end, it sounds more like, *"What were you thinking?"* or *"You clearly made a mistake."* This question forces them to justify their past decisions rather than explore better solutions. Even if their approach has flaws, you don't want to make them feel like they've been doing it wrong. Instead of opening a productive dialogue, this question can trigger a defensive response like, *"Well, this is just how we've always done it."* And once a prospect starts doubling down on their past choices, it's much harder to influence them toward a new perspective.

3. "Why are you currently using your existing solution?"

On the surface, this question seems like a reasonable way to understand a prospect's current situation. However, in practice, it often puts them in a position where they feel the need to *defend* themselves. Imagine telling someone, *"Why are you still driving that car?"* or *"Why do you eat at that restaurant?"* Even if you're just curious, the question carries an implicit suggestion that their choice might not be the best one. And in sales, making a prospect feel like they have to defend their past decisions can backfire quickly. The moment they start reinforcing why they chose their current solution, they are psychologically anchoring themselves to it—making it harder for them to consider switching to yours.

In the delicate dance of building first impressions and overcoming the Asymmetry of Information, "why" questions are the equivalent of stepping on your partner's toes. As the relationship develops, there may come a time when "why" questions are more appropriate and even strategically helpful, but in the initial steps of connecting with prospects, they are to be avoided. **(Check out Strategy #1, Why to What, to avoid this)**

Fastball Question #2: Presumptive Questions

If "why" questions put people on the defensive, presumptive questions take it one step further by accidentally making people feel inadequate, uninformed, or out of their depth. These are the questions that subtly (or not so subtly) assume the prospect already knows something, has a certain level of expertise, or has made a particular decision—whether or not that's actually the case.

The problem? Presumptive questions create an immediate gap between the inquirer and the responder. Instead of inviting the prospect into a conversation, they make them feel like they're being tested—or worse, that they're already failing the test. When a prospect feels like they don't measure up to the expectations implied in your question, they're more likely to retreat, get defensive, or disengage entirely.

Here are three common presumptive questions that salespeople unknowingly use—and why they backfire:

1. "You knew that already, right?"

This question is meant to check for understanding, but it often has the opposite effect. Instead of confirming knowledge, it puts the prospect in an uncomfortable position where they have to either admit they didn't know (which can feel embarrassing) or pretend they did know to save face. Neither outcome helps the conversation move forward.

Think about how it feels when someone assumes you're familiar with a concept you've never heard of. If you admit you don't know, you risk feeling incompetent. If you nod along, you risk getting lost in the conversation. Either way, the question doesn't create clarity— it creates anxiety. And when a prospect feels uneasy, they're less likely to engage and more likely to shut down.

2. "You've handled this before, haven't you?"

This question might seem like a way to build rapport or acknowledge the prospect's experience, but it can quickly backfire. If they have handled it before, the question is redundant. If they haven't, they might feel like they should have, which can lead to feelings of inadequacy or insecurity.

Imagine walking into a gym for the first time and having a trainer say, "You've done this exercise before, haven't you?" If you haven't, you're instantly aware of the gap between where you are and where they assume you should be. Instead of feeling encouraged, you feel behind. In sales, the same thing happens when a prospect is asked a question that assumes experience they don't have—it doesn't make them more open to learning, it makes them feel judged.

3. "You're already familiar with [industry jargon], correct?"

This one happens all the time—especially in industries with technical language, niche concepts, or insider terminology. Salespeople drop an acronym, reference a complex idea, or mention a process as if the prospect should already know what it means. And if they don't? They're left feeling like an outsider.

The ironic thing about presumptive questions is that they are statements masquerading as questions. They are telling the listener something they ought to already know [9], and no one likes to be told or feel they're out of the loop, especially in a sales conversation. And when a prospect doesn't recognize a term, doesn't know a behavior, or is struggling to follow the conversation, they might not ask for clarification out of fear of looking uninformed. Instead, they'll nod along, disengage, or silently start questioning whether they're in the right conversation at all. All while you mistakenly think everything is going great and charge ahead, leaving your prospect further behind. Which is the risk that

"The ironic thing about presumptive questions is that they are statements masquerading as questions."

comes with presumptive questions. **(Check out Strategy #2, Open Ended, to solve this.)**

Fastball Question #3: Questioning Their Motive

The third type of fastball question is particularly destructive—not just in sales, but in any relationship: questioning someone's motive. These questions don't just ask for information; they challenge the prospect's reasoning, decision-making, or judgment. And when that happens, the conversation shifts from being a collaborative exchange to a subtle (or not-so-subtle) confrontation.

When you question someone's motive, you're essentially saying, *"I don't trust your judgment,"* or *"You need to justify yourself to me."* Even if that's not your intention, that's how it feels on the receiving end. The moment a prospect feels like they're being interrogated instead of understood, their walls go up. Instead of opening up and exploring possibilities with you, they shut down or get defensive.

Here are three common examples of questions that unknowingly challenge a prospect's motive—and why they do more harm than good:

1. "Why would you...?"

This question is laced with judgment. It doesn't just ask about a decision—it suggests that the decision was wrong or stupid. The phrasing makes it sound like the prospect made a mistake, which immediately puts them in a defensive position.

Imagine telling a friend about a new restaurant you tried, only to have them respond with, *"Why would you eat there?"* Instantly, you feel the need to explain or justify your choice. In sales, when a prospect feels the need to defend their past decisions, they become less open to discussing new possibilities. Instead of influencing them toward a better solution, you're making them double down on their current one.

2. "What made you choose that ridiculous option?"

While this may seem like an exaggerated example, variations of this question happen all the time in sales. Even if the word "ridiculous" isn't included, the *tone* or context can carry the same condescending implication. If a prospect senses that you're mocking or belittling their choices—whether it's their current provider, process, or strategy—they're not going to feel safe discussing alternatives with you.

When someone has invested time, money, or effort into a decision, even a small hint of criticism can trigger a defensive response. They'll instinctively want to justify their decision, not reconsider it. And once they feel like they need to defend their past choices, they're far less likely to explore something new.

3. "Why haven't you...?"

This question assumes incompetence. It suggests that the prospect *should* have already solved their problem and that they've been negligent in not doing so. It frames them as irresponsible or behind the curve, which instantly creates resistance.

No one wants to feel like they've failed. And when a prospect feels like they're being judged for *not* having solved their issue yet, they're going to be more focused on protecting their ego than considering a solution. Instead of making them feel empowered to take action, this question makes them feel *embarrassed* for not having acted sooner. And embarrassment does not lead to trust or open conversation.

In the Selective Environment, questioning someone's motive is one of the fastest ways to erode trust. Instead of positioning yourself as a helpful guide, you come across as an interrogator—someone who is looking to *catch* them in a mistake rather than *help* them move forward. **(Check out Strategy #3, Conceptual vs Personal, to change this)**

"Once they feel like they need to defend their past choices, they're far less likely to explore something new."

Asking Questions With Curiosity and Connection: It's Time for Some Tee-ball

Now that we've mapped out some examples of what not to do, let's dig into strategies that are more effective in helping you ask questions with curiosity. These Tee-ball questions will in turn build better connections and influence your prospects to see you as the obvious choice.

Tee-ball Question #1: Convert "Why" to "What"

Now that we've covered how **"why"** questions can put a prospect on the defensive, let's talk about an easy way to fix them. Instead of asking **"why"**, shift to a **"what"** question. This small tweak makes a huge difference in how your prospect *experiences* the conversation.

If "why" questions put the burden on the prospect to justify themselves, then "what" questions, on the other hand, create space for them to share without feeling judged. The shift from interrogation to exploration makes prospects feel safer, more open, and ultimately more willing to engage in a meaningful conversation.

Let's Compare
- **Fastball question (why):** *"Why did you choose this approach?"*
- **Tee-ball question (what):** *"What led you to this approach?"*

The first version sounds like a challenge, as if the prospect needs to defend their choice. The second version invites them to share their thought process—without any implied criticism.

- **Fastball question (why):** *"Why haven't you changed this yet?"*
- **Tee-ball question (what):** *"What challenges have made it difficult to change?"*

The first question assumes incompetence. The second question shows curiosity and empathy, giving the prospect a chance to explain without feeling attacked.

- **Fastball question (why):** *"Why do you think this will work?"*
- **Tee-ball question (what):** *"What do you hope to achieve with this plan?"*

Again, the first question demands justification, while the second encourages open reflection.

Why This Works

Can you sense a difference in these questions? If YOU were asked these by a sales professional, how would one question make you feel compared to another?

In the Selective Environment, prospects are already wary of sales conversations. They're evaluating *you* just as much as you're evaluating *them*. If your questions make them feel like they need to defend

"In the Selective Environment, questioning someone's motive is one of the fastest ways to erode trust. "

themselves, they'll shut down. But when you shift to "what" questions, you signal that you're genuinely interested in their perspective—not just trying to prove them wrong. That's the difference between feeling understood vs feeling interrogated.

Tee-ball Question #2: Open-Ended Questions

If there's one habit that can instantly transform the way prospects engage with you, it's asking open-ended questions. Unlike closed-ended questions that force a simple "yes" or "no" answer, open-ended questions create a runway for deeper conversations. They encourage people to share their thoughts, expand on their experiences, and feel truly heard.

When a prospect feels like they are leading the conversation, they naturally open up more. And when they open up, you gain valuable insights into what they care about, what they fear, and what they truly need. This, in turn, allows you to position yourself as the clear, natural choice rather than just another option.

Let's Compare

- **Fastball question (closed-ended):** *"Do you feel ready to move forward?"*
- **Tee-ball question (open-ended):** *"Are there any concerns about moving forward?"*

The first question puts the responder on the spot, which doesn't encourage further discussion. The second invites them to express concerns, giving you a chance to address them proactively.

- **Fastball question (closed-ended):** *"Is this what you were expecting?"*
- **Tee-ball question (open-ended):** *"How does this compare to what you were expecting?"*

Again, the first question shuts down exploration, while the second encourages them to compare and share their perspective.

- **Fastball question (closed-ended):** *"Would you like more information?"*
- **Tee-ball question (open-ended):** *"What additional information would help you feel confident in your decision?"*

Instead of asking for a basic yes/no response, this version encourages them to articulate their needs, making it easier for you to provide exactly what they're looking for.

Why This Works

When someone feels like their thoughts and experiences truly matter, they are far more open to your guidance. Open-ended questions shift the focus from your agenda to their perspective, which fosters trust and collaboration. In fact, researchers discovered that when you ask open-ended questions, it helps people be more honest and feel like they are valued. Closed-ended questions, on the other hand, reduce the amount of trust they feel, and limit the truthfulness they can share [10].

In sales situations, people don't just want answers—they want to feel safe in their decision-making process. By asking open-ended questions, you give them space to process, express their hesitations, and gain clarity—which ultimately makes it easier for them to choose you.

Tee-ball Question #3: Conceptual vs Personal

One of the most powerful shifts you can make in your conversations is moving from personal questions to conceptual questions. Why? Because personal questions can trigger emotional responses, while conceptual questions encourage rational thinking and open discussion. This makes people more open to new ideas because they're discussing concepts rather than defending their own choices.

Let's Compare

- **Fastball question (personal):** *"What do you like about your current approach?"*
- **Tee-ball question (conceptual):** *"What about this approach do you think works well in general?"*

The first question makes the prospect evaluate themselves, which can make them feel like they need to justify their position. The second question moves the discussion to a more neutral space, allowing them to analyze ideas rather than defend their own choices.

- **Fastball question (personal):** *"How do you feel about this proposal?"*
- **Tee-ball question (conceptual):** *"How does this proposal compare to what you've seen before?"*

Again, the first version makes it about their feelings, which can lead to hesitation or defensiveness. The second version shifts the conversation toward objective analysis, making it easier to discuss without emotional resistance.

- **Fastball question (personal):** *"Do you agree with this solution?"*
- **Tee-ball question (conceptual):** *"What aspects of this solution do you think are most valuable?"*

By avoiding a yes/no decision and instead inviting the prospect to analyze different elements, you keep the conversation fluid and exploratory rather than forcing an immediate stance.

Why This Works

In high-stakes conversations, emotional resistance is often the biggest roadblock to progress. When people feel like they need to defend themselves, they shut down. But when the focus shifts from their personal decisions to broader concepts, they engage in the conversation more freely. By making this small but powerful tweak, you make it easier for prospects to reflect, analyze, and explore new possibilities—without feeling like they're being judged or pressured.

The Two Most Effective Questions

Of all the questions you can ask in order to build connection with someone else, there are two that I have found to be the most effective in the shortest amount of time. In fact, these questions have opened more doors for me professionally than any other and are responsible for the continued growth and success of my business.

Let's start with the first question that, for me, is the epitome of the Influence Mindset:

THE MOST EFFECTIVE QUESTION #1:

So what is the biggest obstacle you are facing right now?

When you ask this question, it is an open invitation for the prospect to share their perspective, and it creates a strategic opportunity for you to get a glimpse into their operating reality. More importantly, it instantly and generously puts the power into the hands of the other person and shows that you are genuinely concerned.

Let's break it down to see why, and how it can help us influence people more effectively.

First, starting the question with "what" keeps it objective. I'm inviting them to reflect and to think about what they are facing and am intentionally trying to move all the emotion out of the equation. "What" is also singular: I'm asking them to boil down their thoughts into what single thing matters most for them.

Second, the invitation for singular focus is reinforced with "what is the biggest obstacle." However, notice I didn't say "problem", "issue", "conundrum", "challenge" or any other word. I intentionally use "obstacle". The reason is the words "problem", "issue", "conundrum", and "challenge" semantically have more emotions attached to them and can make a person feel potentially judged. "Obstacle", on the other hand, is more objective, neutral, and removes the hint of judgement. It also reinforces that I am standing on their side looking at it from their perspective.

Third, the end of the question, "facing right now," is both passive and incisive. On the one hand, the word "facing" gives them a wide range of ways they can be encountering the problem. They don't have to be fighting it, they don't have to be tackling it, they can just be looking at it, and I'm not judging them. However, "right now" also invites clarity and focus to bring up the most important thing that is occupying their time at present. It brings immediacy and also hints that I'm interested in jumping in with them in this moment.

When you ask, "So what is the biggest obstacle you are facing right now?" You are creating a safe space for them to drop their walls and empowering them to give you real-time information on what matters most in that moment. Most importantly, you are helping them feel your genuine interest and concern and building a meaningful connection.

The Second Most Effective Question

The other question that I have seen create powerful results in my business is:

THE MOST EFFECTIVE QUESTION #2:

What has been most helpful in our conversation today?

Whenever I wrap up a coaching call, a workshop with high-level executives, or even a simple conversation with a client, I make a habit of ending with this question. This serves two key purposes:

1. It helps me refine and improve by giving me direct feedback on what resonated most.
2. It ensures that the last thing they reflect on is the value they gained from our interaction.

This is important because in business, the most powerful conversation isn't the one you have with your client—it's the one they have about you when you're not in the room. The moment they finish speaking with you, they will unconsciously package the experience into a simple takeaway, something they can easily recall and share with others. And when they talk about you to a friend, a colleague, or a potential referral, what do you want that key takeaway to be?

You can have a surprising amount of influence over the conversations people have about you.

"Attention follows value and connection."

Do you want them to say, "Yeah, they are really good at what they do," or do you want them to RAVE about the insight, clarity, or solutions they walked away with?

Attention follows value and connection. And when your client speaks about you to someone else—likely a trusted friend, colleague, or decision-maker—there is likely already a strong emotional connection in that conversation. Your job is to make sure that when they describe their experience, they aren't just explaining what you do, but instead, they are reinforcing why you were invaluable to them. Hence, the connection and perceived value the prospect feels will combine to increase their attention towards you and see you as the obvious choice.

But there's a deeper reason why this question is so effective.

It subtly re-sells your client on why working with you was the right decision. By asking them to reflect on what was most helpful, you prompt them to actively recall and reinforce the value they received. And when someone consciously reminds themselves of the benefits they gained, they naturally feel more confident in their investment and are far more likely to tell others.

So when you ask, "What has been most helpful in our conversation today?" you're not just wrapping up a meeting—you're strategically shaping the way they remember you. You're making sure they walk away with clarity, confidence, and a compelling reason to share your name the next time someone asks, "Do you know anyone who can help with this?"

How can you ask these 2 powerful questions more in your daily conversations?

Let me know how they help you and your business!

Wrap Up: The Power of Questions Rooted in Curiosity

Marie Tharp changed the way we see the world—not because she sought to reinforce what was already known, but because she asked the right questions and doggedly maintained an open mind. Where others clung to their assumptions, she pursued discovery. Where her colleagues sought certainty, she remained curious. And because of her curiosity, she unexpectedly uncovered truths that redefined our understanding of the planet.

In much the same way, the questions we ask in sales and leadership define our influence. Are we asking questions to confirm our own expertise, control the conversation, or appear impressive? Or are we asking questions that create space for our prospects to feel heard, understood, and empowered? The difference between fastball questions and Tee-ball questions is the difference between reinforcing your own position and fostering real connection.

As we've explored, great questions remove barriers. They decrease the Asymmetry of Information, create a Symmetry of Understanding, and shift conversations away from judgment and defensiveness toward collaboration and trust. When we move from interrogating to inquiring, from certainty to curiosity, we invite our prospects to engage, reflect, and ultimately see us as the obvious choice.

"Great questions remove barriers. In Selective Environments the more control you give to the responder, the more YOU are winning."

Sales, and much of life, is often framed in terms of winning or losing a zero sum game. Any ground gained by you is an opportunity lost by me. Hence, it can be scary to cede control to another. But in Selective Environments, where we listen and ask questions with the intent to build trust and connection, the opposite is true. In these situations, the more control you give to the responder, the more YOU are winning.

Like Marie Tharp, the most influential professionals aren't the ones who insist on their own expertise, but the ones who seek to uncover deeper truths. And when you approach your conversations with the same spirit of curiosity, you won't just get better answers—you'll build stronger, more lasting relationships that lead to success.

How can you ask your next question with more curiosity?

Chapter 7: Key Takeaways

- **Curiosity is More Powerful Than Certainty.** Marie Tharp's discoveries came from a willingness to challenge assumptions, and the same applies to the way we ask questions in sales and leadership.

- **Poorly Framed Questions Create Resistance.** Fastball questions put people on the defensive, making them feel judged, exposed, or inadequate—shutting down productive conversations.

- **The Best Questions Remove Friction and Encourage Openness.** Tee-ball Questions create space for dialogue, helping prospects feel safe enough to share their real concerns.

- **Shifting from "Why" to "What" Makes All the Difference.** "Why" questions force people to justify themselves, while "what" questions invite reflection and insight.

- **Great Questions Build Connection and Trust.** When you ask with curiosity instead of assumption, you move beyond transactions and into relationships—making you the obvious choice.

Bonus

I've created exclusive content to help you apply the principles we cover together. To access them, go to: **www.TheChristianHansen.com/ BookBonus**

SUMMARY TABLE

INFLUENCE FORMULA:	Competence	(Plus) Connection	(Equals) Influence
ENVIRONMENT:	Performance Environment	Relational Environment	Selective Environment
DEFINITION OF SUCCESS:	Where Success Is Based On How Well You Perform	Where Success Is Based On How Well You Connect & Work With Others	Where Success Is Based On Influencing People To Choose You
STRATEGY:	Achievement Mindset	Charismatic Mindset	Influence Mindset
DEFINITION OF STRATEGY:	Success Happens When I Prove My Value Is High	Success Happens When I Am Likable, Relatable, & Win People Over	Success Happens When You Influence Someone To Choose You Over Others
IF INCOMPLETE?	Competence (Without) Connection = Noise	Connection (Without) Competence = Charm	Competence With Connection = Influence
BRAIN'S DEFINITIONS OF SUCCESS:	SURVIVAL BRAIN Success = When I Meet My Brain's Needs For Security, Resources, Novelty, Belonging, & Status…		EXECUTIVE BRAIN Success = When I Meet Their Brain's Needs For Security, (etc.)
STRATEGIES	ACHIEVEMENT THINKING	CHARISMATIC THINKING	INFLUENCE BRAIN HACKS
Competence Strategy #1: LOGIC VS EMOTION	*How Can I Convince Them I'm Qualified & Capable?*	*N/A*	How Can I Also Acknowledge This Person's Emotions Right Now?
Competence Strategy #2: KNOWLEDGE VS INSIGHT	*How Can I Prove I'm Credible & Impressive?*	*N/A*	What Unique Insight Or Perspective Speaks Directly To Their Challenges?

Competence Strategy #3: HERO VS GUIDE	*How Can I Prove I'm The Best Option They Should Trust?*	*N/A*	How Can I Help Them Feel Like The Hero Of Their Story?
Connection Strategy #1: LISTENING	*N/A*	*How Can I Make This Person Like Me Or See Me As Interesting?*	How Can I Help This Person Feel Heard & Understood Right Now?
Connection Strategy #2: QUESTIONS	*How Can I Ask Questions To Be More Impressive & In Control?*	*How Can I Ask Questions To Be Likable & Relatable?*	How Can I Ask My Next Question With More Curiosity?
?	?	?	?
?	?		?

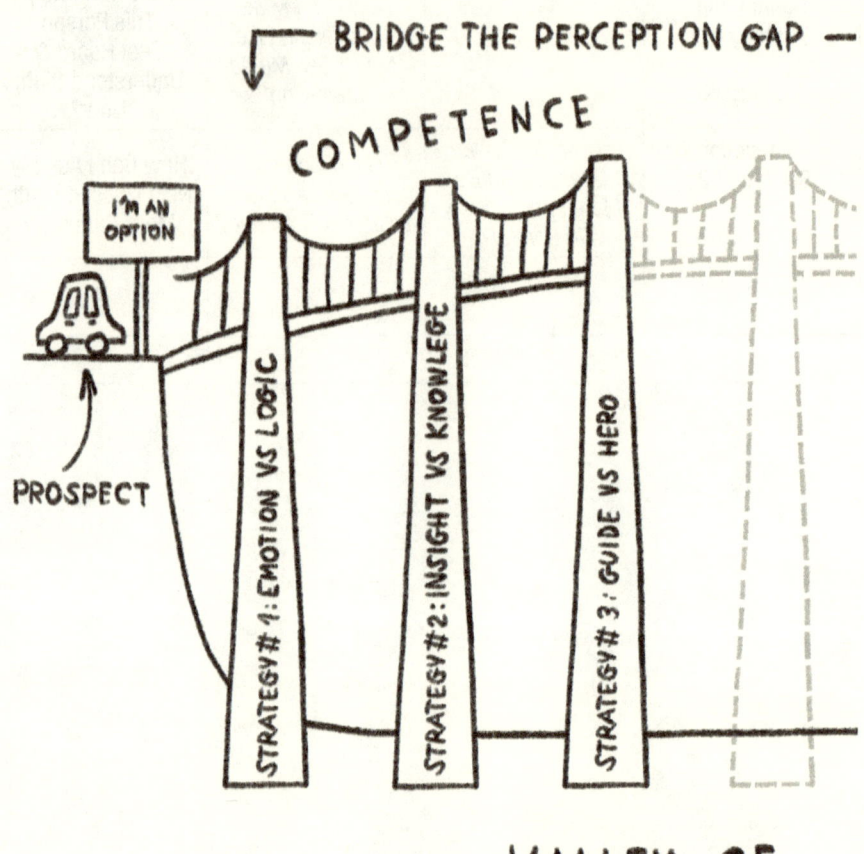

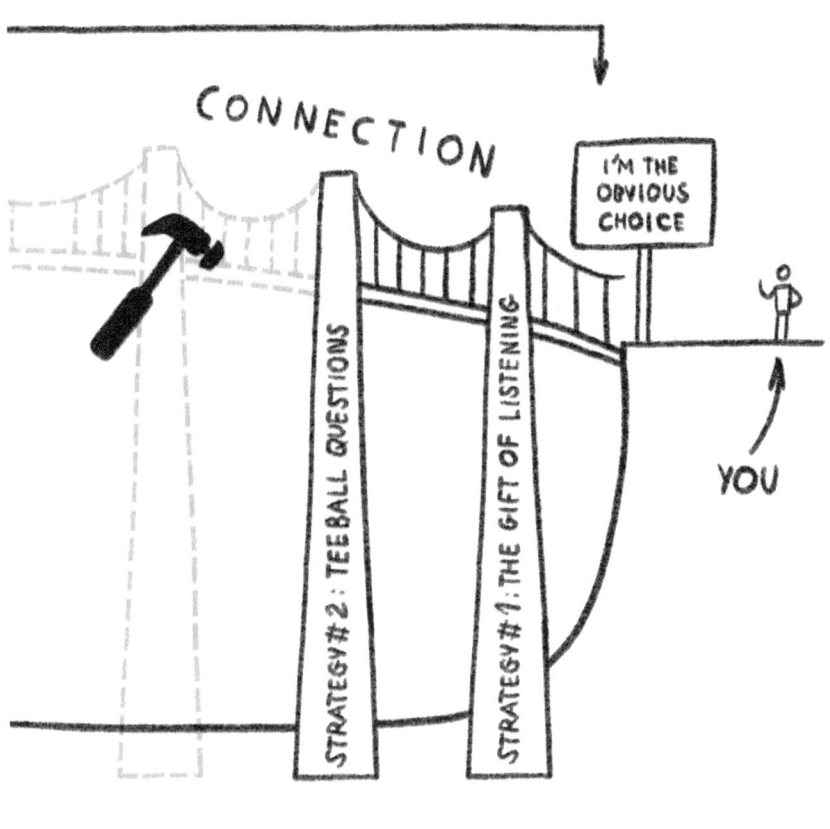

CONNECTION

I'M THE OBVIOUS CHOICE

STRATEGY #2: TEEBALL QUESTIONS

STRATEGY #1: THE GIFT OF LISTENING

YOU

IRRELEVANCE

THE SECRET TO REAL MAGIC

"People will forget what you said, people will
forget what you did, but people will never forget
how you made them feel."

— **Maya Angelou**

When I was in college, I had a secret weapon for surviving those days when life felt overwhelming. Her name was Grandma Jeanine.

Jeanine didn't just know how to cook legendary Sunday meals or always handed you a warm plate of freshly baked cookies as you walked out the door—she had a superpower. She could walk into a room, sit down, and in minutes, leave you feeling like the most capable, brilliant, and important person in the world. And it wasn't just me who felt this way. My friends—people she'd just met—would leave her house awestruck by her uniquely perceptive abilities.

One Saturday afternoon, I decided to test this superpower. A buddy of mine and I were stopping by to visit, and just before we walked in, I stopped him.

"How are you feeling right now?" I asked.

He looked at me, confused by the directness of my question, but said, "Uh, fine, I guess?"

I smiled. "Okay. Now remember that feeling, because when we leave here, I want you to tell me if anything's changed."

He shrugged, and we walked inside.

Grandma greeted us with her usual warmth and modest protests of, "Oh you shouldn't have stopped by! Don't you have anything better to do?" and then led us to the sitting room, where we joined my grandfather who, ailing and blind, was confined to the couch most days listening to the radio or TV. However, despite his physical challenges, he had a brilliant mind and always switched off the media to listen to our conversations with keen interest.

On the surface, if you looked at this couple, you would be forgiven if all you saw were two old people caring for each other in their final years. But the moment you sat down and began speaking with them, this dynamic duo worked wonders.

And that day with my friend was no different.

Grandma started with her usual question, "So tell me about what's happening in your life!"

I shared my updates of how the semester was going, and she listened intently. My grandfather also chimed in with follow-up questions. After we got caught up, she then turned her laser-like gaze to my friend. "And what about you? What are you studying right now?"

As he responded, she poured all her attention into him. "And how did you decide to pursue that?" she asked.

He opened up even more. He shared where he was from and how he had adjusted to college by making friends in his classes. To that she shrewdly added, "Well, you must be gifted in building relationships, or else you wouldn't have been able to make friends so easily."

Surprised at the compliment, my friend's walls came down even more, and he continued. As he spoke, my grandma asked more questions, gently and strategically offering well-placed comments:

- "Well, how creative of you to find that solution!"
- "It's amazing that class came so easily to you. That is a very challenging subject, and not many people have the same abilities as you."
- "I'm so impressed you figured that out. I never would have seen that connection; how insightful of you!"
- "That really shows discipline. You are so dedicated to creating opportunities for your future."
- "How extraordinary. My grandson Christian is lucky to have a friend like you."

Many times she would turn to my grandfather and ask for his feedback, and he would add similarly valuable comments:

- "Well when I was teaching, I rarely had students who had that perspective."
- "That comment you just made reveals a great deal of sensitivity and curiosity. I'm very impressed!"

At which point Grandma would skillfully direct the conversation back to my friend with more open-ended questions. Most people in similar situations would have turned the conversation to themselves at some point. But not Jeanine. No, Grandma had this way of noticing things in people, seeing qualities they didn't even recognize in themselves. Piece by piece, compliment by compliment, she built my friend up—acknowledging not just what he did, but the kind of person he was underneath it all.

As we made our way to leave, my friend didn't walk out. He floated. And when we made it to my car, I asked him the same question: "How are you feeling now?"

He laughed and said, "Amazing. That was incredible! What just happened in there?"

What happened was this: Grandma had a gift for seeing people and validating the best parts of who they were. She didn't just give compliments; she gave people a story about themselves they could believe in—a story they could rise to.

What I didn't realize that day was that Grandma's ability wasn't just a personality quirk or a family trait. It was a skill. And it's one of the most powerful ways to connect with people, influence them, and leave them better than you found them.

What is this overlooked and critical skill in building connection with people? Validation. As we've covered previously, when people feel understood and heard, it has powerful effects on their brain and releases both oxytocin and dopamine. However, when you validate people and their experiences, it speaks to them on a much deeper level.

Let's dig into this and explore why it matters.

Internal Narrative vs External Perception

Disclaimer: *The following technique is a very powerful form of persuasion and influence, and in the wrong hands it can be used to create emotional harm. Use responsibly with great care.*

One of the sources of human emotion is the degree to which our internal narratives are validated (or contradicted) by external perceptions. I know that may seem like a very dense sentence, but to explain how this works, let's assume that I have two internal beliefs about myself:

1. I am a good car driver
2. I am a poor math student

"One of the sources of human emotion is the degree to which our internal narratives are validated (or contradicted) by external perceptions."

One is a positive belief (I'm a good driver), and the second is clearly a negative belief (I'm bad at math). Whether or not these are true statements is not the point, but I believe them, and they shape how I engage with the world and myself. Now let us consider several scenarios and see how these beliefs respond to situations and influence my emotions. To start, let's take my internal belief that I am a good driver and see how that is impacted with two separate stories:

1. One afternoon I got a last-minute call from a friend saying he had two spare tickets to see a popular Broadway musical downtown. Would my wife and I want them? he asked. The problem was,

the theater was 30 minutes away, and the show was ALSO set to begin...in 30 minutes. If we were going to claim the tickets, we needed to get there fast. For the next half hour, I pushed the boundaries of legal driving as I deftly weaved in and out of traffic and triumphantly arrived right on time to catch the first act. This experience validated and confirmed my internal belief that I am a good driver, and I felt really good about myself[1]. Hence, I experienced a *positive* emotion.

2. My wife and I were driving in an unfamiliar part of town and had an argument. Unfortunately, caught up in the moment, I was distracted and missed a stop sign. We entered an intersection just as another car did the same. They had the right of way, and I slammed on the brakes, narrowly missing them. Thankfully the cars didn't hit and no one was hurt, but I was clearly at fault. I sheepishly waved my apologies towards the angry driver. This experience *contradicted* my positive narrative that I am a good driver, and I felt pretty terrible. This created cognitive dissonance, and I experienced a *negative* emotion[2].

In these cases, my POSITIVE internal belief encountered two different sets of external experiences. When my positive internal belief was validated by a similarly positive external perception, I experienced a *positive* emotion. However, when my positive internal belief was contradicted, I felt a *negative* emotion.

But what happens when an internal belief is negative to begin with? Let's take it one step further with my negative belief about math class and how that impacted me in high school.

1. In high school, I dreaded math. I struggled with it, and no matter how hard I tried, it always seemed to evade me. Though I worked with tutors and did extra assignments to get it right, there were so many detailed steps, and I had a hard time keeping

track. Accordingly, when I received bad test scores, it validated my NEGATIVE internal belief and I felt *negative* emotions.

2. One time though, I took a placement exam that assessed my math abilities, and by a miracle of the gods, I scored really high. My teacher looked surprised and congratulated me on my accomplishment (to this day, I still have no idea how it happened). In this instance, my positive math score CONTRADICTED my negative internal belief, and in that moment I felt really happy. I experienced a *positive* emotion.

In these examples, my NEGATIVE internal belief encountered two different sets of external experiences. When my NEGATIVE internal belief was validated by negative external inputs, I experienced negative emotions. However, when it was contradicted, I felt positive emotions.

Do you see the interplay between our internal beliefs and external perceptions? Hence, though there are many factors that can impact how we feel, one of the sources of human emotion is the degree to which our internal narratives are validated (or contradicted) by external perceptions.

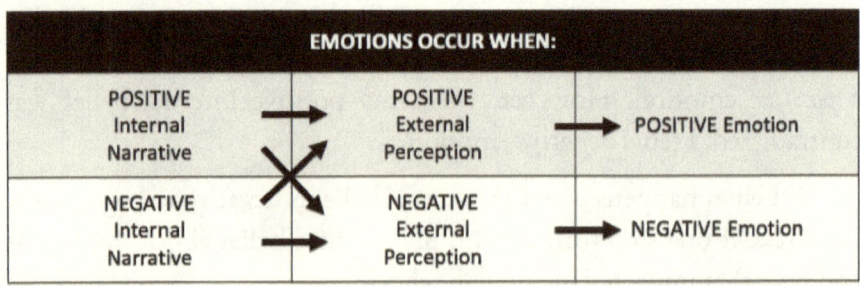

While these two beliefs and accompanying scenarios are just examples, we all carry many internal beliefs that are validated or contradicted by external experiences every day. And just as you and I have a variety of beliefs that are positive and negative, so too do your prospects.

Consider some of the internal beliefs they may have about themselves:

- Some feel as confident as parents. Others anxiously worry that they aren't good enough.
- Some feel that they are successful business owners. Others feel deep personal doubts if they have what it takes.
- Some feel respected in their professional field. Others worry about imposter syndrome.
- Some feel that they can work well by themselves, while others struggle with the guilt of not being able to focus on tasks.

Whatever it is, everyone has deeply held narratives that inform how they view the world and themselves. And they feel intense emotions when these narratives are either validated or contradicted [3].

If we all have powerful internal narratives, and if these narratives react with our external perceptions to create powerful emotions, then YOU have the power to influence the emotions of other people by how you intentionally validate or contradict their internal narratives.

Which is what my Grandmother ingeniously did. As she talked with my friend that Saturday, she noticed he had *negative* internal narratives about his academic abilities. The truth was, he often sold himself short and downplayed his achievements. And so she contradicted them.

- "It's amazing that class came so easily to you. That is a very challenging subject, and not many people have the same abilities as you."
- "I'm so impressed you figured that out. I never would have seen that connection; how insightful of you!"

And so, as his NEGATIVE internal narratives were contradicted with POSITIVE external perceptions, his emotions changed. Similarly,

266 The Influence Mindset

when she perceived his positive internal narratives, she validated them. Take for example the pride he felt when he mentioned how he made friends in different classes:

- "Well, you must be gifted in building relationships, or else you wouldn't have been able to make friends so easily."
- "That really shows discipline. You are so dedicated to creating opportunities for your future."
- "How extraordinary. My grandson Christian is lucky to have a friend like you."

With these comments, she gently and strategically validated his POSITIVE internal narratives. And with this one-two-punch combo of contradicting his negative narratives and validating his positive beliefs, my grandma worked her superpower with soul-transforming results. Like I said, my friend didn't walk out of there. He floated.

Can you see the potential impact if you learned to validate or contradict your prospect's internal narratives? Can you see the results this could have in your personal relationships as well?

But my grandma's magic didn't end there. To her credit, she frequently and intuitively engaged in yet another powerful behavior that changed lives and shaped how people felt around her.

And it took me *years* to figure out.

Giving a Compliment to Live up to

Whenever I would stop by to help her and my grandfather around the house with chores, or whenever I (or anyone else) would bring food for Sunday dinners, she had an odd way of commenting and saying thank you. Instead of saying things like, "That looks lovely," "That smells wonderful," "That looks great," or "What a difference this will make," she said:

- *"How thoughtful of you to notice that needed fixing."*
- *"How creative of you to solve that problem."*
- *"How persevering of you to complete such a challenging task."*
- *"How diligent of you to stick with it until it was done right."*
- *"How kind of you to think of bringing exactly what we needed."*
- *"The care you put into making this just right..."*
- *"How insightful of you to recognize that solution..."*

Do you see a difference?

Rather than, "Good work," "Nice job," or "This will be perfect," she consistently spoke at a higher level. And just like my friend, I watched as she had a similar impact on all sorts of people. No matter their background or relationship to her, they too floated out of her house.

That's why, after years of watching her masterfully influence people, I asked myself, "What is she doing that is having such a powerful effect on others?" And then it hit me:

Instead of complimenting peoples' behaviors, she complimented the attributes the behaviors came from.

Notice her comments above. What attributes was she commenting on?

- *Thoughtfulness.*
- *Creativity.*
- *Perseverance.*
- *Diligence.*
- *Kindness.*

"Instead of complimenting peoples' behaviors, she complimented the attributes the behaviors came from."

- *Care.*
- *Insightfulness*
- *And many many more.*

None of these are direct behaviors. They are attributes that result in behaviors. More importantly, they are desirable qualities we all strive for. Can you see how these spoke to people's internal narratives?

Consider how you would feel if someone took the time to sincerely say you were thoughtful, creative, insightful, smart, and diligent. Would it be meaningful to you? More importantly, would it create a deeper connection between you and the person sharing their insight? My grandma Jeanine knew this. However, she also knew an even deeper truth about communicating and influencing people:

People will rise or fall to the story you give them to tell about themselves.

And she was a master at giving people compliments to live up to.

In my own communication experience, I have found this approach to be profound. Whether in professional environments or in personal relationships, when I've taken the time to acknowledge and validate desirable attributes in others, not only does it create positive emotions, but it can also change their behaviors in deeply impactful ways. Similarly, when you help people build a story they like telling about themselves, the result is nothing short of magical.

Which is the power that validation can have.

But why is attribute-based validation and giving sincere compliments so powerful? When you look at the neuroscience, the research speaks for itself.

The Complementary Findings on Compliments

Researchers have long known that receiving praise from other people:

- Activates the reward parts of our brain [4,5]
- Generates strong feelings of well-being and happiness [6]
- Increases our sense of status [7]
- Helps us feel more attractive to others [8]
- Boosts our self-esteem [9]

But in 2023, scientists wanted to dig a little deeper. They wanted to find out what exactly happens in our brains when we receive compliments [10]. And so they used functional magnetic resonance imaging (fMRI) to observe participants' brain activity as they received compliments from people they trusted. And what the researchers found was powerful.

"People will rise or fall to the story you give them to tell about themselves."

When participants received compliments, the brain's core reward centers became highly active. In earlier chapters we covered how these are the same areas that respond when we experience pleasure, motivation, and deep satisfaction—whether it's from eating our favorite meal, winning a game, or getting a well-deserved promotion.

But that wasn't all. Compliments didn't just make people feel good—they also strengthened social connections. The regions of the brain responsible for emotional awareness and social bonding were also activated. In other words, compliments don't just register as "nice words" in our minds—they signal trust, connection, and validation at a deep neurological level.

And here's where it gets even more fascinating: because these compliments came from trusted sources, they had an even stronger effect. Our brains seem to amplify the impact of praise when it comes from someone we respect or care about. It reinforces not just our sense of self-worth but also our sense of belonging.

Put simply, receiving genuine validation and compliments isn't just a fleeting feel-good moment—it has a measurable impact on our brain, reinforcing both our happiness and our relationships. Science confirms what we've always felt: a well-placed, sincere compliment is a powerful tool to increase the connection and trust we have with others.

But the remarkable findings don't end there.

The Flat Lines of Flattery

In 2023, another group of scientists wanted to take it even further. They asked a simple but powerful question: Does it matter if the praise is real? In other words, if we believe someone's compliment is genuine and deserved, does our brain react differently than if we suspect it's just empty flattery?

To find out, they brought people into an fMRI machine and asked participants to perform different tasks. As they did so, they received two kinds of feedback:

- Sincere praise, where the compliment was actually based on how well they performed.
- Flattery, which was a generic compliment, given regardless of performance.

And the results? It turns out our brains can tell the difference.

When people received sincere praise, as mentioned in the previous study, the reward centers of the brain lit up. When compliments were genuine and felt meaningful and valuable, the brain responded accordingly. Flattery, on the other hand, didn't get the same response. Sure, it was still nice, but the brain wasn't as excited. Without real effort or truth behind it, the compliment lost its power. [11].

But the research gives us one more important insight, which takes this to a completely different level.

"A well-placed, sincere compliment is a powerful tool to increase the connection and trust we have with others."

Choosing YOU with Certainty

If sincere validation strengthens trust, deepens relationships, and activates the brain's core reward centers, then what about situations where uncertainty creeps in? Say, for example, moments where people feel uncertain whether to choose you or not?

This is where validation becomes more than just a tool for connection—it becomes a catalyst for decision-making. Researchers found that affirmation enhances the brain's ability to process uncertainty, making individuals more willing to engage with ambiguous situations rather than avoid them. In essence, when people feel validated—whether through external recognition or affirmation—their brains allocate more cognitive resources to moving forward instead of hesitating [12].

Now, let's apply this insight to sales and influence.

When a prospect is weighing their options, uncertainty is one of the biggest barriers they face. If they don't feel confident in their ability to make the right choice, they may stall, second-guess, or default to doing nothing at all. But when you validate them—not just in their need for a solution, but in their ability to choose wisely—you actively reduce that uncertainty. Instead of feeling lost or overwhelmed, they feel capable and assured, making them far more likely to take action.

In other words, validation doesn't just build trust—it helps people overcome the uncertainty of choosing you over someone else.

So, what do these studies tell us? First, sincerity matters. Our brains don't just crave praise—they crave real praise. When validation is authentic and well-earned, it's processed as a true reward, reinforcing positive emotions and strengthening social bonds. But when it feels fake or self-serving, our brains don't buy in.

Second, when uncertainty is present, authentic validation does more than just feel good; it actively helps people move past hesitation and make confident decisions. It shifts their focus away from doubt and toward action.

Which would you like? Would you like to talk about yourself and stroke your ego...OR...validate your prospect and help them feel more excited, attractive, confident, and certain about choosing you?

The choice is hopefully obvious. But here's the catch: just like compliments, not all validation is created equal.

Which is exactly where the Charismatic Mindset runs into trouble. It recognizes the power of validation but misuses it—turning it into a tool for self-promotion rather than genuine connection.

"Validation doesn't just build trust—it helps people overcome the uncertainty of choosing you over someone else."

The Charismatic Mindset:
Seeking Validation Instead of Giving It

The Charismatic Mindset thrives on attention. It's a mindset that, while often well-intentioned, subtly shifts the focus from validating others to seeking validation for oneself. People with this mindset don't necessarily mean to dominate conversations. In fact, they may be quite fun and engaging to talk to. But their need to be seen, heard, and impressive often outweighs their ability to make others feel seen, heard, and valued.

Instead of using validation as a tool to empower others—like Grandma Jeanine did—it becomes a tool for reinforcing their own social standing. They may give compliments, but their praise feels more like a performance than a genuine recognition of the other person's qualities.

And as the neuroscience research above shows, our brains can tell the difference.

The internal narrative of the Charismatic Mindset is: "How can I look for ways to tell my story?" While it may create a surface-level connection and further a conversation, it often fails to leave a lasting impact. Instead of building people up, it keeps them in a secondary role.

THE CHARISMATIC MINDSET:

How can I look for ways to tell my story?

This is where the Influence Mindset takes a different approach. Instead of seeking validation, it gives it—thoughtfully, strategically, and in a way that reinforces the other person's identity. When you walk into a situation, consider using this simple brain hack: "How can I validate the story this person likes to tell about themselves?" When you listen for the way they frame their role, their values, or their priorities, you can align your validation with what already matters to them. Instead of just agreeing with what they say, you help them see themselves in the best possible light.

THE CHARISMATIC MINDSET:	THE INFLUENCE MINDSET:
How can I look for ways to tell my story?	*How can I validate the story this person likes to tell about themselves?*

That's the core of the Influence Mindset: Validation isn't about making yourself look good—it's about making the other person feel understood. And when someone feels understood, their trust in you deepens.

"In influence, connection beats charisma every time."

And the best part? When you do this authentically with sincerity, they don't just feel validated—they feel a genuine connection with you. And in influence, connection beats charisma every time.

Let's Get Tactical

How does validation work in sales situations? And what are some of the pitfalls? Let's dig into three common behaviors that often get in the way, and then we will explore three strategies that will help you build better connections and influence others to see you as the obvious choice.

Bad Habit #1: Overgeneralized Praise

A few months ago, I attended a business networking event where local entrepreneurs gave short presentations about their businesses. These events are always a great place to connect, learn, and find potential collaboration opportunities. One presenter in particular caught my attention—a consultant who spoke about how small businesses could improve their brand messaging. His delivery was smooth, his points were well-structured, and as he wrapped up, I found myself nodding along, thinking, *That was solid. Maybe we could help each other?*

After the session, I went up to introduce myself. We exchanged pleasantries, and after a moment, he asked, *"So, what did you think?"*

Now, I had enjoyed the presentation, but I hadn't really thought critically about *why* I liked it. So, without much forethought, I said, *"That was great! Really informative."*

He nodded, smiled politely, and responded with a casual, *"Thanks, I appreciate that."*

And just like that...the conversation stalled.

I could tell my response hadn't landed the way I hoped. He wasn't rude, but there was an awkward pause—like he had been expecting more. And he was right to expect more. My feedback was so vague that it didn't give him anything to build on. There was no specific insight, no real connection—just a hollow, obligatory compliment.

The truth was, I was really looking to connect to tell him about ME. I hadn't brought an ounce of curiosity about him. And so, by offering a piece of generalized feedback, I had fallen victim to the Charismatic Mindset without realizing it.

We chatted for another minute or two, but the conversation stayed surface-level. There was no real spark, no momentum, and certainly no lasting impression. As I walked away, I realized I had just wasted an opportunity to make a meaningful connection—all because I fell back on generic, forgettable praise.

And at that moment, I promised myself that next time, I'd do it differently. **(Check out Strategy #1, Attribute-Based Validation, to see how I changed.)**

Bad Habit #2: Forcing a Silver Lining

A while back, I was part of a mastermind group made up of fellow entrepreneurs. We met regularly to share ideas, troubleshoot challenges, and find ways to grow our businesses. It was an invaluable space where we could be open about our struggles and learn from each other's experiences.

At a mastermind event, I grabbed lunch with one of the members to get to know them better. As we ate, we swapped stories about our backgrounds—what led us to where we were, the ups and downs of running a business, and the lessons we had picked up along the way. At one point, I shared a particularly tough challenge I was facing—one that had been weighing on me for a while. I wasn't venting or looking for pity; I just wanted to be real about the obstacles I was working through.

But before I even finished my thought, they jumped in with, *"Well, at least it wasn't worse."*

I paused, nodding politely, but inside, something shifted.

He went on, *"At least you didn't have X problem. That happened to me once..."* and then he shared his own story.

It wasn't that their response was mean-spirited—it was probably meant to be encouraging. But instead of acknowledging what I was saying, it felt like they had brushed it aside, slapping on a quick "silver lining" instead of actually listening. The struggle I had been working through was complex and frustrating, but their response made it feel small—like my obstacle wasn't worth talking about.

Which is what forcing a silver-lining comment can do. It often releases the stress or discomfort of a moment by trying to gloss over it. But more often than not, this serves the person *making* the comment... not the listener.

And that's when I had another realization.

This person was someone I had considered referring business to. I had clients who could have benefitted from their services, and I had been thinking about making an introduction. But if this was how they handled my challenges—glossing over them instead of truly listening to me—how would they handle my clients' challenges? Would they make them feel brushed aside too?

" Their response made it feel small—like my obstacle wasn't worth talking about. "

I left that lunch feeling unseen, and more importantly, unconvinced that this was someone I could trust to serve my clients the way I would want them to be served. **(Check out Strategy #2, Experience-Oriented Validation, to overcome this)**

Bad Habit #3: Self-Centered Validation

After moving to a new town, I was eager to connect with the local business community. I wanted to meet other professionals, build relationships, and see who might be a good fit for collaboration or referrals. So, when I heard that the Chamber of Commerce was hosting a networking event, I jumped at the opportunity.

During the event, I met a mortgage officer who seemed sharp, personable, and knowledgeable about the local market. Since I had family members planning to relocate to the area, I was actively looking for someone I could trust to refer them to. We had a great initial conversation, and I left the event thinking, *Maybe this is someone I should get to know better.*

A few days later, we met over lunch, and that's when things took a turn.

At first, I shared a bit about myself—what had brought me to town, the work I did, and my goals for connecting with the business community. But every time I shared something, they immediately redirected the conversation back to their own past experiences.

I mentioned my extended family's potential move, and they cut in with, *"Oh yeah! I remember when I moved to a new city— boy was that a hard change. I was just a teenager..."*

I talked about a challenge I had faced when expanding my business, and they jumped in with, *"That reminds me of when I hired a new team member last year. That sure threw me for a loop..."*

Every topic, every experience, every piece of my story somehow became a springboard for them to talk about *themselves*. You may recognize this from Chapter 6 as a form of piggybacking, which it was. Now, I get it—sometimes people relate by sharing their own experiences. But there's a fine line between connecting through shared experience and making the conversation all about you.

By the end of the conversation, I realized something: While we had a lively back-and-forth, I didn't feel like they really got to know *me* at all. They were friendly and engaging, sure—but they hadn't taken the time to truly listen. And if they hadn't made the effort to understand *me*, how could I trust that they would take the time to understand my relatives when they needed guidance on buying a home?

So, when the time came to refer someone, I hesitated. Instead of feeling confident that this mortgage officer would take great care of my family, I felt uncertain. And in business, uncertainty kills referrals. **(Check out Strategy #3, Future-Oriented Validation, to see how this was resolved.)**

In each of these situations, I and the individuals I mentioned used other people's stories as platforms to tell OUR OWN stories instead. Whether it was giving generalized praise, forcing a silver lining, or being

"Uncertainty kills referrals."

self-centered in the validation, the speaker entered these interactions to make themselves feel better. The result? The listener felt unheard, and the opportunity for connection was lost.

How can you avoid this? Let's check out some strategies that showcase the influential power of validation...when done right.

Strategy #1: Attribute-Based Validation

A few weeks after my awkward encounter at the business networking event—where my vague compliment had led to a dead-end conversation—I found myself at another entrepreneur presentation. This time, I was determined to do things differently. I had learned that empty praise, no matter how well-intended, didn't create real connection. If I wanted to stand out and make an impression, I needed to be more intentional.

After the presentation, I walked up to the speaker, a business owner who had just given an engaging talk about scaling her company. Instead of defaulting to something generic like, "Great presentation!" I paused and thought about what had really impressed me.

"You know, I was really struck by how clearly you laid out your growth strategy. It's one thing to scale a business, but to articulate it in such a way that makes it feel achievable for others? I was really impressed at the *level of clarity* you brought. Your *insightfulness* reshaped how I am thinking about a problem in my own business."

She blinked in surprise, then smiled. "Wow—thank you. That actually means a lot."

Immediately, the energy of the conversation shifted. Instead of the awkward, polite nod I had received from the last entrepreneur, this time, she leaned in and started sharing more about her experiences. She opened up about how she had struggled early on to communicate her vision and how much she had worked to refine it. Because I had validated specific attributes—her clarity and insightfulness—rather than just giving a vague compliment, she felt seen and understood.

Before I knew it, she asked, "Hey, we should hop on a call sometime. I'd love to hear more about what you do."

That simple shift—from generalized praise to attribute-based validation—made all the difference. Since that conversation, we've stayed in touch, referred business to each other, and even collaborated on a few projects. And all of it started with one well-placed, thoughtful validation.

When you highlight the personal qualities behind someone's success, you're not just complimenting them—you're reinforcing a powerful, positive story they already want to believe about themselves. And in sales, business, and relationships, helping someone see their own strengths more clearly is one of the fastest ways to earn trust and build lasting influence.

What attributes can you compliment in others when you speak to them?

Strategy #2: Experience-Oriented Validation

The day after my disappointing lunch at the mastermind event—where my struggles were brushed aside with a forced silver lining—I found myself in a conversation with another entrepreneur. It was the second day of the event, and this time, I was hesitant to open up. After all, no one enjoys sharing something personal only to have it minimized or

"Helping someone see their own strengths more clearly is one of the fastest ways to earn trust and build lasting influence."

turned into a shallow pep talk. But as I spoke with this new person, something felt different.

I shared a challenge I had faced in my business, a particularly tough season where things hadn't gone according to plan. Instead of offering a premature "look on the bright side" or immediately trying to fix it, this new colleague simply nodded and listened. Then, he said something that completely changed the tone of the conversation.

"That must have been a huge challenge, but you handled it really well. I mean, to pivot like that and find a new direction—most people would have given up. That kind of persistence says a lot about you."

It caught me off guard in the best way possible. He didn't just acknowledge the facts of my story—he recognized the effort, resilience, and creativity it took to navigate it. Instead of feeling dismissed, I felt *understood*. Instead of feeling like I had to defend my experience, I felt *validated*.

"I'm really impressed at how you worked through that," he continued. *"That kind of consistency is rare—it's no wonder you've been able to find success even when things got tough."*

And just like that, the connection deepened. This wasn't someone who was just making small talk or looking for an easy conversation filler—he genuinely saw me and what I had been through. That single moment of experience-oriented validation made me feel like I could trust him, not just as a professional, but as a person. Which is what experience- oriented validation does best. When someone shares their experiences, and when you use those as platforms to help them see themselves in different light? That connection is powerful

Since then, I've referred business to him *constantly*. Whenever someone asks me for a recommendation in his field, he is the first name I give. Not because he had the flashiest pitch or the most aggressive sales tactics, but because he had a rare ability to create trust and connection through how he validated others.

And in sales, influence, and business, *that* is what makes someone the obvious choice.

When someone tells a story about an important experience, what attributes can you notice and highlight?

Strategy #3: Future-Oriented Validation

After my frustrating conversation with the first loan officer—the one who kept turning everything back to himself in Bad Habit #3—I was still searching for someone I could confidently refer to my relatives who were exploring a potential move. A few weeks later, I had lunch with another loan officer. I wasn't expecting much beyond another standard business conversation, but from the very beginning, something about this meeting felt different.

Instead of dominating the conversation with his own experiences, this person asked thoughtful questions. And more importantly, after each answer I gave, he didn't just nod and move on—he reflected back something meaningful about what I had shared.

"It sounds like you've really taken the time to think through all the angles before making big decisions. That kind of strategic thinking will make all the difference for you..."

I hadn't thought of it that way before. I had just been doing my best to figure things out. But he framed my efforts in a way that made me feel capable, prepared, and even more confident in my decisions.

As we kept talking, he continued this pattern of *future-oriented validation.*

"The way you've prioritized things really says a lot. I imagine that kind of intentionality will open up even more doors."

" People aren't looking for solutions, they're looking for affirmation. They want to feel that who they are, what they've done, and where they're going matters. "

"It's clear you care about making the right choices. I have no doubt that the same thoughtfulness you've shown here will continue to create opportunities."

By the end of our conversation, I wasn't just impressed—I *trusted* him. He wasn't just another professional making small talk; he was someone who truly listened, who recognized the effort I had already put in, and who could see how those same strengths would serve me well in the future.

It was an easy decision to start referring him to others. In fact, when my relatives asked me for a recommendation, I gave them his name without hesitation. And today, anytime someone I know needs a loan officer, I tell them, *"You have to talk to this guy."*

Because when someone makes you feel seen—not just for where you've been, but for where you're going—it creates a level of trust and connection that is impossible to ignore. And in sales, influence, and business, that trust is what makes you the obvious choice.

When people share their stories, how can you validate them in a way that makes them feel excited about their future?

Wrap Up: The Magic of Seeing People

Looking back, I realize Grandma Jeanine was one of the great artists of our time. Though she didn't work with chisels or paint, she used words and expertly placed encouragements to sculpt and mold souls. She had the rare gift to perceptively see and amplify people around her, and because she gave people a story to live up to, they left her presence believing more in themselves than when they arrived. My Grandma Jeanine's superpower wasn't just about making people feel good—it was about making them feel seen.

In many ways, this is exactly what the Influence Mindset does. It recognizes that people aren't just looking for solutions—they're looking for affirmation. They want to feel that who they are, what they've done, and where they're going matters. And when you validate those

"Sales professionals who master this skill don't just gain clients; they build relationships. "

things in a meaningful way, you're not just making them feel good for a moment—you're creating a lasting impression of trust and connection.

Sales professionals who master this skill don't just gain clients; they build relationships. They become the obvious choice, not because they pushed the hardest or had the flashiest pitch, but because they made their prospects feel heard, valued, and understood. Validation isn't just a feel-good tool—it's a strategic advantage.

So, the next time you're in a conversation, whether in business or in life, remember the lesson of Grandma Jeanine: People rise to the story you give them to tell about themselves.

Make it a great one.

Chapter 8: Key Takeaways

1. **Validation Isn't Just About Making People Feel Good— It's About Making Them Feel Seen.** Thoughtful, specific validation builds trust and deepens connections.

2. **Generalized Praise Falls Flat.** Compliments are most impactful when they highlight specific attributes, experiences, or future potential.

3. **Forcing a Silver Lining Can Backfire.** Instead of rushing to make someone feel better, acknowledge their experience first. People don't want their struggles dismissed—they want them understood.

4. **Self-Centered Validation Weakens Connection.** Turning every conversation back to yourself may feel relatable, but it often makes the other person feel unheard.

5. **Great Salespeople Validate the Story People Tell About Themselves.** The Influence Mindset doesn't just acknowledge what someone has done—it reinforces who they are and who they are striving to become.

Bonus

I've created exclusive content to help you apply the principles we cover together. To access them, go to: **www.TheChristianHansen.com/ BookBonus**

SUMMARY TABLE

INFLUENCE FORMULA:	Competence	(Plus) Connection	(Equals) Influence
ENVIRONMENT:	Performance Environment	Relational Environment	Selective Environment
DEFINITION OF SUCCESS:	Where Success Is Based On How Well You Perform	Where Success Is Based On How Well You Connect & Work With Others	Where Success Is Based On Influencing People To Choose You
STRATEGY:	Achievement Mindset	Charismatic Mindset	Influence Mindset
DEFINITION OF STRATEGY:	Success Happens When I Prove My Value Is High	Success Happens When I Am Likable, Relatable, & Win People Over	Success Happens When You Influence Someone To Choose You Over Others

IF INCOMPLETE?	Competence (Without) Connection = Noise	Connection (Without) Competence = Charm	Competence With Connection = Influence
BRAIN'S DEFINITIONS OF SUCCESS:	SURVIVAL BRAIN Success = When I Meet My Brain's Needs For Security, Resources, Novelty, Belonging, & Status…		EXECUTIVE BRAIN Success = When I Meet Their Brain's Needs For Security, (etc.)
STRATEGIES	ACHIEVEMENT THINKING	CHARISMATIC THINKING	INFLUENCE BRAIN HACKS
Competence Strategy #1: LOGIC VS EMOTION	*How Can I Convince Them I'm Qualified & Capable?*	*N/A*	How Can I Also Acknowledge This Person's Emotions Right Now?
Competence Strategy #2: KNOWLEDGE VS INSIGHT	*How Can I Prove I'm Credible & Impressive?*	*N/A*	What Unique Insight Or Perspective Speaks Directly To Their Challenges?
Competence Strategy #3: HERO VS GUIDE	*How Can I Prove I'm The Best Option They Should Trust?*	*N/A*	How Can I Help Them Feel Like The Hero Of Their Story?
Connection Strategy #1: LISTENING	*N/A*	*How Can I Make This Person Like Me Or See Me As Interesting?*	How Can I Help This Person Feel Heard & Understood Right Now?
Connection Strategy #2: QUESTIONS	*How Can I Ask Questions To Be More Impressive & In Control?*	*How Can I Ask Questions To Be Likable & Relatable?*	How Can I Ask My Next Question With More Curiosity?
Connection Strategy #3: VALIDATION	*N/A*	*How Can I Look For Ways To Tell My Story?*	How Can I Validate The Story This Person Likes To Tell About Themselves?
?	?		?

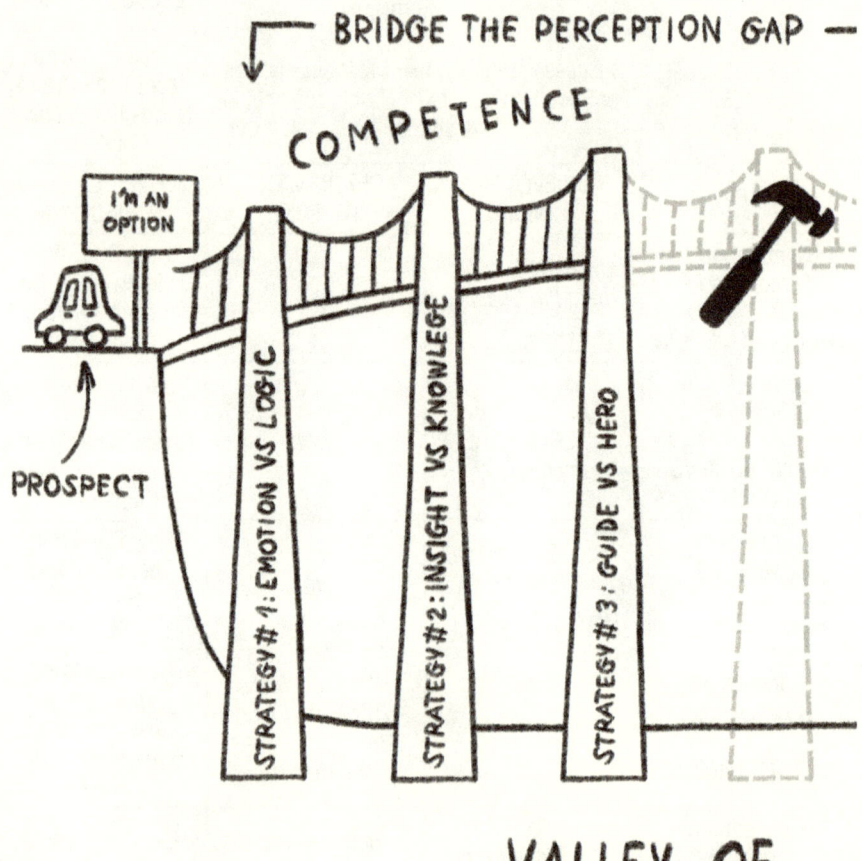

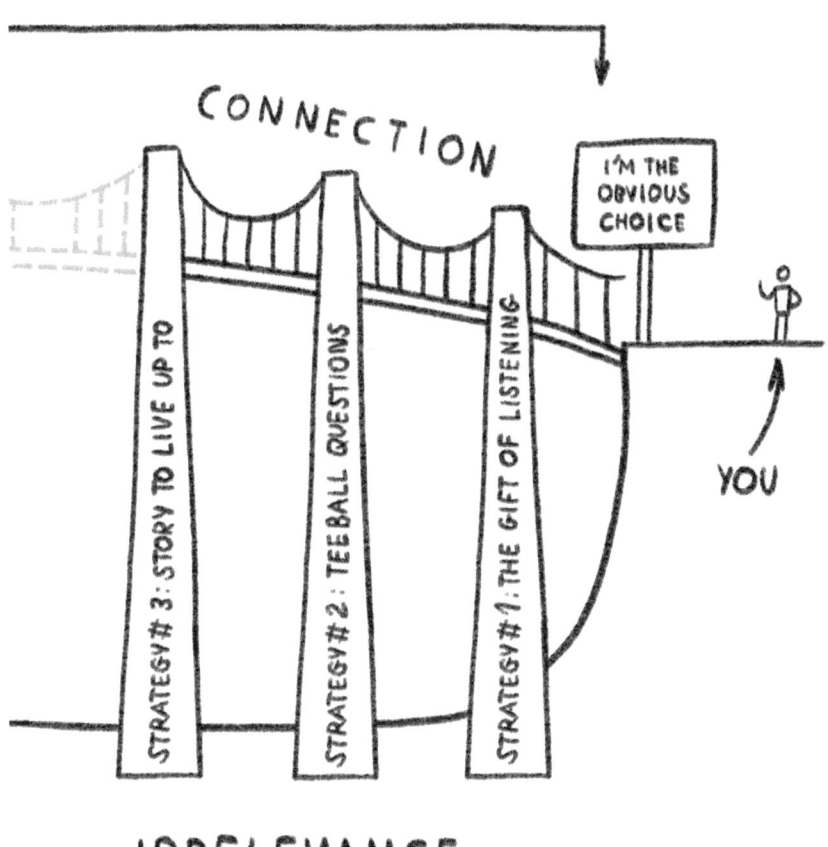

CONCLUSION

BEING THE OBVIOUS CHOICE

The 35-Ton Miracle

"If you saw how much work it took, you wouldn't
call it genius."

— **Michelangelo**

In 1464, the city of Florence had recently finished its cathedral, Il Duomo (The Dome), and wanted a series of statues of Old Testament prophets to guard its majestic roofline. A well-known artist, Agostino di Duccio, was commissioned and tasked with beginning the large project. In an effort to use the best marble possible, he personally traveled to the famous quarries at Carrara to select a block worthy of the endeavor.

After selecting a massive 5-meter, 35-ton stone ideal for his vision, di Duccio carefully followed as it journeyed by oxcart to the sea, where it was then shipped 150 kilometers down the coast and up the Arno river to Florence by barge [1]. Eventually the stone arrived in the heart of the city, and finally...a year after being commissioned...di Duccio began carving his statue for the cathedral.

Except for one problem.

He got stuck. The massive rock had unexpected weak points and impurities he couldn't work around, to say nothing of its formidable size. In an attempt to define where the legs would be, he carved a hole in the middle of the statue, but to no avail. For all his efforts, he was stymied. It was simply too difficult! And so, for a host of reasons, di Duccio gave up after only 1 year of effort.

What about the stone? Il Gigante (or The Giant), as the locals called it, lay on the ground, difficult to move, and scarred with a gaping hole. There it remained in the yard for another ten years, collecting bird droppings and dust, with no one brave enough to work it. Everyone wondered, "Could anything be done?"

Then in 1476, a new artist was chosen: Antonio Rossellino [2]. Filled with creative vision, he threw himself into the rock trying to make headway. He tried to salvage the earlier work completed by di Duccio and made impressive sketches showing his ideas. The city was thrilled that finally their goal of an Old Testament Prophet gracing their cathedral would be fulfilled. However, just like di Duccio, the stone evaded Rossellino's efforts, and he too gave up work after just 1 year.

And so The Giant lay abandoned in the stone yard once again... being *cotto* (cooked) by the weather...for another *25 years*. The problem was, the locals said, it was simply too big! It was difficult to stand up straight, it had impurities, and what about the hole? The multiple failed attempts defaced it to the point of being unworkable. Even the great Leonardo Da Vinci, a fellow Florentine, was consulted, and he walked away shaking his head. Not even HIS great mind knew what to do. And so Il Gigante, twice rejected, remained in the masons' yard for decades.

All that money and work gone to waste.

Then, in 1501, word spread about a young Florentine sculptor who had just finished a masterwork in Rome. His Pietà depicting Mary holding Christ after being lowered from the cross was a marvel in marble and made people weep with its beauty. Maybe he could do something with The Giant? He was awarded the commission, and on September 13, 1501, the 26-year-old artist began to work [3]. For the next three years he would hammer, carve, chip, chisel, grind, cut, shape, sand, and polish his way into the heart of the stone. And the shape that emerged shocked and astonished all who saw it step forth.

And finally, on September 8, 1504...

- 40 years after being carved from the mountain...
- 38 years after being abandoned the first time...
- 28 years after being rejected the second time...

...the stone emerged triumphant as Michelangelo Buonarroti unveiled his colossal 17-foot-tall Renaissance masterpiece: the David.

Today the statue, housed in the Uffizi Museum in Florence, draws millions of visitors each year who marvel at its achievement. And while many people take pictures of its flawless perfection, few know the story of how this era-defining statue came from a twice rejected 35-ton block of stone that nobody wanted for nearly 40 years.

But what does this have to do with you?

You May See the David, But All They Can See is a Rock

People don't choose or reject you. They choose or reject their *perception* of you.

Just like the Florentines who only saw an unremarkable block of stone, the world doesn't automatically see your full value. Not because it isn't there, but because it's obscured by layers of miscommunication, misunderstood signals, and outdated mindsets.

If you can communicate in a way that helps them perceive your value, you will be seen as the obvious choice and people will choose you.

If you can't? Then like di Duccio and Rossellino, your value will remain hidden and people will pass you by. Even though YOU can see your value...clear as day...all your prospects can see is a rock.

Just like everyone else.

In the same way that Michelangelo used his skills and tools to hammer, carve, chip, chisel...and released the David from stone, so too is it your responsibility to find the right words and behaviors that remove all the obscuring layers that prevent people from perceiving you as the obvious choice. In fact, your success hinges on this.

People need to buy into you before they buy from you. Which is where the Influence Mindset comes in.

Throughout this book, we have explored the hidden forces that shape how people perceive you. We have uncovered six powerful tools—six key

"It is your responsibility to find the right words and behaviors that remove all the obscuring layers that prevent people from perceiving you as the obvious choice."

emotional intelligence hacks—that enable you to stand out, connect, and ultimately shape how others see your value. Relying upon the remarkable stories of Ignaz Semmelweis, Malcom McLean, Deloris Peoples Jordan, Marie Tharp, the Wright brothers, and many more, we have revealed the hidden pitfalls of the Achievement and Charismatic Mindsets as well as the psychological needs that drive decision-making. Along the way, we've explored specific strategies that allow you to influence others without resorting to the ineffective approaches of hard selling, pressure, or shallow, self-serving self-promotion.

Which ultimately are what the Achievement and Charismatic Mindsets do. They both operate from the insecure reactions of the Survival Brain, and in one way or another think, "How can I feel more interesting (and secure) by making this conversation about me?"

THE ACHIEVEMENT & CHARISMATIC MINDSETS:

How can I feel more interesting (and secure) by making this conversation about me?

While these approaches certainly help us feel better in the moment, they fundamentally miss our audience's core needs. And so our prospects see yet another indistinguishable block of stone, and pass us by.

Which brings us to the 7th and final emotional intelligence (EQ) brain hack. If you know that success is really based on influencing people to choose you over others, and if you know that their Survival Brains have core needs to be met, then when all else fails, ask this Influence Mindset brain-hacking question: How can I be more interested and make this conversation about them, right now?

THE ACHIEVEMENT & CHARISMATIC MINDSETS:

How can I feel more interesting (and secure) by making this conversation about me?

THE INFLUENCE MINDSET:

How can I be more interested and make this conversation about them right now?

Learning to master this question will create magical results in accelerating your influence and sales. That's because hiding behind it lies one of the great secrets of life: While learning to set your needs to the side and intentionally giving your focus wholly to someone else is one of the most difficult skills a person can learn...it is also one of the most rewarding. In these moments, you are giving them the greatest gift you can offer: the gift of yourself.

And such a gift can be life-changing.

"People need to buy into you before they buy from you."

"In these moments, you are giving them the greatest gift you can offer: the gift of yourself."

Influence is a Mindset and a Skillset

We began this book by outlining this simple formula:

Competence + Connection = Influence

However, we soon discovered that:

Competence (Without) Connection = Noise

And...

Connection (Without) Competence = Charm

No matter what your background is, and no matter if you think you are a good communicator or not, influencing people through demonstrating your competence and creating connection is a skillset that can be learned and improved. You can consistently learn to avoid the ineffective behaviors that are getting in the way, and instead cultivate and sharpen the skills that influence people to choose you.

Specifically, as you ask these "brain-hacking" questions in sales situations, namely:

1. *How can I also acknowledge this person's emotions right now?*
2. *What unique insight or perspective speaks directly to their challenges?*
3. *How can I help them feel like the Hero of their story?*
4. *How can I help this person feel heard and understood right now?*
5. *How can I ask my next question with more curiosity?*
6. *How can I validate the story this person likes to tell about themselves?*

And finally...

7. *How can I be more interested and make this conversation about them right now?*

...You will increase your ability to rise above the noise, stand out from the crowd, and influence people to see you as the obvious choice.

Never Has It Been More Important

In today's world, never has it been more important to stand out from the crowd.

Never has it been more important to communicate your value in a way that resonates emotionally, not just logically.

Never has it been more important to influence others to choose you—not through force or manipulation, but through insight and authenticity.

Because in a world drowning in information and saturated with distracting noise, people are starving for genuine connection.

"When all else is equal, he or she who communicates their value and connects best, wins."

Remember: When all else is equal—when everyone has comparable skills, experience, and qualifications—he or she who communicates their value and connects best, wins.

Regarding another statue, Michelangelo once remarked, *"I saw the angel in the marble and carved until I set him free."* When it comes to your value, you must do the same.

Michelangelo saw the David before anyone else did. And just like Michelangelo, you now have everything you need to remove the barriers, refine the details, and help your value step forward from its captive stone...as the clear and obvious choice.

That is exactly what the Influence Mindset enables you to do. That's because it's not just about standing out. It's about helping others see themselves more clearly—their gifts, their challenges, and their path forward. And at the end of the day, when you help people see themselves with new eyes? When you give them a story to live up to? That's the most important influence of them all.

Your value is already there. The question is, can you help others see it too?

Like the people of Florence all those years ago, I can't wait to see what you're about to share with the world.

May you rise above the noise.

May you stand out from the crowd.

And may your influence rise *ever higher*.

Go influence life, and God bless.

Christian Hansen

"Your value is already there. The question is, can you help others see it too?"

SUMMARY TABLE

INFLUENCE FORMULA:	Competence	(Plus) Connection	(Equals) Influence
ENVIRONMENT:	Performance Environment	Relational Environment	Selective Environment
DEFINITION OF SUCCESS:	Where Success Is Based On How Well You Perform	Where Success Is Based On How Well You Connect & Work With Others	Where Success Is Based On Influencing People To Choose You
STRATEGY:	Achievement Mindset	Charismatic Mindset	Influence Mindset
DEFINITION OF STRATEGY:	Success Happens When I Prove My Value Is High	Success Happens When I Am Likable, Relatable, & Win People Over	Success Happens When You Influence Someone To Choose You Over Others
IF INCOMPLETE?	Competence (Without) Connection = Noise	Connection (Without) Competence = Charm	Competence With Connection = Influence
BRAIN'S DEFINITIONS OF SUCCESS:	SURVIVAL BRAIN Success = When I Meet My Brain's Needs For Security, Resources, Novelty, Belonging, & Status…		EXECUTIVE BRAIN Success = When I Meet Their Brain's Needs For Security, (etc.)
STRATEGIES	ACHIEVEMENT THINKING	CHARISMATIC THINKING	INFLUENCE BRAIN HACKS
Competence Strategy #1: LOGIC VS EMOTION	How Can I Convince Them I'm Qualified & Capable?	N/A	How Can I Also Acknowledge This Person's Emotions Right Now?
Competence Strategy #2: KNOWLEDGE VS INSIGHT	How Can I Prove I'm Credible & Impressive?	N/A	What Unique Insight Or Perspective Speaks Directly To Their Challenges?

Competence Strategy #3: HERO VS GUIDE	*How Can I Prove I'm The Best Option They Should Trust?*	*N/A*	How Can I Help Them Feel Like The Hero Of Their Story?
Connection Strategy #1: LISTENING	*N/A*	*How Can I Make This Person Like Me Or See Me As Interesting?*	How Can I Help This Person Feel Heard & Understood Right Now?
Connection Strategy #2: QUESTIONS	*How Can I Ask Questions To Be More Impressive And In Control?*	*How Can I Ask Questions To Be Likable & Relatable?*	How Can I Ask My Next Question With More Curiosity?
Connection Strategy #3: VALIDATION	*N/A*	*How Can I Look For Ways To Tell My Story?*	How Can I Validate The Story This Person Likes To Tell About Themselves?
CONCLUSION:	*How Can I Feel More Interesting (& Secure) By Making This Conversation About Me?*		How Can I Be More Interested & Make This Conversation About Them Right Now?

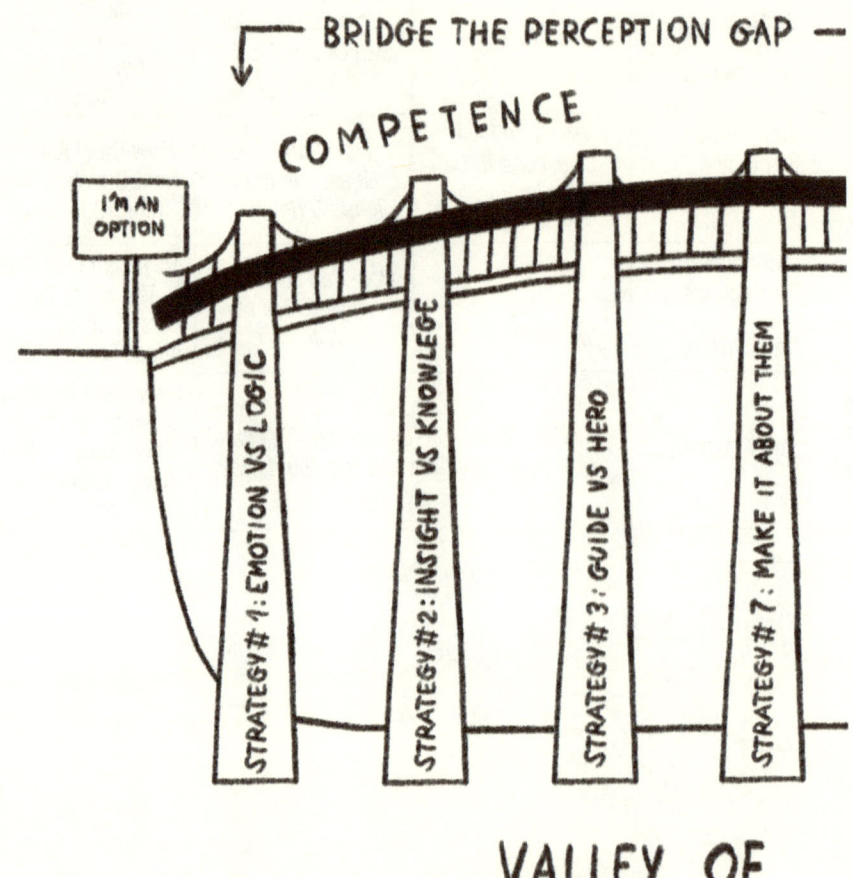

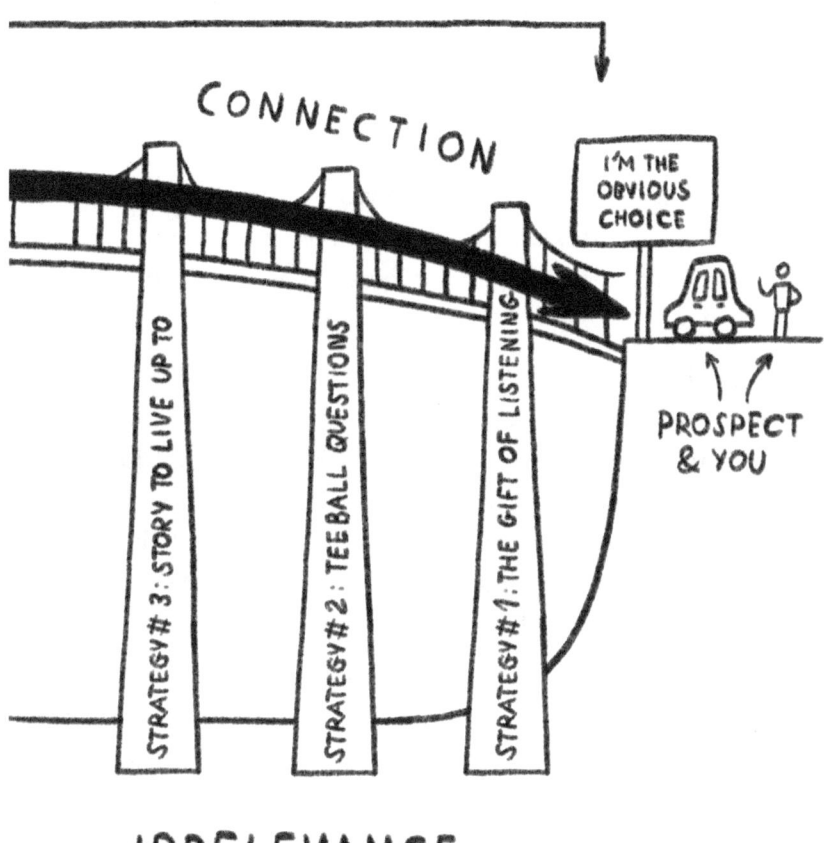

IRRELEVANCE

ACKNOWLEDGEMENTS

On February 5th, 1675, Sir Isaac Newton wrote a letter to fellow scientist Robert Hooke. In it, Newton confessed the now-famous line: "If I have seen further [than others], it is by standing on the shoulders of giants."

When my first book, *The Influence Mindset*, was published in 2021, I had no idea the journey it would send me on. It opened doors I never imagined and introduced me to several remarkable people—individuals without whom this book would not have been possible. Though it would be impossible to name everyone, if this book has helped you in any way, then I must be the first to express my gratitude to the many hands and hearts who shaped it. They are giants to me.

To Brandon Thomas and Suzette Smith—your work as real estate agents for me and my family in a difficult time showed me what was possible when professionals serve others in deeply meaningful and impactful ways. You opened your professional network to me, and helped create relationships I will treasure for the rest of my life. You embody what it means to "go above and beyond" and for me, you will always be the obvious choice when I refer others.

To Natalee Champlin, founder of The Affluent Affect—your deeply insightful and incisive ability to ask questions that get to the heart of any business problem is astonishing as it is illuminating. You were instrumental as a sounding board for many of the ideas presented herein and I am grateful for you and your continued friendship to me and my family.

To my trusted circle of Beta Readers—thank you for showing up. Your feedback, thoughtful questions, and willingness to engage with earlier drafts made this book better in ways that only community can. And to Susan Gaigher—thank you for your keen editorial eye and ability to work through my manuscripts with a fine tooth comb. Your attention to detail is a gift, and I've long admired your ability to polish sentences so they land with even greater impact.

To my parents John and Kathie Hansen, and my uncle Bent Hansen, I am grateful for your examples, encouragement, and support. Your feedback and guidance all these years have been invaluable, and I am who I am today because of you. Thank you for influencing me in the best of ways and for making me better.

And finally, to my wife, Nathalie. It's not easy living with someone who's constantly filtering the world through a lens of metaphors, frameworks, and mid-sentence revelations—especially when those ideas arrive at 4 a.m. or on a weekend getaway. Your patience, your wisdom, your ear for emotion and nuance have shaped this book in ways both seen and unseen.

Though the premise of this book is that Competence + Connection = Influence, I may have missed the mark yet again. Because as I mentioned in my first book Nathalie has proven time and time again that kindness (more so than any other attribute) is truly the greatest influence of all. I love you.

—Christian Hansen

REFERENCES

Section 1: Bridging the Perception Gap

1. "How the World's Tallest Bridge Changed the Map of Europe." *CNN*, Jan. 2025, https://www.cnn.com/travel/millau-viaduct-tallest-bridge-construction/index.html.

2. Martin, Jean-Pierre, et al. "The Design of the Millau Viaduct." *Proceedings of the fib Symposium: Concrete Structures – The Challenge of Creativity*, Avignon, 2004, https://www.afgc.asso.fr/app/uploads/2018/05/Servant.pdf.

3. Nesterova, Mariia, Franziska Schmidt, and Christian Soize. "Probabilistic Analysis of the Effect of the Combination of Traffic and Wind Actions on a Cable-Stayed Bridge." *Bridge Structures*, vol. 15, no. 3, 2019, pp. 121–138.

4. "Viaduc de Millau – Longest Cable-stayed Bridge in the World." *YouTube*, uploaded by Science Channel, Dec. 2022, https://www.youtube.com/watch?v=HYzdwJGJEvw.

Chapter 1: How to Be Irrelevant

5. Hansen, Christian. *The Influence Mindset: The Art & Science of Getting People to Choose You*. CreateSpace Independent Publishing Platform, 2021.

6. Dovidio, John F., Samuel L. Gaertner, and Tamar Saguy. "Commonality and the Complexity of 'We': Social Attitudes and

Social Change." *Personality and Social Psychology Review*, vol. 13, no. 1, 2009, pp. 3–20. https://doi.org/10.1177/1088868308326751.

7. Castro-González, Sandra, Belén Bande, and Pilar Fernández-Ferrín. "Influence of Companies' Credibility and Trust in Corporate Social Responsibility Aspects of Consumer Food Products: The Moderating Intervention of Consumer Integrity." *Sustainable Production and Consumption*, vol. 28, 2021, pp. 129–141.

8. Dowell, David, Mark Morrison, and Troy Heffernan. "The Changing Importance of Affective Trust and Cognitive Trust across the Relationship Lifecycle: A Study of Business-to-Business Relationships." *Industrial Marketing Management*, vol. 44, 2015, pp. 119–130.

Chapter 2: How Not to Crash in the Potomac

1. McCullough, David. *The Wright Brothers*. Simon & Schuster, 2015. Pg 33.

2. McCullough, Pg 80.

3. McCullough, Pg 93.

   a. (Note: Langley himself along with Alexander Graham Bell and other luminaries contributed an additional $20,000 for the construction out of their own pockets.)

4. McCullough, Pg 96.

5. McCullough, Pg 99.

6. McCullough, Pg 108.

7. McCullough, Pg 67.

8. "Patent No. 821,343." *Wright Brothers Aeroplane Company*, https://www.wright-brothers.org/History_Wing/Wright_Story/Showing_the_World/Politics_%26_Patents/Patent_821343.htm.

9. "1906 Wright US Patent #821,393." *The Wright Brothers: The Invention of the Aerial Age*, Mississippi State University, https://invention.psychology.msstate.edu/i/Wrights/WrightUSPatent/WrightPatent.html.

10. Jheeta, Sohan. "The Landscape of the Emergence of Life." *Life*, vol. 7, no. 2, 16 June 2017, article 27. https://doi.org/10.3390/life7020027.

11. Stetka, Bret. *A History of the Human Brain: From the Sea Sponge to CRISPR, How Our Brain Evolved.* Timber Press, 2021. Pg 32.

12. McCullough, Pg 45.

13. McCullough, Pg 43.

14. Gören, Erkan. "The biogeographic origins of novelty-seeking traits." *Evolution and Human Behavior* 37.6 (2016): 456-469.

    a. (This is a fascinating paper detailing the need for exploration in humans and how it has impacted civilization)

15. Stetka, Bret. *A History of the Human Brain: From the Sea Sponge to CRISPR, How Our Brain Evolved.* Timber Press, 2021. Page 51

16. Bohannon, Cat. *Eve: How the Female Body Drove 200 Million Years of Human Evolution.* Penguin Random House, 2023.

17. Stetka, Pg 61

18. Schmelz, Martin, Sebastian Grueneisen, Ayse Kabalak, Joachim Jost, and Michael Tomasello. "Chimpanzees Return Favors at a Personal Cost." *Proceedings of the National Academy of Sciences of the United States of America*, vol. 114, no. 28, 2017, pp. 7462–7467. https://doi.org/10.1073/pnas.1700351114.

19. Wilson, Edward O. *The Social Conquest of Earth*. Liveright Publishing Corporation, 2012. Pg 45.

20. Stetka, pg 62, 79.

21. Donahue, Chad J., Matthew F. Glasser, Todd M. Preuss, James K. Rilling, and David C. Van Essen. "Quantitative Assessment

of Prefrontal Cortex in Humans Relative to Nonhuman Primates." *Proceedings of the National Academy of Sciences of the United States of America*, vol. 115, no. 22, 29 May 2018, pp. E5183–E5192. https://doi.org/10.1073/pnas.1721653115.

22. Friedman, Naomi P., and Trevor W. Robbins. "The Role of Prefrontal Cortex in Cognitive Control and Executive Function." *Neuropsychopharmacology*, vol. 47, no. 1, Jan. 2022, pp. 72–89. https://doi.org/10.1038/s41386-021-01132-0.

23. Carlén, Marie. "What constitutes the Prefrontal Cortex?." *Science* 358.6362 (2017): 478-482.

24. McBride, Thomas, Steven E. Arnold, and Ruben C. Gur. "A comparative volumetric analysis of the Prefrontal Cortex in human and baboon MRI." *Brain, behavior and evolution* 54.3 (1999): 159-166.

25. Stetka, 158.

    a. Emphasis on "newly developed" is my insertion.

26. Arnsten, Amy FT. "Stress signalling pathways that impair Prefrontal Cortex structure and function." *Nature Reviews Neuroscience* 10.6 (2009): 410-422.

Section 2: From Tonic to Iconic

1. "John Pemberton." *Lemelson-MIT Program*, Massachusetts Institute of Technology, https://lemelson.mit.edu/resources/john-pemberton.

2. King, Monroe. "John Stith Pemberton." New Georgia Encyclopedia, last modified Jun 1, 2020. https://www.georgiaencyclopedia.org/articles/business-economy/john-stith-pemberton-1831-1888/

3. Rogers, Staci. "What Doesn't Kill You Only Makes You Stronger: How the Temperance Movement Helped Make Coca-Cola."

Historia, (19) 2010:. 43–59. Eastern Illinois University, https://www.eiu.edu/historia/2010Rogers.pdf.

4. Paul, April L., and Robert D. Gulbro. "Allied Academies International Conference." *International Academy for Case Studies. Proceedings*, vol. 12, no. 2, 2005, pp. 91–94. Jordan Whitney Enterprises, Inc.

5. Rogers, pg 49.

Chapter 3: Emotions Drive Decisions

1. "The Sveriges Riksbank Prize in Economic Sciences in Memory of Alfred Nobel 1978." *NobelPrize.org*, Nobel Prize Outreach, 1978, https://www.nobelprize.org/prizes/economic-sciences/1978/press-release/.

2. Simon, Herbert A. *Administrative Behavior: A Study of Decision-Making Processes in Administrative Organization*. Macmillan, 1947.

3. Lerner, Jennifer S., et al. "Emotion and decision making." *Annual review of psychology* 66.1 (2015): 799-823.

4. Song, Gao. "The Research on Consumer Decision Process and Problem Recognition." *2016 2nd International Conference on Humanities and Social Science Research (ICHSSR 2016)*. Atlantis Press, 2016.

5. Damasio, Antonio R. (2008) [1994]. *Descartes' Error: Emotion, Reason and the Human Brain*. Random House.Arnsten, Amy F.T. "Stress signalling pathways that impair prefrontal cortex structure and function." *Nature Reviews Neuroscience* 10.6 (2009): 410-422.

6. McRae, Kateri, Bethany Ciesielski, and James J. Gross. "Unpacking cognitive reappraisal: goals, tactics, and outcomes." *Emotion* 12.2 (2012): 250.

7. Merkebu, Jerusalem, et al. "What is metacognitive reflection? The moderating role of metacognition on emotional regulation and reflection." *Frontiers in Education,* Vol. 8. Frontiers Media SA, 2023.

8. Zhao, Meina, Jing Wang, and Weiwei Han. "The impact of emotional involvement on online service buying decisions: an event-related potentials perspective." *Neuroreport* 26.17 (2015): 995-1002.

9. Muzumdar, Prathamesh, and George Kurian. "Empirical study to explore the influence of salesperson's customer orientation on customer loyalty." *arXiv preprint arXiv:2103.01220* (2021).

10. Tustonja, Marijan, et al. "Active listening–A model of empathetic communication in the helping professions." *Medicina Academica Integrativa* 1.1 (2024): 42-47.

Chapter 4: Think "Insight" the Box

1. "Issue from April 27, 1956." *The New York Times,* 27 Apr. 1956, https://timesmachine.nytimes.com/timesmachine/1956/04/27/issue.html.

2. https://www.pbs.org/wgbh/theymadeamerica/whomade/mclean_hi.html

3. Levinson, Marc. *The Box: How the Shipping Container Made the World Smaller and the World Economy Bigger.* Princeton University Press, 2006. Pg 39.

4. Levinson, Pg 43.

5. Levinson, Pg 10.

6. Levinson, Pg 49.

7. Ebeling, C. E. (Winter 2009), "Evolution of a Box," Invention and Technology, 23 (4): 8–9.

8. Levinson, pg 85.

9. Levinson, pg 103.

10. Levinson, Pg 48.

11. "Shipping Pioneer Largely Ignored". - The Baltimore Sun. - June 14, 2001. p.23A.

12. Saxon, Wolfgang (May 29, 2001). "M. P. McLean, 87, Container Shipping Pioneer.".\ *The New York Times*.

13. Hansen, Christian. *The Influence Mindset: The Art & Science of Getting People to Choose You.* CreateSpace Independent Publishing Platform, 2021.

14. Cappelli, Peter, et al. "Develop Strategic Thinkers Throughout Your Organization." *Harvard Business Review*, 10 Feb. 2014, https://hbr.org/2014/02/develop-strategic-thinkers-throughout-your-organization.

15. Kounios, John, and Mark Beeman. "The Aha! Moment: The Cognitive Neuroscience of Insight." *Current Directions in Psychological Science*, vol. 18, no. 4, 2009, pp. 210–216. https://doi.org/10.1111/j.1467-8721.2009.01638.x.

16. Oh, Jieun, Christopher Chesebrough, Brittany Erickson, Fanghui Zhang, and John Kounios. "An Insight-Related Neural Reward Signal." *NeuroImage*, vol. 214, 1 July 2020, article 116757. https://doi.org/10.1016/j.neuroimage.2020.116757.

Chapter 5: How to Get a $150 Million Shoe

1. Lazenby, Roland. *Michael Jordan: The Life.* Little, Brown and Company, 2014. Pg 33.

2. Pg 37.

3. Knight, Phil. *Shoe Dog: A Memoir by the Creator of Nike.* Scribner, 2016.

4. Lazenby, Pg 235.

5. Lazenby, Pg 237.

6. Lazenby, Pg 238.

7. Lazenby, Pg 243.

8. Lazenby, Pg 244.

9. Baum, Brent. "How Michael Jordan Revolutionized the Sneaker Industry—and Our Relationship to Shoes." *Temple Now*, 3 Apr. 2023, https://news.temple.edu/news/2023-04-03/how-michael-jordan-revolutionized-sneaker-industry-and-our-relationship-shoes.

10. McAdams, Dan P., and Kate C. McLean. "Narrative Identity." *Current Directions in Psychological Science*, Vol. 22, no. 3, 2013, pp. 233–238. SAGE Publications, https://doi.org/10.1177/0963721413475622.

11. Rogers, Ben A., et al. "Seeing Your Life Story as a Hero's Journey Increases Meaning in Life." *Journal of Personality and Social Psychology*, Vol. 125, no. 4, 2023, pp. 567–589. https://doi.org/10.1037/pspa0000341.

12. Cappelli, Peter, et al. "Develop Strategic Thinkers Throughout Your Organization." *Harvard Business Review*, 10 Feb. 2014.

13. *Oh, Jieun, Christopher Chesebrough, Brittany Erickson, Fanghui Zhang, and John Kounios. "An Insight-Related Neural Reward Signal." NeuroImage, vol. 214, 1 July 2020, article 116757. https://doi.org/10.1016/j.neuroimage.2020.116757.*

14. Schnall, Simone, et al. *"Social Support and the Perception of Geographical Slant." Journal of Experimental Social Psychology, Vol. 44, no. 5, 2008, pp. 1246–1255. https://doi.org/10.1016/j.jesp.2008.04.011.*

15. Rogers, Ben A., et al. "Seeing Your Life Story as a Hero's Journey Increases Meaning in Life." *Journal of Personality and Social Psychology, Vol. 125, no. 4, 2023, pp. 567–589. https://doi.org/10.1037/pspa0000341.*

16. Alexander, Kerri Lee. *"Deloris Jordan." National Women's History Museum,* https://www.womenshistory.org/education-resources/biographies/deloris-jordan. *Accessed. Jan 6 2025.*

17. Jordan, Deloris. *Facebook, uploaded by NBA on ESPN, May 10, 2020,* https://fb.watch/wXKy8l27lT/. *Accessed January 27th 2025.*

Section 3: The Two Doctors Fighting an Invisible Killer

1. Semmelweis, Ignaz (1983). *Etiology, Concept and Prophylaxis of Childbed Fever,* translated by Carter, K. Codell, University of Wisconsin Press. Pg 81.

2. Lane, Hillary J.; Blum, Nava; Fee, Elizabeth (June 2010). "Oliver Wendell Holmes (1809–1894) and Ignaz Philipp Semmelweis (1818–1865): Preventing the Transmission of Puerperal Fever," *Am J Public Health,* 100 (6): 1008–1009.

3. Ataman, Ahmet D., Emine E. Vatanoğlu-Lutz, and Gül Yıldırım. "Medicine in Stamps – Ignaz Semmelweis and Puerperal Fever." *Journal of the Turkish-German Gynecological Association,* vol. 14, no. 1, 1 Mar. 2013, pp. 35–39. https://doi.org/10.5152/jtgga.2013.08.

4. Lepenos, Themistoklis, Despina Sanoudou, Alexandra Protogerou, Konstantinos Laios, George Androutsos, and Karamamou. "Louis Pasteur (1822–1895), Ignaz Semmelweis (1818–1865), Joseph Lister (1827–1912) and the Link Between Their Works Toward the Development of Antisepsis: A Narrative Review." *Cureus,* vol. 16, no. 6, 17 June 2024, article e62543. https://doi.org/10.7759/cureus.62543.

5. Smith, Kendall A. "Louis Pasteur, the Father of Immunology?" *Frontiers in Immunology,* vol. 3, 10 Apr. 2012, article 68. https://doi.org/10.3389/fimmu.2012.00068.

6. Toledo-Pereyra, Luis H. "Louis Pasteur Surgical Revolution." *Journal of Investigative Surgery*, vol. 22, no. 2, Mar.–Apr. 2009, pp. 82–87. https://doi.org/10.1080/08941930902794729.

Chapter 6: Everyone's Favorite Gift

1. De Wolff, Marinus S., and Marinus H. van IJzendoorn. "Sensitivity and Attachment: A Meta-Analysis on Parental Antecedents of Infant Attachment." *Child Development*, Vol. 68, no. 4, 1997, pp. 571–591. https://pubmed.ncbi.nlm.nih.gov/9306636/.

2. Morelli, Sylvia A., Jared B. Torre, and Naomi I. Eisenberger. "The neural bases of feeling understood and not understood." *Social cognitive and affective neuroscience*, 9.12 (2014): 1890-1896.

3. Reis, Harry T., Margaret S. Clark, and John G. Holmes. "Perceived Partner Responsiveness as an Organizing Construct in the Study of Intimacy and Closeness." *Handbook of Closeness and Intimacy*, edited by Debra J. Mashek and Arthur Aron, Lawrence Erlbaum Associates Publishers, 2004, pp. 201–225.

4. Cross, Susan E., Pamela L. Bacon, and Michael L. Morris. "The Relational-Interdependent Self-Construal and Relationships." *Journal of Personality and Social Psychology*, vol. 78, no. 4, 2000, pp. 791–808.

5. Oishi, Shigehiro, Joanna Schiller, and Erica B. Gross. "Felt Understanding and Misunderstanding Affect the Perception of Pain, Slant, and Distance." *Social Psychological and Personality Science*, vol. 4, no. 3, 2013, pp. 259–266.

6. Buffini, Brian, host. "Episode 026: Mastering the Art of Listening." *It's a Good Life*, featuring Steve Shapiro, episode 26, 15 Nov. 2016. Apple Podcasts, https://podcasts.apple.com/nz/podcast/episode-026-mastering-the-art-of-listening/id1089027054?i=1000377868308.

7. Triana-Del Rio, Rodrigo, et al. "The modulation of emotional and social behaviors by oxytocin signaling in limbic network." *Frontiers in Molecular Neuroscience,* 15 (2022): 1002846.

8. Kawamichi, Hiroaki, et al. "Perceiving active listening activates the reward system and improves the impression of relevant experiences." *Social Neuroscience,* 10.1 (2015): 16-26.

Chapter 7: How to Explore the Ocean Floor

1. Heezen, Bruce C. "The deep-sea floor." *Continental Drift* 3 (1962): 235-288.

2. Barton, Cathy. "Marie Tharp, oceanographic cartographer, and her contributions to the revolution in the Earth sciences." *Geological Society, London, Special Publications* 192.1 (2002): 215-228.

3. Higgs, Bettie Matheson. "Understanding the Earth: The Contribution of Marie Tharp." *Geological Society, London, Special Publications,* vol. 506, 2021, pp. 231–243. https://doi.org/10.1144/SP506-2019-248.

4. Ewing, Maurice, and Bruce C. Heezen. "Oceanographic research programs of the Lamont Geological Observatory." *Geographical Review* 46.4 (1956): 508-535.

    a. Note: Notice how Marie is not mentioned anywhere in this paper.

5. Evans, Rachel. "Plumbing Depths to Reach New Heights: Marie Tharp Explains Marine Geological Maps." *Library of Congress Information Bulletin,* Nov. 2002, https://www.loc.gov/loc/lcib/0211/tharp.html.

6. Sweller, John. "Cognitive load during problem-solving: Effects on learning." *Cognitive Science* 12.2 (1988): 257-285.

7. Edmondson, Amy C. *"Psychological Safety and Learning Behavior in Work Teams."* Administrative Science Quarterly, Vol. 44, no. 2, 1999, pp. 350-383.

8. Heritage, John, and Steven Clayman. *Talk in Action: Interactions, Identities, and Institutions.* Wiley-Blackwell, 2010.

9. Schein, Edgar H. *Humble Inquiry: The Gentle Art of Asking Instead of Telling.* Berrett-Koehler Publishers, 2013.

10. Semyonov-Tal, Keren, and Noah Lewin-Epstein. "The Importance of Combining Open-Ended and Closed-Ended Questions When Conducting Patient Satisfaction Surveys in Hospitals." *Health Policy Open*, Vol. 2, 2021, article 100033.

Chapter 8: The Secret to Real Magic

1. Swann, William B., Jr. "Self-Verification Theory." *Handbook of Theories of Social Psychology*, edited by Paul A. M. Van Lange, Arie W. Kruglanski, and E. Tory Higgins, vol. 2, Sage Publications, 2012, pp. 23–42.

2. Harmon-Jones, Eddie, and Judson Mills. "An Introduction to Cognitive Dissonance Theory and an Overview of Current Perspectives on the Theory." *Cognitive Dissonance: Reexamining a Pivotal Theory in Psychology*, 2nd ed., edited by Eddie Harmon-Jones, American Psychological Association, 2019, pp. 3–24. https://doi.org/10.1037/0000135-001.

3. Cascio, Christopher N., et al. "Self-affirmation activates brain systems associated with self-related processing and reward and is reinforced by future orientation." *Social Cognitive and Affective Neuroscience* 11.4 (2016): 621-629.

4. Izuma, Keise, Daisuke N. Saito, and Norihiro Sadato. "Processing of Social and Monetary Rewards in the Human

Striatum." *Neuron*, vol. 58, no. 2, 2008, pp. 284–294. https://doi.org/10.1016/j.neuron.2008.03.020.

5. Lin, Alice, Ralph Adolphs, and Antonio Rangel. "Social and Monetary Reward Learning Engage Overlapping Neural Substrates." *Social Cognitive and Affective Neuroscience*, vol. 7, no. 3, 2012, pp. 274–281. https://doi.org/10.1093/scan/nsr006.

6. Burnett, P. C., and Mandel, V. (2010). "Praise and feedback in the primary classroom: teachers' and students' perspectives." *Aust. J. Educ. Dev. Psychol.* 10, 145–154.

7. Lin, Alice, Ralph Adolphs, and Antonio Rangel. "Social and Monetary Reward Learning Engage Overlapping Neural Substrates." *Social Cognitive and Affective Neuroscience*, vol. 7, no. 3, 2012, pp. 274–281. https://doi.org/10.1093/scan/nsr006.

8. Yatsenko, Olga. ""How Do I Look?" The Impact of Compliments on Self-Perceived Attractiveness." *Inquiries Journal* 5.09 (2013).

9. Modigliani, A. (1968). "Embarrassment and embarrassability." *Sociometry* 31, 313–326

10. Eckstein, Monika, et al. "Neural Responses to Instructed Positive Couple Interaction: An fMRI Study on Compliment Sharing." *Social Cognitive and Affective Neuroscience*, Vol. 18, no. 1, 2023, article nsad005.

11. Fujiwara, Shotaro, et al. "Sincere Praise and Flattery: Reward Value and Association with the Praise-Seeking Trait." *Frontiers in Human Neuroscience*, Vol. 17, 15 Feb. 2023.

12. Gu, Ruolei, et al. "Self-affirmation enhances the processing of uncertainty: An event-related potential study." *Cognitive, Affective, & Behavioral Neuroscience* 19 (2019): 327-337.

Conclusion: The 35-Ton Miracle

1. Barron, A.J. Mark. "Carrara Marble." *Mercian Geologist*, Vol. 19, 2018, pp. 188–194. https://www.researchgate.net/publication/338480228_Carrara_Marble.

2. Attanasio, Donato, Platania, Rosario, and Rocchi, Paolo . "The marble of the David of Michelangelo: a multi-method analysis of provenance." *Journal of Archaeological Science* 32.9 (2005): 1369-1377.

3. Weinberger, Martin. *Michelangelo the Sculptor.* Columbia University Press, 1967.

ABOUT THE AUTHOR

Christian Hansen is an international thought leader and bestselling author specializing in empowering individuals and organizations to communicate their value, stand out, and be the obvious choice in competitive markets. As the author of *The Influence Mindset*, a #1 bestseller and LinkedIn's Top Ten Marketing Books selection, Christian combines academic rigor with practical insights to transform how people approach influence and connection. His expertise spans talent acquisition, global marketing strategies, and leadership development, gained through roles at top organizations and academic institutions.

Christian holds degrees from Brigham Young University and The London School of Economics, where he developed a deep understanding of organizational behavior and international business culture. He has impacted thousands of lives as a coach and speaker, equipping them with tools to rise above the noise and become the obvious choice in their fields. Fluent in English and Korean; Christian's global perspective informs his work, making his strategies universally applicable.

His proprietary methods have helped students secure spots in top universities, professionals achieve career breakthroughs, and teams improve sales performance. Christian's work emphasizes the intersection of competence and connection, showing that influence stems from mastering both. He is the founder of www.TopCollegeGuru.com, a platform that demystifies the admissions process for students and families as well as www.TheChristianHansen.com a place for professionals who want to upgrade their influence and stand out from the crowd.

Christian is passionate about sharing insights through keynote speeches, where he often integrates his musical talent to create memorable experiences. He is also a proud member of the Tabernacle Choir at Temple Square, embodying a commitment to excellence and creativity. Christian resides in Utah with his wife, an avid traveler always on the hunt for the world's best taco.